BEHIND A WIRE FENCE

BEHIND A WIRE FENCE

MY TRAVELS DURING A SEASON
IN THE CLASS A
NEW YORK-PENNSYLVANIA LEAGUE

Martin D. Cox, Ed.D.

PALMETTO
P U B L I S H I N G
Charleston, SC
www.PalmettoPublishing.com

Hardcover ISBN: 979-8-8229-5734-3
Paperback ISBN: 979-8-8229-5735-0
eBook ISBN: 979-8-8229-5736-7

To my home team: my wife, Mary Beth, and my children, Hillary, Kevin, and Abigail.

TABLE OF CONTENTS

INTRODUCTION

The snow was falling lightly outside the sliding glass door of my home in the Upstate New York town of Walworth, located thirty minutes east of Rochester. Christmas had just passed, and New Year's 1993 was less than a week away. It was right around this time of the year that I got the itch for our national pastime of baseball. The World Series had been over for two months, spring training was still a long way off, and the upcoming season could not get here soon enough.

For some reason, this winter led me to reflect on where I was ten years earlier and where I was right now. An aspiring baseball-radio play-by-play announcer who was just two years out of college in 1983, I was in my second year as the public address announcer for the Redwood Pioneers, an affiliate of the California Angels and a member of the Class A California League. During that summer of 1983, the Redwood ball club suddenly woke up from the dead in mid-July after a horrendous first half of the season when they finished ten and a half games behind the division winner, Stockton. Fortunately, the California League schedule was devised so that after the first seventy-one games, the "second half" of the season began, and everyone in the league started over with a 0-0 record. Amazingly, the Pioneers caught lightning in a bottle, winning thirteen of sixteen games, and went on to win the North Division title in the second half of the season with a 40-30 record.

Stockton, which finished 35-35 and five games behind Redwood in the second half, won the opener of the best of three division series behind the pitching of Bill Wegman, who would soon find his way to the team's major league affiliate in Milwaukee. The Pioneers, however, then won the next two games, pounding out twenty-one hits in a 13-6 drubbing of the Ports in the decisive Game Three in Rohnert Park, the home base for the Redwood club. Stockton shortstop Dale Sveum would eventually make it to Milwaukee as well, but on this night the headlines belonged to the Redwood designated hitter Dennis Gilbert, who had five hits in five at bats, including a pair of home runs, and five runs batted in. First baseman Terry Harper, his teammate, was three for three at the plate, with a home run and two runs batted in. Redwood's Tony Mack was the winning pitcher. Mack was promoted to the Angels in 1985 and pitched in just one game in the major leagues. I was in attendance for the game on July 27, 1985, when he gave up four runs on eight hits through two and one-third innings pitched in a loss to the Blue Jays at Exhibition Stadium in Toronto. He was then sent back to the minor leagues and never pitched again in the major leagues.

In the 1983 California League Championship Series, the Pioneers beat the Visalia Oaks, a team that easily won both editions of the South Division schedule—the first half of the season as well as the second half. The Oaks had a center fielder named Kirby Puckett, and the Pioneers countered at that position with Mike Madril. In the end, Puckett would go to the majors, but a championship ring would go to Madril and his Redwood teammates, a 3-1 winner against Visalia in the best-of-five championship series. In Game Four of the series, the Pioneers won 5-3, scoring all their runs in the seventh inning, catcher Rick Turner leading the way with a three-run homer. Tim Kammeyer was the winning pitcher for Redwood, a team that won its first California League Championship in just its fourth year of existence. On that championship Sunday of the 1983 Labor Day weekend, few took notice, however, as a crowd of only 661 came out to Rohnert Park Stadium to watch.

And now, here I was, watching the snow come down just over nine years later, home during Christmas break as an elementary school teacher but with the urge to get back to the low minors of professional baseball during the coming season in one way or another. In an instant, I informed my wife, Mary Beth, I wanted to visit all fourteen ballparks of the Class A New York–Pennsylvania League when school let out, and the 1993 NY-P League season began in June.

Surprisingly, she agreed.

Now all I had to do was wait for winter to end and the baseball season to begin.

The reality is that I have felt this urge for baseball to return during the dead of every winter since I was a little kid.

The affection for the game began when I was growing up in the Rochester suburb of Greece, the youngest of five children. I have a sister, Carol, and three brothers, Ron, Buzz, and Benny. My brothers and my dad were always willing to play a game of catch with me on the front lawn of our modest ranch house on McGuire Road. Most memorable were the times when Buzz, eleven years my elder, would hit grounders to Benny, Ron, and me. Buzz would start out easy, but within moments, he would hit us hard grounders and screaming line drives with a wooden bat. Years later, we still laugh about the balls that would fly over our heads, hitting the telephone wires above us that draped between the street pole and our neighbor's house. On cue, the homeowner would open her window and yell at us, often saying, "If you hit that wire again, I'm going to call the police." My brothers and I would look at each other and shake our heads in disbelief. We could not understand how such a threat could be coming from a neighbor who also happened to be our Aunt June. If we were not playing catch or fielding grounders in the front yard, we would drop our makeshift bases a fair distance apart and play games of hot box, with a fielder guarding each base and one or two runners trying to advance from one base to the other. When three tag outs were made, the runners and fielders would switch, and a new game would begin.

My father was a big baseball fan, having played the sport for Charlotte High School in Rochester in the 1930s before serving in the United States Army in World War II as an infantry soldier while stationed in Northern Africa and Sicily. He would often play catch with my brother Benny, three years my elder, and me during the baseball season and shoot baskets with us on the driveway during basketball season, nailing one shot after another with his 1930s "set shot." On Sunday, following mass at Our Mother of Sorrows Church, my dad would occasionally take Benny and me to the Maplewood Diner on Ridge Road in Rochester, where the three of us would sit in silence eating our eggs, bacon, and toast while splitting the Sunday *Democrat and Chronicle* sports section into thirds, passing the sections around our booth to each other when finished. My dad was a Pete Rose fan because he admired his hustle and referred to him as "Rose Bud." It was common for him to break the silence in our booth with comments such as, "Rose Bud had two hits last night," or, "Rose Bud is batting over .330."

One of my favorite stories involving baseball centers on my mother and goes back to 1967 when I got off the school bus one October afternoon as a third-grade student at Our Mother of Sorrows School. When I entered the kitchen, my mother greeted me by saying, "You should go to the living room, because there is something there you will want to see." Not having any idea what was awaiting me while walking around the corner through the dining room of our modest, three-bedroom ranch house, I first noticed that the black-and-white television that was always stationed on its magazine cart in the far corner of the living room was unplugged and moved to the center of the room. The old black-and-white television was now directly in front of what my mother referred to as the "picture window." Taking its place in the corner was a wooden, floor-model, Zenith colored television. Staring into my living room was Bob Gibson, pitcher for the St. Louis Cardinals, who was throwing fastballs at the Boston Red Sox lineup in the 1967 World Series. Gibson and the Cardinals were wearing bright red hats, with two red Cardinals positioned at each end of a bat on the front of their jerseys. My jaw dropped at the beauty of the colors, the red of the Cardinals, the navy-blue of the Red Sox, and the emerald-green grass of Fenway Park in Boston. I had never imagined our family having a color television. The black-and-white TV with the rabbit-ear antennas we constantly fiddled with for a clearer screen was part of family history. Now, here I sat on the couch looking at the beauty of color on a baseball field at the outset of the World Series. Eventually, I turned around as my mother stood behind me, apron tied around her waist, watching her youngest son completely enthralled with his first-ever view of a baseball game on a colored television. "I knew you would like this colored TV," she said, "and just in time for the World Series."

The love of the game was enhanced every time my dad, mom, or brothers would take me to my favorite address in Rochester, 500 Norton Street on the city's northeast side, the site of Red Wing Stadium and the home of the Rochester Red Wings of the Class AAA International League, the top affiliate of the Baltimore Orioles. It was there that I remember being about five or six years old when my dad first walked me up the ramp that led from the concession area under the steel girders supporting the grandstand and into the concourse of the stadium that wrapped around the box-seat section. The venue was inappropriately named because it was not really a stadium but instead a ballpark. The fences were tall wooden structures covered with advertisements promoting local brands and businesses, including French's mustard, Tobin's First Prize hots, and Bob Hiatt's stereo, to name a few. A triple-layering of signs was situated in left field, the bullpen area where relief pitchers from both clubs used to start bonfires inside steel barrels to stay warm during those cold April evenings in the 1960s and 1970s. The fence also included a tall scoreboard in straightaway center field, a hand-operated structure that had the operator viewing the game from an empty square in the column showing run totals per inning. At the very top of the scoreboard was a wooden duplicate of the clock that was situated in the center of Midtown Plaza in Downtown Rochester. The grandstand included steel beams supporting the overhanging roof, the beams becoming obstacles to your view of the field, depending on where you sat in the cheaper general admission seats. Benny and I were always certain to position ourselves in seats so that the nearest beam did not obstruct our view of the pitcher and the batter.

I saw several major league prospects come through the ballpark for the Red Wings and the visiting ball clubs as well: Carlton Fisk (Louisville Colonels), Gary Carter (Peninsula Whips), Dave Cash (Columbus Jets), Ralph Garr (Richmond Braves), Dusty Baker (Richmond Braves), Jon Matlack (Tidewater Tides), Jon Milner (Tidewater Tides), Willie Randolph, Richie Zisk, Omar Moreno, and Dave Parker of the Charleston Charlies, and Jim Rice, Fred Lynn, and Juan Beniquez of the Pawtucket Red Sox. The Rochester list was a long one that included Mike Epstein, Don Baylor, Bob Grich, Al Bumbry, Rich Coggins, Mike Ferraro, Merv Rettenmund, Tom Shopay, Mike Flanagan, Rich Dauer, Wayne Garland, Jim Fuller, and Johnny Oates, to name just a few.

It wasn't just the players who appeared to be headed toward successful major league careers who caught my attention, but the role-players and fringe players as well: Rick Bladt, Frank Tepedino and Mario Guerrero of the Syracuse Chiefs, Buzz Capra and Jim Bibby of the Tidewater Tides, Boots Day of the Winnipeg Whips, Coco Laboy of the Peninsula Whips, Wayne Comer of the Toledo Mud Hens, Rowland Office of the Richmond Braves, and Sam Parilla and Larry Johnson of the Red Wings. And of course, the most fringe player of them all, Mario Mendoza, a shortstop with the Charleston Charlies in 1974 who would go on to become a career .215 hitter in the major leagues and is the subject for the reference "the Mendoza Line." Supposedly, a few of Mendoza's teammates with the Seattle Mariners coined this phrase. The "line" refers to players above or below a batting average of .200 when listed in the sports section of the Sunday newspaper. Since Mendoza often hovered around .200, the hope was to find your name above "The Mendoza Line" of .200 each Sunday.

I came to know the names and faces of the Rochester players when my dad would take us to the ballpark early, just as the gates opened, so Benny and I could scamper down to the railing of the box seats, where we'd beg players for baseballs and hawk autographs. We always came away with autographs, and occasionally, we'd get some baseballs as well. Somehow, as the shyest kid at Our Mother of Sorrows School in Greece, I had a different personality in a ballpark. I was not hesitant at all to ask players if they could give me a baseball. I was denied almost every time, but one time, Wayne Garland, a pitcher with the Red Wings in the mid-1970s, was in a generous mood before a game and surprised me when he answered my request by flipping a ball right at me.

I would often spend time by the visiting dugout to increase my chances of a souvenir, because the larger throng of kids congregated by the Red Wings dugout, a move that paid dividends one Sunday afternoon prior to a game against the Richmond Braves in the early 1970s. Three of the Braves were playing a game of pepper to the side of the dugout in foul territory between the third-base coach's box and the front row of the box seats where I stood. One of the Richmond players fouled off the ball, and it went into the box-seat area right next to me, a section completely unoccupied. I quickly ducked under a few bars that separated the seats and picked up the ball. I looked up at the Richmond players, gesturing that I would throw it back to them, but they had already put another ball into play during their game of pepper and waved me off, a motion that meant, "Keep the ball, kid."

The high-water mark of my baseball childhood took place during the summer of 1971. I had just completed the sixth grade at Our Mother of Sorrows School, and both my brother Benny and I were playing Greece Little League baseball, he in the senior division and me in the majors division. I was the catcher for Security Trust, and our ace pitcher, Johnny Hendry, lived next to the house behind mine. Hendry and I spent a lot of time playing baseball together in 1971. In fact, we spent more time in the backyard playing than we did as teammates during our games with Security Trust, a team that was managed by his father, Tom Hendry. Johnny and I had our routine that summer, one that began each day when he came knocking on my porch door at 8:30 a.m. We would move a shopping cart that had over twenty-five baseballs in it to the backyard, where we'd start with a game of catch and then get right into numerous rounds of batting practice. I would pitch to him, and then he would pitch to me. The baseballs would go flying everywhere, and fortunately, the poplar and willow trees would knock down our line drives and prevent us from breaking the neighbors' windows. The workout would include hitting grounders to each other along with fly balls. As the day progressed, the venue would change to the wide-open fields behind nearby English Village Elementary School for games of home-run ball with my brother Benny and some of his friends, such as Scott Root and Steve Makowiecki. When those games would end, we would often cool off by getting back on our bicycles for a quick ride to the 7-Eleven that was across the street from Northgate Plaza, where we'd quench our thirst by purchasing a Slurpee. The slushy drinks were served in plastic cups with a cartoon drawing of a major league player, along with his statistics and a short biography. I would stack my collection in the form of a pyramid on top of my bedroom dresser, prompting my mother to often say, "Take inventory by putting those cups away; they're nothing but dust collectors!"

In the early days of our summer vacation in '71 when the school year ended, Hendry called me on a Friday night to inform me that

he read an advertisement in the Rochester *Democrat and Chronicle* stating that the Altier's shoe store at Northgate Plaza would host two members of the Rochester Red Wings the following morning. Visitors to the store would receive a free Red Wings shirt and autographs from the players. I told Hendry to come by on his bike and we would be on our way to Northgate, our home away from home, and the plaza where the two of us bought our packs of baseball cards at Key Drugstore.

The following morning, when Hendry and I walked into Altier's shoe store, we introduced ourselves to the Red Wings players, shortstop Bobby Grich and first baseman Larry Johnson. Grich was in his second season at Triple-A Rochester after batting .383 with the Red Wings in sixty-three games during the 1970 season.[1] Both Grich and his Red Wings teammate Don Baylor had outstanding seasons in 1970, Baylor hitting twenty-two home runs with 107 runs batted in to go along with his .327 batting average.[2] Despite the stellar offensive numbers both Grich and Baylor had posted in 1970, there was no room on the parent Baltimore Orioles roster following the 1970 World Series title the team won against the Cincinnati Reds in five games.

So here was the twenty-two-year-old Grich, back in Rochester, still ripping the cover off the ball and leading a Red Wings team that was loaded with talent, including that of his twenty-two-year-old teammate, the left fielder Baylor. Grich's teammate at Altier's on this day, Larry Johnson, was a reliable player that season, playing in ninety-two games and batting a respectable .307.[3] Both Grich and Johnson were congenial with Hendry and me as we lingered in the store long after other kids had come and gone. Here we were, the

1   Grich, Bobby. *Baseball Reference*. "Bobby Grich." 5 August 2024, (https://www.baseball-reference.com/register/player.fcgi?id=grich-001rob

2   Baylor, Don. *Baseball Reference*. "Don Baylor." 5 August 2024, https://www.baseball-reference.com/register/player.fcgi?id=baylor001don

3   Johnson, Larry. *Baseball Reference*. "Larry Johnson." 5 August 2024, https://www.baseball-reference.com/register/player.fcgi?id=johnso003lar

batterymen for the Security Trust entry in the Greece Little League, telling the two Red Wing players everything we could about our team while asking them anything we could think of as it pertained to life in the minor leagues. I distinctly remember Grich sizing up my skinny, wiry frame and telling me that I was too small to be a catcher, advising me instead to put the catching gear away and to play second base.

Hendry and I eventually said goodbye to the two players, but within a few days, I found myself in an interesting position when I was sitting on the bleachers at the Ed Nietopski Baseball Camp at nearby Cardinal Mooney High School in Greece. Nietopski, a former Red Wings infielder during the 1950s when the ball club was affiliated with the St. Louis Cardinals, was a well-respected baseball and basketball coach at Mooney. He was also the athletic director and a theology teacher. He still had connections with the Red Wings and informed us at the outset of the week that he had planned for Red Wings players to visit us each day as guest instructors. On the second day, there came Grich, walking across the dusty diamond wearing street clothes and toward our group of kids awaiting his arrival in the bleachers. The closer he came, the more I realized it would be necessary for the shy catcher to find the courage to say hello. And just as he approached, it came out: "Hey, Bobby, remember me? Marty, from Altier's!" Grich responded with a greeting and a smile, and my fellow campers were astonished that I was on speaking terms with the starting shortstop for the Rochester Red Wings.

Later in the same week, Nietopski brought in one Red Wings player after another, including catcher Johnny Oates and the left fielder Baylor, both going on to play and manage in the major leagues. I distinctly remember Oates talking to us about the mental aspects of hitting, saying that if you went to the plate thinking you might strike out, it was highly probable that you would. Instead, he told us to believe in ourselves, to tell yourself you were going to get a hit, and that things would work out fine.

The visit by Baylor was by far the most memorable.

The baseball field at Cardinal Mooney was situated behind the large school and parking lot, and the campers and I were immediately impressed when Baylor started walking through the outfield toward our bench. Baylor was an imposing figure who was in amazing shape with huge arms. Surprisingly, he visited us not with a baseball bat, but instead with a golf club. He held a wooden driver in one hand and a blue golf ball in the other. Baylor motioned for the campers to follow him to the middle of the infield, where we all took a seat on the grass near the pitcher's mound. Baylor then placed the blue golf ball on a tee, and we thought for sure that he was going to take a swing at it while he moved into his stance and addressed the ball with a swagger of the club. I was thinking that he could easily hit the school if he connected, if not on the fly, then certainly on a few bounces across the paved parking lot.

Much to our disappointment, he never took a swing.

Baylor's message was simple. In golf, he said, nobody is stopping you from hitting the ball; it is just sitting there for you on a tee. But in baseball, he reminded us that when the pitcher throws it, you must be thinking whether it will be a fastball or a breaking ball. The message was appreciated, but not exactly something we did not already know. Instead, I'm certain we would have truly enjoyed seeing how far he could drive that blue golf ball.

Grich, Johnson, Oates, Baylor, and the rest of the Red Wings, including Mike Ferraro, Richie Coggins, Fred Beene, Roric Harrison, and Mickey Scott, went on to win the International League Pennant with a record of 86-54 after starting the season with a record of 0-5. Led by manager Joe Altobelli, the Red Wings won the Governor's Cup playoffs, defeating the Tidewater Tides in the championship and then the Denver Bears of the American Association in the Junior World Series. Due to a conflict with the other tenant of Mile High Stadium, the Denver Broncos, the Bears were bumped out of their home field and forced to play the best-of-seven series with every game scheduled in Rochester. The Bears had Tom Grieve on their roster along with a slugger named Richie Scheinblum, who batted .388 during the regular season with twenty-five home runs and 108 runs batted in.[4] Rochester led the series 3-1, but Denver stayed alive by winning Game Five by a score of 9-5. After the game, the parent Orioles called to inform Altobelli that Grich would need to join the parent club after shortstop Mark Belanger went down with an injury against the Tigers in Detroit. As the story unfolded over the years, Grich supposedly informed Altobelli that he wanted to stay until the Red Wings won the series with Denver, but Baltimore manager Earl Weaver was not interested. Grich needed to pack his bags and join the Orioles immediately. Grich batted .336 in Rochester that year, hitting thirty-two home runs and driving in eighty-three runs. When he cleaned out his locker at 500 Norton Street following Game Five, it would mark the last time he would play minor league baseball.

Rain fell in Rochester for the next two days, but when the skies cleared, my brother Buzz took me with him and his friends to watch Game Six. Grich's replacement in the lineup for that night was a utility man named Ron Shelton who played in sixty-six games during the regular season and batted .260. Years later, it turned out that Shelton was keeping a journal during the 1971 season and would use his anecdotal notes to help him write the screenplay *Bull Durham*, a 1988 box-office hit about life in the minor leagues.[5] Game Six turned out to be a slugfest, won by Denver 12-11, to force a seventh and final game of the series. Rochester would win the finale 9-6 behind the starting pitcher Beene, who drove in the tying run in front of 9,043 fans.

Baylor would follow Grich to Baltimore after the Junior World Series ended, as both players embarked on what would become

---

4   Scheinblum, Richie. *Baseball Reference*. "Richie Scheinblum." 5 August 2024,
     https://www.baseball-reference.com/register/player.fcgi?id=schein001ric
5   Shelton, Ron. Wikipedia, *The Free Encyclopedia*. 7 July 2024, https://en.wikipedia.org/wiki/Ron_Shelton

successful major league careers. Altobelli remained in Rochester through the 1976 season, which was his best yet from the perspective of a regular season record. The Red Wings posted a record of 88-50 but were swept in the playoffs by the Richmond Braves.[6] When the season ended, Altobelli was named manager of the San Francisco Giants.

Hendry and I continued our daily routine throughout the summer of '71, taking far more swings of the bat in my own backyard than in all the games combined as teammates for Security Trust. As the summer wore on, it was clear that our ball club would stay in a race for first place in the Greece Little League with the pesky Mr. Steak entry that included catcher Paul Brigandi and a crafty left-handed pitcher named Bob Locke. On paper, I thought for certain that Security Trust had the better team. Our offense centered around a power hitter named Joe Bianchi, who crushed his share of home runs that summer, the best ones being those that cleared the left field fence and rolled onto the middle of the infield at the adjacent diamond, located on the English Road fields. When Joe Bianchi was not hitting tape-measure shots, his younger brother John was hitting line drives all over the field as he sparked the offense along with Hendry as our two most consistent hitters. We also had a first baseman named Randy Jensen who kept the team loose and had some pop in his bat as well.

The Bianchi brothers, meanwhile, made it a family affair, as their dad was Mr. Hendry's assistant coach. Both coaches were stern taskmasters with a no-nonsense approach to the game. They wanted us to play hard and show good sportsmanship and had little interest in hearing excuses. Mr. Bianchi was a tall man with a tightly cropped crew cut, and just like Mr. Hendry, he had no tolerance for anybody "dogging" it on the field, expecting us to always hustle. My

---

6   1976 International League. *Baseball Reference.* 5 August 2024, https://www.baseball-reference.com/register/league.cgi?id=cd0245ac

teammates and I respected both Mr. Hendry and Mr. Bianchi, as they instilled a sense of pride in us to play the game with hustle, passion, and good sportsmanship. I distinctly remember Mr. Bianchi being slightly tougher on his own two kids than the other players. If he hit a ground ball during infield practice and the ball was not cleanly fielded by John, which was a very rare occurrence, we could expect Mr. Bianchi to yell, "Stay down on the ball, pork chop!"

When I look back on my five years of Greece Little League, two years in the majors, and three in the seniors, it was this team during the summer of 1971 that I considered to be the best. In the end, however, it did not turn out that way, as our team finished behind the eventual league-champion Mr. Steak by just one game in the final standings.

A year later, in 1972, the Bianchi brothers were in the senior division while Hendry and I had one more year left in the majors with Security Trust. His arm now stronger with age, I distinctly remember many batters hesitantly stepping into the batter's box, their legs shaking, and afraid to hit Hendry, who struck out one hitter after another. It is funny, but I remember less about that season of '72 even though Hendry strapped us to his back and led us to the league title that eluded us in the summer of 1971.

A year later, in 1973, I was at Cardinal Mooney High School again, not to attend Nietopski's baseball camp but to enroll in the coeducational Catholic high school in Greece where my sister Carol and brother Buzz had graduated in the 1960s. My oldest brother Ron graduated from Aquinas Institute, and Benny graduated from Greece Arcadia. I was still a shy kid, sweeping a broom in the hallways after school as a member of the Student Workers program that provided students with jobs so that their "earnings" could be used as a tuition deduction. I even came in to work on Saturday morning, when from 9:00 a.m. to 12:00 p.m., a group of about ten students would mop all the hallways and the cafeteria. The Scotto brothers, Joe and Larry, were student supervisors of the program and had keys to the elevators that led to the fourth floor of the building. This was

important, because the Sisters of Mercy lived on the fourth floor of one side of the building while the Brothers of Holy Cross lived on the other. Each Saturday, about midway through the morning, I would pester one of the Scotto brothers, asking them if it was time yet for us to make our annual Saturday visit to the top of the building to find out if the Sisters had any baked goods awaiting us. The Sisters rarely disappointed with this ritual, and one Saturday in particular, I remember being greeted by my English teacher, Sister Margaret Mary, who told me to wait in the kitchen because she had something I might like.

She returned from her room, and when she entered the kitchen area, told me, "I know how much you like listening to sports, so I want you have this radio." Sister Margaret Mary presented me with a large, high-powered radio that she told me was able to pick up radio stations far away. She was right. Over the course of the next year, I had marked the radio dial with pen and call letters for a variety of channels that allowed me to listen to my beloved Baltimore Orioles on WTOP Radio along with the channels that carried the Cleveland Indians, Detroit Tigers, and much more. I would sit in my bedroom and keep score of the games, tuned to my favorite radio voices such as Chuck Thompson of the Orioles, Joe Tait of the Indians, and of course, the legendary Ernie Harwell of the Tigers.

I would share game highlights, statistics, and trivia about the Orioles with my childhood friend Pat Cavanagh at the high school bus stop on the corner of McGuire Road and Woodbriar Drive in the morning. Pat was, and still is, a big Boston Red Sox fan. This banter about our Orioles–Red Sox rivalry began during our days at Our Mother of Sorrows School when we would walk home from school together on occasion and go position by position—Mark Belanger vs. Rico Petrocelli, Geoge Scott vs. Boog Powell, Paul Blair vs. Reggie Smith, and more—while trying to one-up each other to prove which team was better. One of our shared baseball highlights took place on April 22, 1977, opening day of the Red Wings home season with the visiting Charleston Charlies in town. In the bottom of the first inning, Red Wings infielder Blake Doyle hit a foul ball toward our seats in the top row of the general admission section. Pat raised his hands in the air and deflected the ball, and I secured the ball off the deflection. Our Cardinal Mooney crew that was in attendance in our group all signed the ball—Pat Cavanagh, Jim Fulda, Tim O'Keefe, Joe Shufelt—and I still have the souvenir forty-seven years later.

Arguably the most talented baseball team I ever played on was the Cardinal Mooney junior varsity team in 1974 during my freshman year. Coach Dennis Oldenburg told us at the end of practice when a cut list was going to be posted the following morning in the gymnasium. I have vivid memories of my heart pounding each time I opened the door to the gym for a round of three cuts and continued to see the name "Cox" on that list. When tryouts concluded, I made the team, and was a back-up second baseman to sophomore Tim Caufield.

In addition to Caufield, my teammates included Tim Kick, Tom Kick, John Bianchi, Tim O'Keefe, Pete Cumbo, Dave George, Art Eichas, Todd Eichas, Kevin Dennis, Dave George, Randy Delgatti, Jim Hauss, and Tony Agostinelli. I saw limited playing time and struggled to bat above .200.

It didn't matter.

I was proud to be teammates with this talented group of ballplayers while wearing the baggy, gray flannel uniform with "Cardinals" written across the front of the jersey. Coach Oldenburg mirrored Coach Nietopski with his teachings, all centered on hustle, sportsmanship and respect for the game. We sprinted on and off the field and were in the "ready" position on defense during every pitch. We hustled down the first base line on every ground ball, our shirts were always tucked, nobody wore their hats backward, everyone wore black cleats, and we did not argue with umpires.

I don't recall Coach Oldenburg placing a big emphasis on winning. Instead, he taught us the fundamentals of the game and did not tolerate anyone "dogging it." As the season progressed, the players on the team began to manage each other and placed an emphasis on always being positive, especially my classmate Randy Delgatti, a left-handed pitcher and first baseman. Randy came from a good baseball pedigree. His older brother, Scott, was a Mooney graduate and a pitcher who had advanced to Triple A in the New York Yankees farm system. Randy was not hesitant to speak his mind if he saw any of his teammates engaging in "bush league" conduct.

We boarded the bus for each game with an air of confidence, and my teammates broke out into a chorus while singing top hits of the 70s during the ride home following a win. The singing occurred often as the team posted a 16-3 record. We split our six games against the three Catholic schools, Aquinas, Bishop Kearney, and McQuaid Jesuit. The team scored 10 or more runs during 12 of those 16 wins, including a 13-2 defeat of the crosstown Greece Arcadia Titans. We lost the three games by a combined total of only four runs.

A few years after I was married in 1987, I received a surprise phone call from my former teammate Dave George. He was calling simply to share his fond memories of this positive experience we had in the spring of 1974, cherishing the time we spent together and our interactions as teammates. I echoed his sentiment, and only wished that my shyness would not have prevented me from joining my teammates, who created a loose atmosphere on the bus, while singing those songs.

While attending Cardinal Mooney, I began to dream about becoming a major league baseball radio play-by-play announcer. It all made sense to me at the time. I loved the game of baseball, and so why not make a living describing the action from a press box across the radio airwaves?

Following graduation from high school in 1977, I enrolled at Niagara University but transferred to Ohio University for my last two years as an undergraduate student, where I majored in radio/TV broadcasting in the communications program. The school's campus

radio and television stations afforded me broadcasting opportunities I never had imagined. I was able to write scripts at the WOUB
newsroom for both radio and television sports broadcasts. Along
with several other students who were aspiring sports broadcasters
and actively involved in the newsroom, I had various radio time slots
that allowed for me to read the sports on the radio while providing listeners throughout Athens County the latest updates on OU
Bobcat athletics. During my senior year, I was able to secure more
opportunities as the sports anchor for WOUB-TV. I would prepare
scripts, gather video clips, and be on the set alongside student news
anchors during a ten o'clock weekday TV broadcast.

The newsroom was led by three adults who had paid positions and were responsible for the management of the student news
and sports reporters. Our leader was a gentleman named Bruce
Cuthbertson, who was a hard-core news hawk who had minimal
time for giving warm fuzzies to the students under his charge. For
some reason, I always felt like I was on his good side and able to fly
under his radar. During my senior year, I was living off campus in
a house at 150 Mill Street in Athens, and when spring recess came,
I did not have the money to go to Florida for spring break, nor did
I have the desire to go home to Rochester to watch the snow melt.
Instead, I stayed at the house on Mill Street, eating my steady diet of
macaroni and cheese while gaining more radio and television broadcast time. I did the TV sports-anchoring on WOUB the entire week
and was preparing my audition tapes that I would use to land a TV
job if I could not hook up with a ball club as a radio announcer.
One day during that spring break, Cuthbertson leaned over while
sitting at his news desk and asked, "Cox, want to get some experience on the news side? I am heading up to Steubenville to do a story
on the coal miners and their contract." Next thing I knew, I was
riding in a green, state-issued, WOUB news car with Cuthbertson
and heading north for the West Virginia panhandle. We arrived at
the union headquarters of the local coal miners in the Steubenville,

Ohio area, and Cuthbertson was chomping at the bit for a big story. As for myself, I was wondering who was pitching for the Baltimore Orioles that night. We sat around in the lounge area of the union shop for what seemed like an eternity. I was bored out of my mind, knowing at once that I had no interest in being a news reporter. Eventually, there was a big stir, and Cuthbertson alerted me to get the camera ready, because "the Channel 10 chopper is flying in from Columbus!" The chopper landed, and as planned, the coal-mining union workers took a copy of the contract they were offered by management and showed the cameras from Channel 10 in Columbus what they thought of its content. They threw it into a bonfire pit in the front yard of their union headquarters.

My other highlight as a student at Ohio University came during that same spring when the sports director of WATH Radio, the local commercial radio station in Athens, offered me and a few others from WOUB the chance to broadcast some innings of OU baseball games. I jumped at the opportunity and made sure that my housemates Jeff Flinn and Ralph Wagenhoffer were recording the games back at 150 Mill Street so I could use the tapes later when looking for a job.

And that's exactly what I did when I headed to Hollywood, Florida, in December of 1981 for the annual baseball winter meetings following my graduation from Ohio University that summer. I walked the floor of the Diplomat Hotel, approaching general managers of minor league teams across the country and asking if they were hiring a play-by-play announcer. Instead of staying at a cheap hotel on the strip along the ocean, I slept in a pup tent that I took with me on my flight from Rochester. I would either catch a bus or hitchhike the six miles or so that covered the distance between my campground and the Diplomat, the headquarters for the meetings. I remember seeing Billy Martin wearing his feathered cowboy hat and Sparky Anderson sporting his plaid jacket. I engaged in a conversation with Baltimore manager Earl Weaver at the Topps Baseball Card hospitality booth. When I asked if he could assist me in any way with my desire to find a minor league play-by-play radio job, he responded by saying, "I don't know much about the minors and not too much about the majors. I just put nine names on a lineup card and go out and manage."

I had an interview with the Lynchburg Mets, a Class A team in the Carolina League that was in search of an announcer for the 1982 season. There were a few other contacts that I made as well, but in the end, when I pulled up the stakes to my tent and flew north to Rochester, I left the Sunshine State without a job in professional baseball and had very few prospects.

During the winter months of 1982, I continued to pound out cover letters on my manual Royal typewriter to minor league teams across the country while living at home with my mother in Greece. One day, the phone rang, and it was Kathy Leonard, general manager of the Redwood Pioneers, calling to offer me a job. The Pioneers were based out of Rohnert Park, California, about an hour north of the Bay Area, and were the Class A affiliate of the California Angels. After listening to Leonard's offer, I was a bit confused. "So, is this a job to do the games on the radio?" I asked. "No," she said. "We don't have a contract with a radio station. This job is to be the public address announcer. It will pay $1,000 for the season, but we should be able to assist you with housing. Families in the community take in the ballplayers at minimal, if any, cost for rent, and we'll look to find a family for you as well."

I did not have to think twice. I told Leonard I would accept.

When I hung up, I excitedly told my mother of my first job offer as a sports announcer.

She was immediately confused.

"You're going all the way to California to take a job that pays $1,000 for five months?" she remarked. "What are you, crazy?"

I was not. Instead, I was headed for the Golden State as the next public address announcer of the Class A Redwood Pioneers of the California League. I was now employed by a professional baseball club.

My siblings (left to right) at the Baseball Hall of Fame, Cooperstown, NY: Ron, Carol, Buzz. My mother is holding my brother Benny.

The author at a young age swings the bat on his front lawn in the Rochester, NY suburb of Greece.

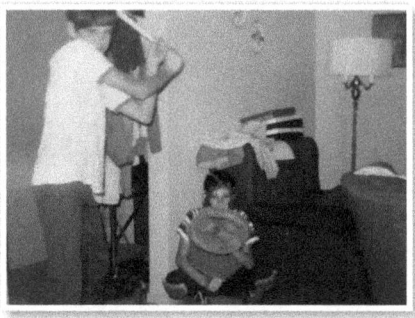

My brother Benny and I played a lot of baseball together in our youth. My catcher's equipment in this photo was made by my brother Buzz.

I caught more pitches from Johnny Hendry while wearing my gear than any other pitcher.

*I was a back-up catcher on the
1971 Greece Little League All-Star Team.*

*Front row (left to right) Jim Johnson, Tom Rzepka,
Marty Cox, Johnny Hendry, Matt Zapf, Jeff Corbett.*

*Back row (left to right) Coach Danny McDonald, Roy
Holland, Kevin Shaughnessy, Joe Bianchi, Jerry O'Neill,
John Bianchi, Joe Pierce, Eddie Sellon, Coach Tom Hendry*

*Ed Nietopski, Cardinal Mooney Varsity Baseball
Coach and former minor league shortstop in
the St. Louis Cardinals organization*

Sister Margaret Mary, my English Teacher at Cardinal Mooney High School, gave me a high-powered radio so I could listen to more ballgames.

I am on two knees in the middle of the front row, a back-up second baseman to Tim Caufield on the 1974 Mooney JV team. Coach Oldenburg, top row, far left, taught us how to respect the game of baseball. The result was a 16-3 record.

*Posing with my dad on Graduation Day
from Cardinal Mooney, June 1977.*

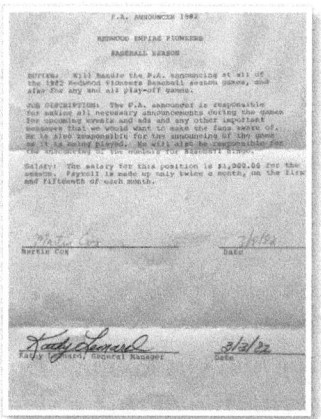

*"What are you, crazy, man?" That's what my mom
asked when I informed her of the $1,000 offer to be the
PA Announcer for the Redwood Pioneers in 1982.*

*I always showed up early to watch batting practice
as the Redwood Pioneers PA Announcer.*

*Yes, it's California, but Rohnert Park, California
required jacket attire during a summer evening.*

The Redwood Pioneers beat Kirby Puckett and his Visalia Oaks teammates in the 1983 California League Championship.

Redwood General Manager Bernie Smith (foreground) takes in the championship trophy celebration on September 4, 1983.

CHAPTER ONE:

OPENING NIGHT
IN AUBURN

June 17, 1993—Auburn, New York

My red Suzuki Samurai entered the sleepy village of Newark, New York, on a sunny June afternoon when the memories from a family vacation twenty years ago began to stir.

It was twenty years ago, during the summer of 1973, when my dad planned a family vacation in this area at a nearby lake. When I was younger, he took the entire family to Canada or the Adirondack Mountains, where he had rented us a cottage so my older siblings could fish. In 1973, three of the older siblings, Ron, Buzz, and Carol, were out of the house, and the vacation was set for a week at a small private lake north of the Thruway between Geneva and Lyons, New York. This family vacation included my parents, my brother Benny, and me.

Benny was going to be a junior at Greece Arcadia High School that fall, and I would be entering my freshman year at Cardinal Mooney High School. We did not know it at the time, but it would be the last summer vacation the four of us would spend together. My dad's health was in decline as high blood pressure and a few strokes had already disabled him from his job at Eastman Kodak Company, where he drove a bulldozer at the Weiland Road landfill in Greece. His disability, which began when I was in the fourth grade, confused me at first. I simply did not understand how he could go from *throwing* a baseball with me in the yard to *watching* us play. My brothers and I were actively playing on the front lawn, but now, my dad was a spectator from his new vantage point: a rocking chair in front of the living room picture window.

My father's physical and cognitive abilities were declining each year. During that

vacation in 1973, I was hoping the fish would bite on a lake I had never visited. As it turned out, they did. Benny and I competed all week long, keeping a tally of the bass we were catching, and often, our dad was there in the boat, smiling each time we would hook a fish. As the week wore on, however, I needed a baseball fix. I glanced at the local newspaper and told him that a New York–Pennsylvania League game was being played that night at Colburn Park in Newark. The hometown Newark Co-Pilots were playing the Elmira Pioneer Red Sox.

My dad did not even flinch at the request, and we were on our way to Newark.

The Co-Pilots starting shortstop that evening was a seventeen-year-old named Robin Yount, who would finish his first and only minor league season with a .285 batting average in 1973.[7] The next year, Yount made the quantum leap from the tiny Upstate New York village of Newark to County Stadium in Milwaukee, where he became the starting shortstop for the Milwaukee Brewers as an eighteen-year-old.

Twenty years later, here I was again, approaching Colburn Park on State Route 31 in Newark. Unfortunately, minor league baseball

---

7   Yount, Robin. *Baseball Reference.* "Robin Yount." 5 August 2024. https://www.baseball-reference.com/register/player.fcgi?id=yount-002rob

was not playing any longer in this small village alongside the Erie Canal. The marquee at the entrance to the park announced to passing motorists that a local rock-and-roll band was playing instead, the sign reading, "Sky Coasters, Here Tonight." Baseball was not playing tonight in Newark, but it was in seven cities across the New York–Pennsylvania League, and I was less than an hour away from one of them: Auburn, New York, home to the Auburn Astros.

Twenty minutes west of Syracuse at the north end of Owasco Lake sat the city of Auburn, home of a maximum-security New York State Prison, the Auburn Correctional Facility. Located on State Street just off the main thoroughfare of Routes 5 and 20, the prison was an

imposing site with tall, gray cinder block walls that rose among a residential and commercial section of the city. The prison was the site of the first execution in the world via electric chair when it happened to inmate William Kemmler on August 6, 1890.[8] Eleven years later in 1901, inmate Leon Czolgosz, the assassin of President William McKinley, was also executed by the electric chair.[9]

Sitting atop the apex of the turret at the front of the prison wall was a large statue of a Revolutionary War soldier named Copper John. The soldier stood at attention with a rifle and bayonet attached to his left arm. Copper John received its nickname when the original soldier, made from wood, became weatherworn and needed to be replaced. The new replica was made of copper at the prison foundry and given the nickname Copper John.

Minutes away from the prison, on a residential section of North Division Street, was another landmark in Auburn: Falcon Park, a rickety wooden grandstand built in 1927 and one of the oldest ballparks in the country. Falcon Park had seen better days, and the

---

8   Auburn Correctional Facility. Wikipedia, *The Free Encyclopedia.* "William Kemmler." 26 July 2024, https://en.wikipedia.org/wiki/Auburn_Correctional_Facility
9   Auburn Correctional Facility. Wikipedia, *The Free Encyclopedia.* "Leon Czolgosz." 26 July 2024, https://en.wikipedia.org/wiki/Auburn_Correctional_Facility

baseball fans of this city in Central New York would be best served if the park was leveled and replaced with a new one.

The history of baseball in Auburn included the nicknames of Yankees, Mets, Twins, Phillies, Sunsets, Red Stars, Americans, and, dating back to the 1982 season, the current name of Astros. Among the Auburn baseball alumni who went on to play in the major leagues are Jim Bouton, Cleon Jones, Ed Kranepool, Tug McGraw, Joe Pepitone, Mel Stottlemyre, Jim McAndrew, and Jerry Koosman.

One of the best eras of baseball in Auburn would be the period of 1962–66 when the team was affiliated with the New York Mets and brought home the New York–Pennsylvania

League championship three times, in 1962, '64, and '66. The ball club in 1966 was one of the best, finishing with a record of 80-49. Two of the top pitchers on the team were Jerry Koosman (12-7) and Jim McAndrew (11-7), who just three years later were both members of the Miracle Mets team that won the World Series in five games against the Baltimore Orioles.

Longtime Auburn Mets fans, however, might tell you that the ace of the '66 staff was neither Koosman nor McAndrew but instead a right-hander from Whittier, California, named Al Schmelz who had a 12-0 record and 2.23 earned run average. While Koosman and McAndrew would go on to pitch a combined twenty-six years in the major leagues, Schmelz was a September call-up to the Mets in 1967 when he pitched a combined total of three innings over two games and never pitched in the big leagues again.[10]

When I walked through the front gate at Falcon Park some two hours before opening night against the visiting Watertown Indians, my first glimpse at the park made me understand why residents there wanted a new ballpark. Falcon Park was comprised of two covered wooden grandstands, one of them behind home plate and another

---

10   1966 Auburn Mets. *Baseball Reference*. 5 August 2024. https://www.baseball-reference.com/register/team.cgi?id=901b96c4

adjacent to the first-base line. The fragmented configuration also included an uncovered set of wooden bleachers on the third-base side. Everything about the ballpark appeared old, run down, and in need of repair or replacement. The press box sat atop a set of steel girders behind the bleachers, resembled a game booth at an amusement park, and was large enough to house a public address announcer, official scorer, a writer and not much more.

The dugouts were as decrepit as the rest of the facility, built at field level and exceedingly small. I worked hard to find appealing characteristics and was able to do so when I discovered ivy hanging over the left-field fence and trees surrounding the ballpark at every angle. I was also attracted by the fact that the seating area was remarkably close to the playing field, giving the park an intimate feeling.

Long before the opening pitch, the entire first-base grandstand was vacant except for two elderly men. One of them was a man wearing glasses and a blue Auburn Astros warm-up jacket and cap. His eyes were focused with intensity on the playing field where the Watertown Indians were taking batting practice. I introduced myself to the man, sixty-three-year-old Bobby Cross, a member of the Auburn Astros Booster Club. My very first interview during the start of a summer-long journey of baseball at the lowest rung of the minor league ladder would later prove to be my shortest interview of all.

Cross was candid and brief with me when I inquired about his interest in the ball club, stating that he did not miss a game and had been coming here "a long time, every year."

Cross continued to observe batting practice while I introduced myself to the less intense and more sociable John A. Hermann of the Freeman Bus Corporation in Watertown. Hermann was the person responsible for transporting the Indians across the fourteen-city league from now through Labor Day. Hermann was wearing the blue company uniform with a tag on his chest bearing his name.

"I enjoy it," he said of his job driving the back roads of the bush leagues. "They're a nice bunch of kids. You see them go up to the bigs. I'm not good on remembering names, (but) Moises Alou is one."

During trips, Hermann said players would pass time by sleeping, reading books, listening to music, or playing cards. He said some players would get to know his name as the season progressed but that others would not.

"It doesn't bother me being called 'Bussie,' as long as they don't call me 'late for dinner,'" said Hermann.

During this visit to Auburn, the Indians were in town for just one game and would not be staying overnight. Schedules in the low minors, depending on the geography of the league, were arranged in a much different manner than higher levels of the minor leagues. Playing just one game in Auburn, the Indians left town afterward and saved money by not staying in a hotel. Instead, the Astros would get up early and depart for Watertown and the second game of a home-and-home series against the Indians at Duffy Fairgrounds.

When the schedule warranted the need for the ball club to stay overnight, the travel routine was very different.

"At 9:00 a.m. (the day after a game), I take the trainer to get the laundry done, then I clean the bus," said Hermann. "After that, I watch TV. You leave for the park at 4:00 p.m. We have a lot of idle time. That part, I don't enjoy so much."

Hermann said that his most important relationships were with the trainer and the manager.

"Jeff Cox, he seemed to look after me," Hermann said of the former Watertown manager of a few years ago when the team was affiliated with the Pittsburgh Pirates. "He ran a good ship with the players. The bus was always clean. I'm close to the trainer because I take him to the laundromat every day."

While I watched the Indians take their cuts during batting practice, I began to browse today's edition of the *Auburn Citizen* sports section that showed a picture of Nate Peterson, a twenty-two-year-old outfielder from Melbourne, Australia. Shortly thereafter, I had the opportunity to meet Peterson after he finished infield practice. On this first day of the regular season, Peterson was working alongside two other Auburn catchers. Baseball in America was not new to Peterson, who played his college ball at Fresno State. He spent the past winter playing in his home country, in the Australian Baseball League, but when comparing the game in both countries, there was no comparison.

"It's much more professional here," said Peterson. "Over there, you play three days per week and have a job. Even when I played at Fresno State, baseball was a full-time job."

The same Houston scout who saw Peterson as a prospect, Bob King, was in uniform tonight and working with the Auburn ball club as a traveling instructor for the next two weeks. King was Houston's West Coast scouting director, based out of California, and had spent parts of the past two years in the Land Down Under, researching the Australian Baseball League while combing the baseball diamonds across Australia in search of prospects. When King discovered Peterson, he liked what he saw in the left-handed hitter.

"It's a compact swing, and he uses the whole field," said King, who signed Peterson as a free agent the previous January. "We'd like to have a left-handed hitting catcher who can steal a base. You conceptualize these things to create a future." Transforming Peterson from an infielder to a catcher would be advantageous for the organization, because as King explained, left-handed hitting catchers were a commodity in the major leagues.

King and other major league scouts were spending more time in Australia, a land that he viewed as fertile ground for baseball prospects. "Baseball in Australia is exciting," said King. "They're really inspired to come over here. They've been playing other things. Cricket is the national pastime, but thousands of kids are playing T-ball. They have to fill the gap, and baseball can win that battle."

Peterson was happy to be back in the States playing the American version of baseball. But he also admitted to missing his family, Australian Rules Football, and meat pies, a pastry consisting of meat and gravy.

Thirty minutes before the start of the game, I knocked on a door located in the rear of the concession stand, the locker room for the umpiring crew. When the door opened and I introduced myself as a freelance writer, I was invited to enter by Shawn McAnally and his partner Mike Shields. There was barely enough room for a third person to be in the cramped quarters, but neither umpire seemed fazed at all by the conditions. Shields was busy tugging at his brand-new hat, bending the brim while trying to give shape to the dark blue cap that read "NY Penn" on the front. McAnally, meanwhile, was busy sitting in a chair in the corner of the room rubbing mud on a few dozen baseballs. This was a nightly ritual for professional baseball umpires across the country, a job responsibility of the home-plate umpire.

Among the two umpires, McAnally had more experience as he suited up for his second tour of duty in the league. The twenty-four-year-old from Philadelphia started umpiring high school baseball while attending college at Montclair State in New Jersey.

"I thought, this is something I wanted to do," said McAnally of his decision to become a professional umpire. "My first year in baseball was developmental. I feel like a better umpire. It should be that way every year."

His partner, Shields, a fellow Pennsylvanian, was twenty-three years old and a 1992 graduate from Grove City College, where he majored in marketing. Shields, a native of Pittsburgh, had experience umpiring Little League and high school baseball. He also had experience as a bank teller.

"In my junior year in college, I talked to a couple of ex–minor league umpires, and they talked me into it," said Shields. "I knew I wanted to be in baseball."

Shields listened to his gut instinct, and in January of 1993, he attended the Harry Wendelstedt Umpiring School in Daytona Beach, Florida. When school ended, he was among the few candidates selected to work minor league baseball for the 1993 season. His first taste of professional baseball came at extended spring training in Florida, an extra session of baseball for minor leaguers who broke camp without an assignment to a team within an organization. Instead, the prospects stayed at the minor league complex and played sixty to seventy games during the months of April and May, an experience that Shields said gave him the confidence he needed heading into tonight's opener.

The future of baseball in Auburn was mentioned during the pregame ceremonies when Auburn Astros president Mike Chamberlain, who headed the board of directors for the community-owned team, stood near home plate with microphone in hand, making a plea to the opening-night crowd of three thousand fans.

"Spend twenty-nine cents to write a letter to the mayor (Guy Cosentino) and tell him we want baseball in Auburn," said Chamberlain.

As the national anthem began to play over the public address system, two members of the local American Legion Post stood on the warning track in left field with an American flag in their hands. While the anthem played, the flag began to rise the pole on cue. But

halfway up the pole, the flag stopped rising, and the anthem continued to play. Watching this proceeding unfold from the concourse area behind the home plate screen was the Auburn general manager Derek Duin, who was in his second year running the show for the Auburn ball club. As the taped recording of the anthem ended, the flag was stuck halfway up the pole. Duin watched from afar with a look of distress, staring at the ground while placing his hand over his forehead. Hopefully, this was not a sign of what was to come at North Division Street during the summer of '93. For the Auburn faithful, last year was a season to forget when only 21,200 clicked the turnstiles to watch the Astros compile a dismal record of 32-41.[11]

Things could only get better a year later.

Out on the field, Nate Peterson's catching debut in an Auburn uniform would have to wait as Brett Callan took the warm-up pitches on this opening night from pitcher Kendall Rhine. First-year manager Manny Acta had penciled Peterson into the lineup as the designated hitter and had the Australian batting fifth in the order.

As Rhine was warming up, I was busy filling up a cardboard food holder at the concession stand behind home plate. Determined to be in my seat by the first pitch, I hurried toward the third-base bleachers while Rhine was getting his signs from Callan. Walking up the bleachers, I tripped over a steel girder that ran underneath the open-air plastic benches. I then braced myself after falling, leaving one leg dangling through the bleachers while spilling my soda all over my hamburger. It could have been worse had a nearby fan not grabbed me, preventing me from falling further through the crevices between the benches.

"That's going to smart," he said as we both glanced at my shin that was scraped and quickly turning a shade of purple.

"He's a reporter," snickered another fan.

I regrouped quickly, ate the soggy hamburger, and recorded a strikeout in my scorebook for Watertown leadoff hitter Rich Prieto.

The 1993 New York–Pennsylvania League season was underway.

The Indians went down in order in the first inning, as did the Astros in the bottom half against Watertown starter Craig Sides. In the second inning, Sides found himself in a jam when Auburn's Noel Rodriguez led off with a single and Peterson reached based on an error by Sides. Another error, this one by the second baseman Prieto,

---

11 1992 Auburn Astros. *Baseball Reference.* 5 August 2024, https://www.baseball-reference.com/register/league.cgi?id=408b8984

a balk, and a single by John Vindivich brought home Rodriguez and Peterson to give the Astros a 2-0 lead.

Through four complete innings, the Indians could not reach Rhine as the twenty-two-year-old from Liburn, Georgia, had not allowed a hit. The only batter to reach base was Bryan Garret in the third inning when he was hit by a pitch.

In the bottom of the fourth inning, Shields had his first close play of the young season, a bang-bang play at second base that from a distance was close enough to the casual observer to have gone either way, safe or out. Peterson was attempting to steal second base, and when the dust settled, Shields came up big with his arms extended in both directions, "selling" his safe call as Peterson slid under the tag, just beating the throw of Watertown catcher Bob Lewis.

Somewhere in the Auburn dugout, King had to be smiling about Peterson and his scouting report as a base-stealing threat.

Just behind me in the rear of the third-base bleachers, fans were so close to the elevated press box that I could hear the Auburn play-by-play radio announcer mention that he had a conversation with Rhine before the game and that the Astro starter had predicted he would throw a shutout. Rhine lost his shutout in the fifth when the Indians reached him for two runs on one hit, a walk, an error, and a wild pitch.

Midway through this game that was moving at a snail's pace through five innings, neither team seemed relaxed as a total of *seven* errors had already been committed, four by Watertown and three by Auburn.

"It's the first professional game for a lot of these guys," Acta would say later. "They're pressed, they have a crowd. It's always impressive, their first pro game."

The game was still tied, 2-2, entering the seventh inning, and Rhine had allowed just one hit. But his outing began to unravel when he walked Jeff Haag and then hit his second batter of the night, George Curtis, with two outs, causing Acta to go to the bullpen in favor of the nineteen-year-old left-hander Kevin Smith. Oddly enough, despite tossing a one-hitter through a total of six and two-thirds innings pitched, Rhine left the game without having a chance to get the win, but it was still possible he could be tagged with the loss.

As it turned out, Smith could not slam the door on the Watertown rally. He walked the bases loaded and then gave up back-to-back hits, a two-run single by Prieto, and a run-scoring double by Brian Lefevre, which put the Indians ahead 5-2. Just like that, the home team saw its starter exit the game with a one-hitter, and minutes later, the Astros were trailing by three runs.

During the seventh inning stretch, the traditional song at ballparks across America, "Take Me Out to the Ball Game," was replaced over the loudspeaker by John Denver's "Thank God I'm a Country Boy." The Auburn fans did not seem to mind, because as the song played, two middle-aged gentlemen, William Jayne and Nathaniel Burke, met in the aisle on the concourse of the home-plate grandstand and danced side-by-side with each other. The crowd loved it and began to clap along as the song and the dancing by the two fans was entertaining to the hometown fans.

The Astros scored twice in the home half of the seventh and were trailing 5-4 entering the bottom of the ninth inning. Rob Augustine was now pitching for the Indians, and with one out, he gave up a single to Masalis Basey, who then advanced to second base on a wild pitch and to third base on a passed ball. Steve Verduzco then struck out for the second out, and the Indians were one out away from winning the game. Augustine would not get the chance to finish it, because the Watertown manager Mike Young came out of the dugout and replaced him with his fourth reliever of the night, Dalton Dempsey.

The first batter Dempsey faced was Tim Forkner, who hit a ground ball to second base that was mishandled by Prieto, allowing Basey to score from third to tie the game at 5-5. Dempsey got Rodriguez to look at a third strike to end the inning, and as the game entered the tenth inning, the Indians now had more errors, a total of six, than runs scored.

In the bottom half of the tenth, the game was still tied, 5-5, when Peterson led off, still in search of his first professional hit. He was hitless in four at bats but had reached base three times on Watertown errors. Peterson would have to wait longer as he flew out to shortstop Curtis. Dan Graphenthien then followed with a walk and was replaced by pinch runner Edward Cedeno.

Vindivich came to the plate and reached base on the seventh Watertown error of the night, this time, it being the shortstop Curtis who booted a ball, advancing Cedeno to scoring position at second base. In an opening night highlighted by eleven combined errors for both teams and a parade of relief pitchers, Watertown manager Mike Young went to the bullpen again, bringing in reliever number five in the form of Roberto Garza. Callan greeted Garza with a double to score Cedeno, and the Astros gave a crowd of 2,889 a 6-5 win to start the season.

As I added up the numbers in my scorebook while seated in what was quickly becoming a vacant bleacher section, the numbers were not pretty: five runs, five hits, and seven errors for the Indians and six runs, eight hits, and four errors for the Astros. The game lasted three hours and ten minutes, partly due to the worn-out path from both bullpens as a total of eleven pitchers were used by the two teams.

The Auburn fans were going home happy, however, and as the stands emptied and the players exited the field, they all came together within one crowd in the concourse area between the home-plate grandstand and third-base bleachers. The players were trying to make their way to the cinder block clubhouse situated inside the front of the ballpark and the fans were moving toward to the street exits. Such a sight, fans and players walking together at the end of the game, was part of the allure of the minor leagues. The stands were so close to the field that you could almost reach out and touch the players during the game, and the fans *were* standing right next to the players while clustered together *after* the game.

In the Auburn clubhouse, Acta was answering questions from a local reporter while seated in a chair behind a desk in his office.

"It feels pretty good," said Acta of the opening-night win.

"It's always a pleasure," he continued, "to win the first game right out of the shoot. These guys showed me they've got some heart. If we lost, I'd still be happy. They never gave up."

I did not move quickly enough, however, to get commentary from Young, the Watertown manager, and his players.

The Indians were nowhere to be found in the visiting clubhouse as I entered. I could easily understand why the ball club opted to make the drive back to Watertown while wearing their uniforms. Inside the visiting clubhouse, the only attraction was the Coke machine. Several of the wooden lockers were destroyed, the shelving broken or in need of repair. In the bathroom, the lone sink was supported from below by a pair of wooden two-by-fours, and the shower room had wooden planks on top of the floor.

The Indians were already boarding the bus that Hermann had revved up, ready to head east on the New York State Thruway toward Syracuse and then north on Interstate 81 to Watertown, a drive that would take approximately two hours. Somewhere in between, Hermann would pull over so the players could eat a late-night meal.

Some players would stay awake, and others, according to Hermann, would fall asleep.

"When they're all asleep, I usually wake them up beforehand," said Hermann about his eventual arrival at Duffy Fairgrounds. "Usually, they have pillows in their hands."

Upon arrival in Watertown, Hermann says that the players will disperse into the night.

"They have cars, call cabs, or hitch rides," he says.

With the game over now for thirty minutes, I figured that Shields and McAnally had enough time to discuss their game from the umpiring perspective, so I gave a knock at the door to their locker room.

I was surprised to find two other New York–Pennsylvania League umpires visiting, because I did not envision the room being large enough to hold four people. The two-man crew had come to watch the game after opening their season during a day game earlier that day, just down the road at McDonough Park in Geneva. The four minor-league umpires were now trying to figure out where they would go to eat in Downtown Auburn.

"It's nice to see other umpires," commented Shields. "When you see the same person, day in and day out, you try to take advantage of this."

McAnally and Shields did not have a lot of time to discuss the game with me.

"If we didn't have another crew here, we'd like to talk," said McAnally.

The next day, the two umpires would travel in Shields' Saturn vehicle to another ballpark in another city, making their way through three states—New York, Pennsylvania, and Massachusetts—and the province of Ontario during a seventy-seven-game minor league journey. It would be Shields taking his turn at dipping his hands into the tin can of Delaware River mud tomorrow night while rubbing up dozens of baseballs in preparation for calling balls and strikes behind the plate, his professional debut as a home-plate umpire.

"I'll call home after my first plate appearance," he said. "Working the plate is what it's all about."

The journey began on June 17, 1993 at
Falcon Park in Auburn, NY.

John A. Hermann, Watertown Indians Bus
Driver, Opening Night in Auburn, NY.

Auburn Astros warming up on Opening Night.

Mike Shields, NY-P League Umpire on Opening Night in Auburn.

*Auburn fans watch Opening Night from
the Home Plate Grandstand.*

*(left to right) Umpire Mike Shields, Leo Pinckney, and Umpire
Shawn McAnally prepare for Opening Night in Auburn, NY.*

(left to right) Mike Shields, Auburn Manager Manny Acta (14), Watertown Manager Mike Young, and Shawn McAnally share lineup cards.

The Auburn Astros dugout on Opening Night

The Falcon Park Press Box

A view of the Falcon Park grandstands on Opening Night

CHAPTER TWO:

BASEBALL ON THE PENINSULA

June 18, 1993—Welland, Ontario, Canada

The following night, I found myself across the border in Ontario, Canada, navigating the Suzuki Samurai on Niagara Street, a busy strip in Welland lined with fast-food restaurants and stores. Away from the bustle and off the main drag was Quaker Road and the Welland Sports Complex, a facility dotted with recreational softball fields. At the rear of this expansive facility was Welland Stadium, home of the Welland Pirates.

As I entered the ballpark, everything about Welland Stadium and the surrounding area was exactly the opposite of Falcon Park in Auburn just twenty-four hours earlier. At the Welland Sports Complex, the parking lot was paved and exceptionally large. In Auburn, I parked on a gravel-covered lot across from the ballpark adjacent to some houses. There were no houses surrounding the ballpark in Welland—instead, several recreational softball diamonds that appeared to be better groomed than the playing field in Auburn.

The outside of Welland Stadium was neatly manicured with meticulously landscaped bushes in front of a brick façade at the stadium entrance. Inside, I stood on a paved concourse that was situated at the top of the seating area, a semicircle concrete bowl that contained silver aluminum bleachers wrapping around the playing field from the first base to third-base side. All the bleachers were the same, except for a small area directly behind the plate that had back supports. I would not have to worry about falling through bleachers in this ballpark as all the benches were attached to the concrete semicircle.

The ballpark shone and was clean as a whistle. A spacious press box, located at the very top of the concession stands, quickly caught my attention. I glanced inside the structure from where I stood on the concourse below and noticed a lengthy room with knotty pine paneling inside and enough room to house a large contingent of writers, radio crews, and television cameras.

The ballpark appeared brand new. Later, during the game, I discovered that there was so much space between the rows of benches that I could not even reach the bench in front of me while extending my legs. If Falcon Park was old, run down, decrepit, and in need of demolition, Welland Stadium was the exact opposite: new, clean, spacious, and shiny. Despite the comparison, however, it did not take me long to realize that I liked the facility in Auburn better. Falcon Park was a dump, but it had character. Welland Stadium glistened, but it was sterile. It simply did not have the "feel" of a ballpark. It was more than just the concrete bowl with the silver bleachers that did not do it for me. There was no roof above the seating area in Welland like there was in Auburn. I liked ballparks with a roof above the seats and had no problem with having my view of the field blocked by beams that support a grandstand rooftop.

My jaded thoughts about vantage-point obstructions were traced to my upbringing at Red Wing Stadium in Rochester. As a kid, depending on where I sat, I would lean to the left or right of the red steel girder a few rows in front of me to see the action on the field,

whether it was Freddie Beene in the middle of his windup or Al Bumbry shagging a fly ball in center field.

The open-air facility here in Welland must have posed an interesting dilemma for fans when the skies opened and the rain fell. Fans would either pop open their umbrellas or head to the exits. At places like Falcon Park, you would not have to move. When I was a kid watching games at Red Wing Stadium, a rain delay meant that it was time to watch the ground crew go to work while spreading the tarp over the infield. Benny and I would ride out the delay with our dad by looking at stat sheets, reading the program, and listening to the stories the radio announcer, Joe Cullinane, would share over the airwaves. The entire time, we were protected from the rain thanks to the roof that completely covered the general admission seats.

Tonight, would be the home opener for the Pirates after losing 8-2 last night at St. Catharines against the Blue Jays. A day later, St. Catharines made the twenty-minute commute on Route 406 to complete the home-and-home series to start the season.

An hour before the start of the game, the Blue Jays were on the field taking batting practice. Both teams were wearing uniforms that were exact replicas of their major-league affiliates, St. Catharines wearing road gray uniforms with "Blue Jays" written across the front on an arc. The scene resembled a spring training game because of the size of the ballpark and the major league replica uniforms being worn by the players.

Off to the side of the visiting dugout on the first base side, the St. Catharines trainer was busy giving a Blue Jays player a rub down on his right arm. I opened my Welland program, which had a picture of a black Welland hat and a rose resting atop some bats with the caption reading, "Welland Pirates—Fifth Anniversary." The roster sheet inside identified the player as catcher Joe Durso and the trainer as the twenty-nine-year-old Scott Shannon. I went down to the gate separating the grandstand from the playing field and introduced myself to the young trainer.

As Shannon and I began to talk, I learned that he was now in his fourth season as the St. Catharines trainer and his seventh in the Toronto organization. A native of Montreal, his career path had been intriguing, because unlike most trainers, he started at the top of the ladder in the major leagues with the Toronto Blue Jays instead of at the bottom of the ladder at Medicine Hat, Alberta, in the Pioneer League.

Shannon's big break came when he graduated from college and was working as a volunteer trainer for the Toronto Argonauts of the Canadian Football League during their spring camp in 1987. At that time, the Blue Jays trainer Tommy Craig needed extra help during home games. Fred Dunbar, the Argonauts trainer, mentioned Shannon's name, and just like that, Shannon's foot was suddenly in the door of major league baseball.

"Fred recommended me for the job," said Shannon. "Tommy (Craig) called me at 1:30 a.m. Somebody got hurt that night, Jeff Musselman. A batted ball hit him on the elbow, and Tommy needed some extra help."

Shannon jumped at the opportunity.

He was at the Blue Jays offices at Exhibition Stadium visiting with club officials later that day. "It was unbelievable," said Shannon. "I sat down with Pat Gillick (general manager), Gordon Ash (assistant general manager), and Craig. I had no clue I'd start that night."

Shannon worked for the Toronto ball club during home games for one season and part of another. Then, surprisingly, he was reassigned within the organization and sent to Medicine Hat in the Pioneer League. Just like that, Shannon had gone from the major leagues to baseball's port of entry, from riding charter flights to riding the buses between Great Falls, Montana, and Boise, Idaho. Shannon chose not to discuss the reasoning behind this assignment and did not seem bitter about having to go to the low minors after a taste of the major leagues.

"If I stay in St. Catharines five years, it doesn't bother me," said Shannon. "This is a great organization. I hear everybody talk, but nothing compares to the Toronto organization, from follow-ups in the winter to what goes on in the clubhouse."

As Shannon and I talked about the health of today's ballplayers, I wondered why so many players seemed to find their name in the agate print of the sports section under the category "Disabled List." Were the modern-era ballplayers less willing to play through injuries? I wondered. Did today's players seem to want to protect their minor injuries more often to protect their market value?

"Personally, back then, I don't think they had people to say that we need to shut you down for a while," said Shannon. "People are more aware today. Money is a factor. If you have a million-dollar athlete telling you he's sore, you have to go with what he tells you. It's like a racehorse. *These* horses, though, tell you when they have problems."

As tonight's opening pitch came closer, the pregame ceremonies on the field became more unique by the minute. A gate opened down the left-field line in foul territory where a pickup drove onto the field near third base. The tailgate opened and a series of exercise mats were placed on the field. Next, a group of young female gymnasts began doing a routine of flips and tumbles while music blared through the loudspeakers. A sparse crowd sat and watched, and when the routine ended, the mats and the gymnasts left the field. What exactly this routine had to do with the start of the fifth season of Welland Pirates baseball, I did not understand.

Next, a group of local high school cheerleaders came out on the field in front of home plate with yellow pom-poms and three placards. Their short cheer concluded when they held up the placards that read, "Go, Fight, Pirates."

Members of the Royal Canadian Mounted Police came out onto the field for the playing of the national anthem. The RCMP looked sharp in their bright-red jackets, shiny black boots, and brown hats. They held the red-and-white Canadian flag with the maple leaf in the center and were very professional while marching in unison to honor the country's anthem and colors.

Welland mayor Jon Richard Reuter threw out one of the ceremonial pitches, and Welland native Paul Beeston, the vice president of the Toronto Blue Jays, threw out the other. Beeston is the answer to the following trivia question: Who was the first employee ever hired by the Toronto Blue Jays? It was Beeston, who had been with the ball club since its inception as an expansion franchise in 1977. Two things stood out about Beeston that I noticed while he was walking off the field and toward a gate down in front of me: he had two exceedingly long cigars in his front shirt pocket, and he was not wearing socks. I suppose when you are the president of the 1992 World Series Champions, whether you wore socks did not necessarily matter.

Beeston was immediately approached by a TV crew when he came off the field, not a local television sports crew, but instead an independent firm called Ballpark Pictures, a group that was filming a documentary about the St. Catharines Blue Jays. The producer was a man named Peter Raymount, and his crew was already in St. Catharines for last night's opener at Community Park. I was told that the crew would follow the ball club around the league throughout the season with plans to air the documentary in the fall on the Canadian Broadcasting Company.

St. Catharines was managed by J. J. Cannon, a former major league outfielder who played two years with the Houston Astros and two more with the Blue Jays. Cannon, whose initials stood for Joseph Jerome, played his best season in the minor leagues in 1978 with the Charleston Charlies of the Triple-A International League. He hit .306 and stole thirty-nine bases, and the Charlies won the Governors' Cup, the trophy that was presented to the winning team in the four-team postseason playoffs. His numbers in the majors, however, were not the same. His career batting average over four seasons was .176.[12]

---

12   Cannon, Joe. Wikipedia, *The Free Encyclopedia.* "Joe Cannon." 5 July 2024, https://en.wikipedia.org/wiki/Joe_Cannon_(baseball)

In 1983, Cannon entered the coaching ranks within the Blue Jays organization when he was named player-coach at Kinston of the Class A Carolina League. He spent the next seven seasons as a coach at Knoxville in the Class AA Southern League and made his managerial debut at St. Catharines last season while posting a 33-42 record.[13]

The pregame ceremonies now completed, the game began with two scoreless innings before the Blue Jays scored three runs in the third inning, two of them coming off a single by Sean Hearn. The third hitter in the Blue Jays lineup, Hearn was an imposing figure, standing at 6'3" and weighing two hundred pounds. The twenty-two-year-old Hearn played his first year of professional baseball at Medicine Hat in 1992 where he played in only thirty-five games and compiled a .217 batting average with one home run and five runs batted in.[14] Hearn drove in three runs during last night's opener, and now in his sixth at bat of the season, he already had five runs batted in, matching his season total from a year ago.

The circus atmosphere appeared to be a common marketing theme as the game progressed at Welland Stadium. Vendors walked through the stands selling food and beverages while wearing clown costumes. Count Dracula was selling cotton candy, and over on the first-base side, a court jester was hawking Coca-Cola. During the top of the eighth inning, a cake was lit with candles and brought to the top of the Welland dugout where a woman led fans in singing "Happy Birthday" to celebrate the franchise's fifth season in the league.

The Blue Jays would receive an impressive outing from their pitchers tonight, starter Alonso Beltran giving up just one run on three consecutive hits in the sixth inning and reliever Jay Maldonado throwing two innings of shutout baseball in the seventh and eighth

---

13   1992 St. Catharines Blue Jays. *Stats Crew*. (2024). https://www.statscrew.com/minorbaseball/roster/t-sj14711/y-1992

14   Hearn, Sean. *Baseball Reference.* "Sean Hearn." 5 August 2024 https://www.baseball-reference.com/register/player.fcgi?id=hearn-002sea

innings. In the ninth, Dilson Torres retired the Pirates, and the Blue Jays won 6-1. Maldonado picked up in 1993 where he left off just one year ago, recording a perfect 0.00 Earned Run Average in sixteen innings pitched in the Class A Gulf Coast League.

Just like at Falcon Park in Auburn last night, the players on both ball clubs tonight would have to disperse from the field and into a crowd of spectators to make their way to their respective clubhouses. At Welland Stadium, this route consisted of players leaving the dugouts and climbing the steps in the aisle past fifteen rows of aluminum bleachers to the clubhouses situated adjacent to the concession stands on the third-base concourse. Most of the Blue Jays had quickly entered the visitor's clubhouse, a spacious, clean facility and quite different from the broken-down facility at Auburn Park last night that had the busted locker stalls. Some of the Blue Jays were still among the crowd in the concourse area when the trainer Shannon emerged from the clubhouse and signaled for them to enter the room where their manager Cannon was waiting.

Shannon informed me later that Cannon conducted brief meetings with his ball club after every game of the season, win or lose. He talked about various aspects of the game while trying to focus on situations that needed to be addressed.

"The meetings usually aren't long, especially after a win," said Shannon. "The meeting gives them something to think about on the bus ride home."

The Blue Jays' bus was parked just outside the gate by the clubhouse and already warming up, the side compartments wide open and awaiting the deposit of equipment bags. Only ten minutes after Shannon had closed the door to the visiting clubhouse, the doors opened, and the Blue Jays were ready to depart for the short trip down Route 406. Each player seemed in a hurry as they exited, walking briskly out the door and toward the bus while carrying their own duffel bags, a customary practice in the minor leagues. Within minutes, the compartment doors were closed, and the bus rolled out

of the parking lot. There was no time to talk to Cannon or any of his players. I will catch up with the team tomorrow when I visited Community Park, where the Blue Jays were scheduled to play the Batavia Clippers in a Saturday-night game.

June 19, 1993—St. Catharines, Ontario, Canada

During my first overnight of the season, I opted for the accommodation of my domed Eureka Tent at Four Mile Creek Campground near the banks of the Niagara River in Youngstown, New York. I spent most of the morning and afternoon updating my journal from the night before and was in and out of the tent due to the rain that was off and on throughout much of the day. The voices of Tom Cheek and Jerry Howarth, the radio play-by-play announcers of the Toronto Blue Jays, kept me company throughout the afternoon hours, my transistor radio tuned into CJRN Radio 710 AM out of Niagara Falls, Ontario, for the broadcast of the game against the Boston Red Sox. Both Cheek and Howarth worked magic together over the airwaves: excellent voices, eloquent deliveries, good humor, and most of all, neither one of them was what I referred to as a "homer," an announcer who called the game as if he was a fan while watching from a bar stool. Cheek had been with the ball club since its inception in 1977 after being a swing man announcer for the Montreal Expos while commuting from his home in Burlington, Vermont.

There was more about Cheek that I knew, however, and it had nothing to do with his skills as a broadcaster. I had tremendous respect for the Blue Jays announcer after I met him while job-hunting for a radio play-by-play job in the minors at the baseball winter meetings at Houston in 1984. I was working as a weekend TV sports anchor at KTSM-TV in El Paso at the time, and when the winter meetings came to Houston in December, I was on a flight with my briefcase and audition tapes in hand, dreaming of becoming a baseball radio play-by-play announcer. Cheek was among the baseball personnel

I met during my visit, and I was immediately impressed with how humble he was and that he took the time to give me advice on how to pursue a play-by-play career. Just like the winter meetings of 1981 in Hollywood, Florida, I left Houston without any job prospects. I stayed in touch with Cheek, and when I relocated to New York State the following year, I met him again at Exhibition Stadium in 1985. The Knoxville Blue Jays of the Class AA Southern League had a radio opening for the 1986 season, and the ball club was owned by the parent Blue Jays. I had an interview with executives of the Knoxville ball club, and before the game, I was able to visit Cheek in his broadcast booth at Exhibition Stadium. Once again, Cheek was as congenial and supportive as one could expect, especially considering he was busy preparing to announce a ball game. In the end, the job offer never came from Knoxville, but I appreciated Cheek's hospitality and encouragement.

Now, eight years later, I thought it was ironic that when I walked into the clubhouse at Community Park in St. Catharines today, one of the first players I met was Jeff Cheek, Tom Cheek's son, a St. Catharines relief pitcher who was in his second season with the organization.

Community Park was located off Seymour Avenue on Merritt Street, adjacent to Merritton High School where the classroom windows looked dangerously close and within striking distance of foul balls. Near the front gate to the ballpark at the corner of Seymour and Merritt was the Merritton Lawn Bowling Club, where elderly men wearing white shirts and white pants rolled bocce balls over lush rectangular strips of low-cut grass.

As I was walking toward the front gate of the park, I heard a voice call out to me and noticed that it was Chad Brown, a left-handed relief pitcher for the Blue Jays, who was in street clothes and walking toward the clubhouse as well. I met him briefly last night before the game in Welland when he was badgering me to interview David Pearlman, his roommate last year with the Gulf Coast Blue

Jays. Brown was staring at the men in the white outfits at the lawn bowling club while we walked through the front gate to the ballpark.

"They're doing that again," he said, shaking his head in disbelief at the game of lawn bowling. "I'd rather roll marbles."

My third ballpark in three days, Community Park had a playing field that looked as lush as the grass at the lawn bowling club next door. I did not notice a single brown spot on the entire field. As for the seating area, it was nothing spectacular, just three sets of separated aluminum bleachers, one behind the plate and two more along the first- and third-base sides. The seating arrangement there was different than Welland. The ballpark was comprised of aluminum bleachers you would see at a high school field, the kind supported by girders with no roof overhanging the seating area. At best, the ballpark was a makeshift arrangement of three bleachers surrounding a very green field.

One small concession stand sat inside the front gate adjacent to a large barbecue pit. It was hours before game time, and all was quiet at Community Park. I walked into the clubhouse and there were two players with the trainer Shannon. Brown was one of the players, and he introduced me to the other.

"This is Jeff Cheek," Brown said. "His father announces the Blue Jays games."

Here I was in this tiny clubhouse of the St. Catharines Blue Jays, nine years after meeting Tom Cheek at the Houston winter meetings in 1984, now introduced to his son, Jeff, a Blue Jays farmhand in his second season with the organization.

The younger Cheek was lying down on the trainer's table at the end of the clubhouse wearing a pair of shorts, a T-shirt, and shower sandals. He stood six feet tall, weighed 195 pounds, and was seven days away from his twenty-third birthday. While his age may have seemed young, it was considered slightly old by Class A minor league standards.

Cheek signed last June with the Blue Jays and appeared in twelve games at the organization's port of entry, its Gulf Coast League team in Florida where he was 4-4 with a 2.30 earned run average.[15] Today, while sitting on the trainer's table, he was watching golf, the third round of the US Open from Baltusrol Golf Club in Springfield Township, New Jersey. Interestingly, the volume of the television set was mute. While Cheek watched the golf on TV, he was also listening to the radio, his father's broadcast of the last few innings of the Blue Jays vs. Red Sox game that I was following back at the campground.

"It was great growing up," said Cheek. "Before the rule about kids in the clubhouse, I'd poke around in there. It was as if I had a coach at the calling: Buck Martinez, Sully (John Sullivan), Al Widmar. That was a big thrill, and over the years, I learned to love it. During the summer, I'd go to a lot of games. I'd get to be bat boy or shag flies during batting practice."

Getting into the booth alongside his dad, however, was not as easy.

"I used to have to beg him to let me in the booth," said Cheek. "At Exhibition Stadium, there was only room for him, Jerry Howarth, and Early Wynn. I'd get up there as much as I could. I enjoy watching him and the writers work. I have respect for what he and the others do. It's a long day and a hard job. It helped me pick my major. If baseball doesn't work out, it (the media) intrigues me. I like sports journalism. I can't just walk into it, being the son of Tom Cheek. You have to have talent for it. I'd be stupid to say his association with the Blue Jays hasn't helped me. Sometimes, I wish someone else would've picked me up, but I think I have some merits. I want to think they saw a little bit of talent in me."

Right now, a career in broadcasting was not the top priority for the younger Cheek. Instead, making it to the big leagues was the

---

15   Cheek, Jeff. *Baseball Reference*. "Jeff Cheek." 5 August 2024, https://www.baseball-reference.com/register/player.fcgi?id=cheek-001jef

goal, and if it were to happen with the Blue Jays, it would be a dream come true for the entire family.

"That would be the ultimate for my dad, me, and the family," said Cheek. "That would be the greatest scenario. I'll stick it out until they say I can't play anymore."

To date, Tom Cheek had yet to see Jeff Cheek pitch in a professional game due to his 162-game broadcasting schedule. But father and son stayed connected, and it did not take long for the elder Cheek to learn that Jeff had been thrown out of a game last season in the Gulf Coast League.

"There was a message on my machine," said Cheek, "(He said) if you're going to be a bench jockey, there is an art to it. That was him calling from Minnesota. He finds out things quickly."

Sitting nearby in the St. Catharines clubhouse was Brown, who had been keeping busy by doing arm curls with a hammer.

"The hammer is for the elbow," he said. "It strengthens the muscles and ligaments in the elbow."

Brown spent his first year of minor league baseball in Medicine Hat, Alberta, in the Pioneer League, where the bus trips were long. Lethbridge was the only other team located in Alberta, and four of the teams—Helena, Butte, Great Falls, and Billings—were in Montana.

"That was the biggest thing, getting used to the travel," said Brown. "The bus trips get to you after a while. Fourteen hours to Salt Lake City and not getting off the bus—it kills you. They had a TV with a VCR and you'd listen to your music. Or you'd play cards and tell jokes: some stupid, some funny and some not. It was hard to sleep. People slept on the floor. It takes a toll on you.

"Medicine Hat was culture shock. I'm used to living where everything is close together. This is a big difference (in St. Catharines), a population of 120,000. Medicine Hat was only 30,000. In Medicine Hat, there were a lot of bugs. The mosquitoes there were bad."

Brown told me that his father played minor league baseball as well, in the 1960s with the Pirates, but that his career ended when a ligament in his elbow popped, causing his arm to blow. Coincidentally, while Brown was telling the story about the injury causing the demise of his dad's career, he was curling that hammer to strengthen his own elbow.

It became obvious, looking out the clubhouse door, that there would be no batting practice before tonight's game due to the wet grounds from the steady rain earlier today. Several bags of dirt were being applied at various parts of the ballpark, particularly in the Blue Jays' bullpen down in the right-field corner. The Blue Jays' pitching coach was Reggie Cleveland, a former big-league pitcher who spent thirteen years in the major leagues, including a start in Game Five of the 1975 World Series for the Boston Red Sox.[16]

Today, here was Cleveland talking with Greg Taylor, a member of the grounds crew, while expressing his disappointment over finding so much new dirt on the bullpen pitching mounds.

"You should have just left it," Cleveland told Taylor. "If you were going to put the Diamond Dry on, you should have done it at 8:00 a.m. A player gets hurt, then the Blue Jays find out. They tell JJ, then he tells me, and I tell you."

Cleveland was not the least bit happy with the maintenance of the bullpen mounds, because the additional amounts of dirt had not made for a good blend with the already-wet surface. The young groundskeeper, Taylor, listened carefully to Cleveland and then commented to me, "Well, at least I found out now instead of later in the season."

Cleveland and I spoke while standing in the right-field corner as his pitchers ran the foul poles from right field to left field, and back again, while staying on the warning track.

---

16   Cleveland, Reggie. Wikipedia, *The Free Encyclopedia*. "Reggie Cleveland." 9 July 2024, https://en.wikipedia.org/wiki/Reggie_Cleveland

"We run the poles, foul line to foul line," he said. "They run fourteen poles followed by a half-dozen sprints to stretch the muscles."

The native of Moose Jaw, Alberta, and the first Canadian pitcher to start a World Series game when he threw against the Cincinnati Reds in 1975, Cleveland explained to me his disdain for the mismanagement of the bullpen mounds.

"I need those mounds serviceable," he said. "Six guys need to throw. I sunk my ankles trying to pitch off it."

The way Cleveland explained it, when a starter pitches his turn in the rotation, he takes the next day off and throws the following day for ten minutes. The pitcher rests the next two days and takes his start again on the fifth day. When the mounds are not available due to the conditions, it creates a glitch in the routine.

"Over 125 years of baseball, that's the best way," said Cleveland. "Today, they know of more injuries. With the money involved, you can't afford to have a guy get out. They have to pay him. If he goes down, they pay him and the guy you bring in. The legs are very important.

If you throw 120 pitches over nine innings, see how your legs feel. They feel like rubber, and they quiver from pushing off the mound and landing."

As Cleveland emphasized his point, that was where the running came into play and the need for his pitchers to be running the foul poles daily.

Game time was approaching on "Mr. Sub Night" at Community Park, and two Blue Jays players were stationed at the entrances to the ballpark where the first one thousand fans entering would receive a free vinyl duffel bag sponsored by the Canadian sub shop.

I made my way to the press box, a small wooden structure located above the fifteenth row of home-plate aluminum bleachers, where I met Chris Jeanneret, who was getting ready to broadcast the play-by-play of tonight's game for the Blue Jays. He informed me that tonight was his first-ever broadcast of a professional baseball game that would be carried over the airwaves of CJRN Radio, the same station that carried the Blue Jays–Red Sox game earlier in the day. Jeanneret was the son of the legendary Rick Jeanneret, who had been the hockey radio broadcaster for the Buffalo Sabres since the 1971–72 season.[17] Within the past two hours, I had now met the sons of two of the best radio play-by-play announcers in professional baseball and hockey.

Sitting to my immediate right in press row was the young A. J. McKay, a reporter for CHSC Radio in St. Catharines. McKay had a portable phone and a stat sheet that he would use to call live reports as the game progressed. He told me that his assignment was extra duty for the station, where he worked as program director and disc jockey.

"I don't even get a day off," said McKay. "If I could get it so I work less than sixteen hours (per day), I'd be happy. I can't complain. I celebrate my one-year wedding anniversary tomorrow, and I have a job."

The start of tonight's game was delayed for a few minutes, because the ground crew was still adding more dirt to various wet spots around the infield. Then when the game started, a slight mist began to fall, and the idea of playing a complete game tonight seemed to be questionable. Later, in the fifth inning, with Batavia leading by a score of 3-1, the light mist suddenly changed to a downpour, causing two things to happen: the fans began to vacate the ballpark because there was no roof above the bleachers, and puddles formed quickly across the infield since there was no tarp to cover it. The umpires called for a rain delay, but the process had little promise without a tarp. Some of the diehard fans stuck around, waiting under the bleachers, but there was little relief to be offered, because they were still getting wet from the rain making its way through the cracks in the bleachers.

17　Jeanneret, Rick. Wikipedia, *The Free Encyclopedia*. "Rick Jeanneret." 1 February 2024, https://en.wikipedia.org/wiki/Rick_Jeanneret

Back in the press box, McKay had already sent in a voicer to the radio station, telling the CHSC Radio listeners that the game had been delayed by rain. Next, he made a second call, this one to his wife, informing her that he may have been coming home sooner rather than later as the prospects of a cancellation seemed imminent. Moments later, Ellen Harrigan Charles, the St. Catharines general manager, who was soaking wet, climbed the steps to the press box and made the following announcement to the small press contingent: "Unofficially, the game is suspended, and will be continued from this point on July 3. It will start at 7:05 p.m., and the next game will follow. I can't bump this game back earlier, because I have a promotion scheduled for 6:00 p.m."

A few moments later, the two umpires made an appearance on the field and were examining the numerous puddles that had formed on the infield dirt. Both managers, Cannon and Al LeBouf, stood with the umpires as a signal was made to the press box, a gesture that officially made the contest a suspended game.

On cue, McKay then called the radio station for his final voicer of the night. When he completed the report, he turned off his phone, got up from his chair, and prepared to leave the press box.

"Time to get some sleep," he said.

June 20, 1993—Niagara Falls, New York

Today was getaway day for me as the stakes came out of the ground and the tent was folded up at Four Mile Creek Campground in Youngstown. I would attend the 6:00 p.m. ball game tonight between the Niagara Falls Rapids and Jamestown Expos, and there would be enough time to pass between now and then. With the lunch hour approaching, this meant only one thing for sure: a visit to the Press Box Lounge for some of the finest food in Niagara Falls.

As a former student at Niagara University from 1977–79, my friends and I would make occasional visits to the Press Box to wrap our hands around one of the largest hamburgers I have ever held. The restaurant was nothing more than a no-frills, seedy, hole-in-the-wall. But once inside, the food, especially the size of the helpings, did not disappoint.

The Press Box was located on Niagara Street a few doors down from the offices of the *Niagara Gazette* and across the street from the convention center. Not more than a mile away was the Rainbow Bridge and the historic Niagara Falls. Judging from the outside, a tourist would continue walking past this restaurant with absolutely no reason at all to be curious about this local eatery. But those who knew better would be sure to stop in for a hearty meal, and that was what I did by entering an establishment that appeared frozen in time from when I last entered in the late 1970s.

The walls were covered with paper currency from both the United States and Canada with the signatures of the patrons written on the respective bills. The ordering process was still the same as it was fourteen years ago, and wanting to act like I knew exactly what I was doing, I went straight to the kitchen in the back of the restaurant where I wrote my order on a pad. Most curious about this process was that the pad was located on a counter right next to where the cooks were cooking and where the servers were chopping up lettuce for salad bowls. I was amazed at the low, reasonable prices and wondered how much they had changed, if at all, since 1979. I ordered the famous Pittsburgher, the large hamburger that included a mammoth piece of ground beef with bacon, cheese, lettuce, and tomato for just two dollars and an order of French fries for eighty cents. Upon placing my order, I found myself a seat at one of only ten small tables that were situated in the tight confines of the restaurant.

I immediately noticed that the elderly woman who always wore a black dress with black shoes and sat at a table right in front of the kitchen door was not in her familiar place as she was when I visited during my college days. As a student, I did not know if she was the owner, cook, or manager. I only knew that I could count on her being at that table, usually with a dog at her feet while counting money right among the patrons. My curiosity led me to inquire with a young busboy, who had no idea about the person I mentioned. A nearby waitress, however, overhead the conversation and jumped right in to provide me an update.

"That's my great-grandmother Mary," she said. "She died a few years ago at the age of ninety-three."

When I walked out of the Press Box, I knew that my dinner would not have to come until a late hour, because I was stuffed by having finished the famous Pittsburgher and was barely able to have room for the fries.

Sal Maglie Stadium, home to the Niagara Falls Rapids, was in Hyde Park, a large park on the east side of the city right off Hyde Park Boulevard. The park included picnic areas, a golf course, a swimming pool, the ballpark, and a large water fountain that had attracted several youngsters on this hot June afternoon. It seemed odd that the kids needed to use the fountain to stay cool while the large swimming pool, located directly in front of the ballpark, sat empty with just a small puddle of rainwater in the deep end.

Inside the main entrance to the ballpark was a barber's chair and pole, a shrine to the city's famous son, Sal "the Barber" Maglie, a major league pitcher who earned his nickname for his numerous brushback pitches in the 1950s for the New York Giants. They called him the Barber because those high and inside fastballs were known to have given batters a close shave.

The inside of the ballpark was just as strange looking as on the outside. Based on the appearance of the long, brown, cement grandstand that did not wrap around the diamond, it was obvious that the facility was built for football and not baseball. A chain-link fence had been extended from the grandstand down each foul line, and fans were permitted to stand alongside it during the game, giving them a closer view of the action than those who were sitting in the far-removed grandstand. The dugouts looked like bunkers dug into the walls of the grandstand with a walkway leading to clubhouses that upon inspection were decrepit and in need of repair. Later, during the game, *Niagara Gazette* writer Ken Fox informed me that "the Rapids' clubhouse leaks like a sieve when it rains."

If there were any positive attributes of the home ballpark for the Detroit Tigers' entry in the New York–Pennsylvania League, they would be the playing field and the press box. The field looked immaculate, and the press box was large enough to hold twenty or more people.

The manager of the Rapids was Larry Parrish, a former third baseman and outfielder who spent fifteen years playing in the major leagues, most of that time spent with the Montreal Expos and the Texas Rangers. The husky six-foot-three Parrish hit 256 home runs during his major league career.[18] I found him prior to the game wearing sweat shorts and a white T-shirt with a Detroit Tigers logo. Parrish was talking to Tim Torricelli, the twenty-eight-year-old manager of the Jamestown Expos, a former minor league catcher who spent four years in the Milwaukee organization. Torricelli had the look of a catcher, standing at just five-foot-eight and weighing 175 pounds.[19]

During this Father's Day afternoon, Parrish took time to reflect about his own dad, Alton Parrish, while growing up in Winter Haven, Florida, the spring home of the Boston Red Sox. As Parrish told the story, his dad would take him to spring training games in Winter Haven and throughout the state of Florida.

"My team was the Yankees in the 1950s," said Parrish. "They were the best team—Yogi Berra, Mickey Mantle, Moose Skowron. I remember guys that did not even play because I kept their stats: Phil

18   Parrish, Larry. Wikipedia, *The Free Encyclopedia*. "Larry Parrish." 20 July 2024, https://en.wikipedia.org/wiki/Larry_Parrish

19   Torricelli, Tim. *Baseball Reference*. "Tim Torricelli." 5 August 2024, https://www. baseball-reference.com/register/player.fcgi?id=torric001tim

Linz, Johnny Blanchard, Hector Lopez, they'd come off the bench. Blanchard hit about twenty home runs as a third string catcher in the early 1960s. I used to follow them every day in the paper. If you wanted to know what Bobby Richardson was hitting, I could tell you."

Parrish kept accurate statistics. My visit to the baseball encyclopedia later would show that Blanchard hit twenty-one home runs in only ninety-three games as a backup catcher for the Yankees in 1961.

As a kid, it was more than just keeping the statistics of his beloved Yankees: Parrish had dreams of playing in the major leagues, and his father supported his aspirations.

"He never was too tired to go out and hit me ground balls and give me a chance to hit," recalled Parrish. "He expected me to play hard and play hurt. My dad wasn't too big on mechanics. He used to say, 'Hey, just get comfortable. See it and rip it.'"

When Parrish was playing with Montreal, his dad made the trip from Florida to Atlanta one day to watch his son when the Expos were in town. The younger Parrish was certainly comfortable at the plate on that day. He saw it and he ripped it, clubbing three home runs in one game while driving in seven runs.

Parrish was a dad himself, and his family was in attendance for today's game. His wife Jenny and daughters Amanda and Jessica were in the grandstand while his son Josh was close to his side, working as the batboy for the Rapids.

Parrish's most productive season was in 1979 with the Expos when he batted .307 with thirty home runs and eighty-two runs batted in. He was picked up by the Boston Red Sox during a pennant drive in 1988 and played in the American League Championship Series before being eliminated by the Oakland Athletics. The playoff experience marked the end of his playing career in the majors, a fifteen-year stretch that began at age twenty and included a .263 batting average along with those 256 home runs. The following year, in 1989, Parrish and his family packed their bags for Japan, where he played the next two seasons in the Japanese Central League with the

Yakult Swallows and Hanshin Tigers.[20] When he joined the Hanshin Tigers before the 1990 season, he filled the roster spot that had been vacated by Cecil Fielder, who moved back to the States to play for the Tigers of Detroit following a one-year hiatus from the major leagues. Fielder returned with a bang, belting fifty-one home runs and driving in 132 home runs, numbers that paled in comparison to his previous high of fourteen home runs and thirty-two runs batted in for the Toronto Blue Jays in a part-time role in 1987.[21]

"The kids went to school there," Jenny Parrish said of the two-year stay in Japan. "The language was the toughest part. We got used to the food. I missed it when we got back here."

Jenny Parrish met her husband while he was playing in the major leagues. When she came to Sal Maglie Stadium last season during Larry's debut season as manager of the Rapids, it was her first taste of life in the minor leagues.

"I missed baseball a bit when he retired," she said while pulling money from her purse so her four-year-old daughter Amanda and her twelve-year-old Jessica could visit the concession stand to buy ice cream. "It's hard for the children because of their ages. They're into activities, but it's nice to get away from the heat in Florida."

After the LaSalle Middle School band played the national anthem, the Rapids were off and running. They played an aggressive brand of baseball under Parrish, stealing five bases on the night and riding the strong pitching of starter Brian Moehler and relievers David Rodriguez and Rod Jackson. Moehler gave up just two hits through five innings while the two relievers spread out just three more hits across the remaining four innings in a 6-1 win for the home team.

---

20   Parrish, Larry. Wikipedia, *The Free Encyclopedia*. "Larry Parrish." 20 July 2024, https://en.wikipedia.org/wiki/Larry_Parrish

21   Fielder, Cecil. Wikipedia, *The Free Encyclopedia*. "Cecil Fielder." 30 July 2024, https://en.wikipedia.org/wiki/Cecil_Fielder

During the game, I was amused at the public address announcer Doug Smith, who on occasion would add commentary over the loudspeakers based on what was happening on the field. For example, when a batter drew a walk, Smith added the comment, "Base on balls," so that the sparse crowd of 878 fans could be reassured of what was happening when the count reached ball four.

The game also included the event I had hoped for since the opening pitch: a foul ball landing in the swimming pool. With windows in the back of the press box, I could keep watch on this event when balls would go flying over our booth. The moment I had been waiting for occurred in the top of the seventh inning when Jorge Moreno of the Rapids was at the plate. Moreno lofted a ball over the press box that landed in the shallow end of the vacant pool and proceeded to roll down the sloped cement to the deep end. Soon thereafter, a fan climbed the fence outside the pool to give chase to the souvenir. It was an amusing sight to watch the fan climb down the ladder into the empty pool and then walk into the deepest part of the pool to retrieve the ball.

"They fill it later in the summer," said Fox. "Right now, it catches foul balls."

Welland Stadium, Ontario Canada – Opening Night, 1993

Paul Beeston (center), Toronto Blue Jays Vice President

Scott Shannon, St. Catharines Blue Jays Trainer

*St. Catharines ballplayers relax among fans
in the grandstand, Welland Stadium.*

*Welland ballplayers relax among fans in
the grandstand, Welland Stadium.*

*The aluminum grandstands of Community
Park, St. Catharines, Ontario Canada*

Young Blue Jays fans prior to a game in St. Catharines

St. Catharines Pitching Coach Reggie Cleveland (40), the first Canadian to be the starting pitcher in a World Series.

St. Catharines Manager JJ Cannon (20)
is surrounded by his Blue Jays.

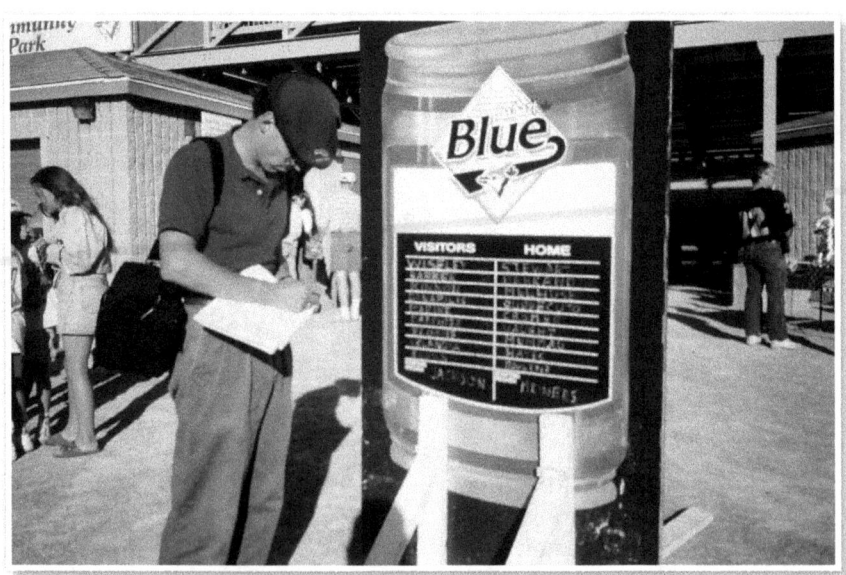

The Author writes the lineups in his scorebook
prior to a game in St. Catharines.

Reggie Cleveland discusses the conditions of the Community Park bullpen with members of the grounds crew.

St. Catharines relief pitchers Chad Brown (left) and Jeff Cheek relax before a game in the home clubhouse.

The pup tent provided me with my lodging at
Four Mile Creek Campsite, Youngstown, NY.

My cot provided me comfort in the pup
tent at Four Mile Creek Campsite.

Sal Maglie Stadium in Hyde Park is named after the Niagara Falls native who played in the Major Leagues.

Larry Parrish is the manager of the Niagara Falls Rapids

A Jamestown Expos player takes his cuts in the batting cage.

Players from Jamestown and Niagara Falls converse prior to a game on June 20, 1993.

CHAPTER THREE:

GEORGE LEVERING, THE TRAVELING MAN

June 23, 1993—Geneva, New York

At the very north end of Seneca Lake in the Finger Lakes region of New York State was the city of Geneva, a resort area that was the home to Hobart and William Smith Colleges, and as the sign indicates when entering the city, "the Lake Trout Capital of the World." Seneca Lake was host to the National Lake Trout Derby; an annual event held on Memorial Day weekend. Seneca Lake was the largest of the Finger Lakes, a group of lakes that stretched across the western-central region of the state between Rochester and Syracuse. The name came from the layout of the lakes, some small, others large, but when viewed on a map give the appearance of a hand. Stretching from west to east, in order, the names of the lakes included the following: Conesus, Hemlock, Canadice, Honeoye, Canandaigua, Keuka, Seneca, Cayuga, Owasco, Skaneateles, and Otisco. Of the eleven lakes, Seneca and Cayuga were the longest, both being thirty-eight miles in length but never more than four miles wide. Seneca Lake was not only long, but it was deep, as in, 618 feet at its deepest point with an average depth of 291 feet.[22] The federal government took advantage of this resource by using the lake as a training site during World War II. The Sampson Naval Training Station was created on the east side of the lake in 1942. The base would eventually be converted to a state park.[23]

On the opposite northwest side, the downtown buildings of the city of Geneva came close to the edge of the lake, but a spacious, wide-open park had been preserved at the very north end of the city where residents and tourists could walk, run, and ride bicycles along sidewalks that provided a terrific view of the beautiful lake. One of the nicest areas in the city was where Route 14 separated Hobart and William Smith Colleges from a group of row houses situated on a hill overlooking the lake to the east.

Along the north edge of the city, in a residential section at the corners of Nursery and Lyceum Streets, was McDonough Park, home of the Geneva Cubs, the 1992 New York–Pennsylvania League champions. How it came about that the Cubs won the league championship was worth a closer look, one that should have made league officials reconsider the configuration of the postseason playoffs. Geneva had finished the regular season with a 41-34 record to win the Pinckney Division, one of three divisions in the league. The Cubs then defeated Utica, winners of the McNamara Division, in just a one-game playoff. On that same night, meanwhile, the Hamilton Redbirds, who ran away with the Stedler Division title while posting a 56-20 record, were facing the Erie Sailors, the team that finished sixteen and a half games behind the Redbirds during the season. Erie (4-37) had the fourth-best record in the league to earn the wildcard playoff spot and made the most of this opportunity by defeating the Redbirds 5-2, earning the right to face Geneva in the league

22   Finger Lakes. Wikipedia, *The Free Encyclopedia*. "Finger Lakes." 7 July 2024, https://en.wikipedia.org/wiki/Finger_Lakes

23   Sampson Air Base. Wikipedia, *The Free Encyclopedia*. "Sampson Air Base." 8 February 2024, https://en.wikipedia.org/wiki/Sampson_Air_Force_Base

championship after being in the rearview mirror of the Hamilton ball club for the entire season.

During the championship series, Geneva went on to sweep Erie, winning two straight games in the best-of-three games series. One must wonder, however, how many people in Geneva took notice and cared. In 1992, only 328 fans clicked the turnstiles for the season opener, and the overall attendance was 32,075, second-last to Auburn's total of just 21,200 for the season.[24]

The ballpark and the franchise here in Geneva came with some rich history. This was the place where Pete Rose broke into professional baseball, playing for the Geneva Red Legs in 1960 when he batted .277 and had a teammate named Tony Perez.[25]

It was also the ballpark where Bernice Gera wrote a chapter in baseball's history books by becoming the first female to umpire a professional baseball game between the host Geneva Rangers and the visiting Auburn Phillies in the first game of a June 1972 doubleheader. While working the bases, Gera called an Auburn runner safe at second base, but then she reversed her call. An argument ensued, and Gera proceeded to eject the Auburn manager, Nolan Campbell, from the game. In between games, Gera resigned out of frustration stemming from her perceived lack of cooperation and support on the part of her fellow umpires.[26]

More recently, history was made here in a unique way in 1988 when the Geneva general manager, twenty-three-year-old Ken Shepard, made a promise after the team lost its sixth game in a row. Shepard had vowed to sleep in the McDonough Park press box until the losing streak ended. The Cubs responded by losing twelve more games in a row, an eighteen-game skid that led Shepard to receive

24 1992 New York-Pennsylvania League. *Baseball Reference.* 5 August 2024, https://www.baseball-reference.com/register/league.cgi?id=408b8984

25 Rose, Pete. *Baseball Reference.* "Pete Rose." 5 August 2024, https://www.baseball-reference.com/register/player.fcgi?id=rose--003pet

26 Gera, Bernice. Wikipedia, *The Free Encyclopedia.* "Bernice Gera." 11 July 2024, https://en.wikipedia.org/wiki/Bernice_Gera

national media attention by taking up residence in the booth with just blankets, a pillow, a clock radio, and not much more. He also drew the attention of the Geneva Police Department during the early days of the stunt when a police officer on patrol noticed a light on within the press during the early morning hours long after the game had ended. The officer decided to look and was surprised to see Shepard trying to get some sleep in the cramped space of the press box.

When I walked up to the main gate outside McDonough Park today, I noticed an elderly man wearing a teal Elmira Pioneers baseball cap, standing alone, waiting to get inside. George Levering, a sixty-five-year-old fan of the Elmira ball club, was wishing he was inside the park where his beloved Pioneers were taking batting practice.

"I'm a nut," said Levering, who had been resting in his car across the street in the grass-covered parking lot following a three-hour drive from his home in Sayre, Pennsylvania. Levering explained that he attended all the home games at Dunn Field in Elmira and that he often made trips throughout the season to watch the Pioneers on the road.

"A couple of years ago, I lost my wife," said Levering. "We were coming back from the Blockbuster Bowl after watching Penn State and Florida State. She died in the car. We were thirty-five miles from home. We had just eaten lunch and were laughing and joking. She said she felt ill, so we drove to the hospital. She said, 'I think I'm dying.' And bang, she was gone. I miss her."

Levering and his late wife, Jane, had six children and fourteen grandchildren with another grandchild on the way when she passed away at age sixty-three. Levering had worked at IBM in Owego, New York, but retired ten years ago so that he and Jane could spend more time traveling.

"As it turned out, it was a godsend," said Levering. "She loved Penn State football. I'm doing this right now because I'm alone. I'm used to traveling. I wouldn't have done this before because we were busy doing other things."

During the fall, Levering traveled to State College, Pennsylvania, where he had been a season-ticket holder of Penn State football since 1978 and says he "will remain one until I die." In the summer, he rarely missed a baseball game and last year attended twenty-five of the thirty-eight road games played by the Pioneers. Dunn Field, home of the Pioneers, was his favorite park, but next in line was Donovan Field in Utica, home to the Utica Blue Sox, an affiliate of the Boston Red Sox.

"I like the layout of the field," he said about the Utica ballpark, "and out front, they have this board with the lineups. At some places, you wait until they announce the lineup. I look for the condition of the field, the seating. Personally, I don't like sitting behind a screen."

Levering was quick to rate Auburn's Falcon Park as the worst venue in the league.

"One reason," he said, "is that the screen (at Falcon Park) is all the way around. On the right-field side, the bars go across, and you have them in front of you."

Levering had made his rounds across the NY-P circuit, having watched games in St. Catharines, Welland, Niagara Falls, Batavia, and Oneonta. Damaschke Field in Oneonta, according to Levering, had an unusual characteristic. "It's kind of a strange field," said Levering. "There is a tree that's out there in right field. I don't know if it hangs over the field, but it's awfully close."

A trip to Welland, Ontario, Canada, meanwhile, required extra bug spray for protection against the mosquitoes.

"I got eaten alive there last year," said Levering.

At Dunn Field in Elmira, Levering described himself as a fixture. He told me the story of the time he was thirty minutes late for a game because he had a chicken bone caught in his throat while eating dinner. When he arrived at the ballpark, the usher at the front gate wondered where Levering had been.

"These kids are great," said Levering of the Elmira ball club. "Last year, I made friends with ballplayers and their parents."

Levering's love of baseball started long ago as a child.

"My parents were baseball nuts," he said. "We used to go up to Elmira when it was in the Eastern League. I saw Earl Weaver, Sal Maglie, and Chet Covington. Weaver had good ball clubs. He was always fiery."

If Levering rated Auburn Park as the worst venue in the league, McDonough Park would have been a close second. Inside the cinder block walls on Nursery Street was a ballpark that consisted of a small, roof-covered bleacher behind home plate along with smaller, open-air bleachers on both foul lines. The field already had brown spots before the scorching summer days in July had arrived. The dugouts were small and consisted of one deep step between the field level and the dugout floor. Glancing around the park, the only positive characteristic I could find was the relatively new clubhouse facility that had been built for the home team down the right-field line—a spacious facility and a major upgrade from the decrepit cinder block confines adjacent to the concession stand that formerly housed the minor league Cubs.

Lynn Jones was the manager of the Elmira ball club, an affiliate of the Florida Marlins following a lengthy partnership with the Boston Red Sox. The forty-year-old Jones was wearing a black jersey and sunglasses and holding a fungo bat while having a brief meeting with his players in front of the dugout before infield and outfield practice. He played eight seasons in the major leagues and still looked fit enough to be playing professional baseball. Jones broke into the majors in 1979 with the Detroit Tigers when he batted .296 in ninety-five games. He stuck with the Tigers through the 1983 season and went to the Royals in 1984 via free agency. The timing of his departure from Detroit could not have been worse, as the Tigers began the season on a torrid pace, winning thirty-nine of their first forty-four games while cruising to the American League and World Series titles.[27]

27   Jones, Lynn. Wikipedia, *The Free Encyclopedia*. "Lynn Jones." 30 July 2024, https://en.wikipedia.org/wiki/Lynn_Jones

"I have no regrets about 1984," said Jones. "The reason I have no regrets is being with the Royals, I had an opportunity to play."

Not only did Jones get his chance to play, but he also found himself with a pennant contender during the 1985 season. The Royals won the AL West title by one game over the California Angels. The team was on the brink of elimination in the American League Championship Series, trailing the Toronto Blue Jays three games to one before winning three straight games and a trip to the World Series.

"We weren't supposed to be there," said Jones. "A team not supposed to be there is relaxed. Anything happens in a short series. When we were down three games to one, there was no pressure on us. Each game we won put more pressure on Toronto. We were as loose as you could get. We came everyday thinking, 'We're here, we'll enjoy it as much as we can.'"

The Royals had their backs against the wall in the World Series as well, trailing the St. Louis Cardinals 3-1 before coming back again to win the Series in seven games. Jones had two hits—a double and a triple—in three at bats against the Cardinals.

"That's got to be the pinnacle of anyone's career," said Jones, "to get to the World Series, to play in it, and to win it."

His teammate, shortstop Buddy Biancalana, a .178 hitter during the regular season, was a World Series hero, batting .278 while anchoring the defense with a steady glove. "Funny you bring him up," said Jones. "I talk to him all the time. He had a good series. He was key in our rise. He played good defense, and between him and Onix Concepcion, we needed guys who could catch the ball. You don't know when you'll ever be in that situation again."

As for Biancalana, history would show that he capitalized when opportunity knocked. He was traded to Houston in 1987, and after just eighteen games with the Astros, he never played in the major leagues again. Biancalana never batted higher than .245 in any regular season and finished with a career batting average of .202.[28]

Jones had fond memories of Dick Howser, the Kansas City manager in 1985 who died just two years later from a brain tumor. Howser had previously managed the New York Yankees and had the unique distinction of being fired after leading his team to an impressive 103-59 record. It happened in 1980, in a season that ended for Howser and the Yankees when they were defeated in the American League Championship Series by the Royals. Yankees owner George Steinbrenner became upset in that series during Game Two when third-base coach Mike Ferraro waved home Willie Randolph only to watch him get thrown out at the plate during a one-run game in the eighth inning. Demanding that Ferraro be fired by the manager after the game, Howser refused Steinbrenner's request. The Yankees lost that ALCS to the Royals, who advanced to the 1980 World Series where they lost to the Philadelphia Phillies. Despite the team's outstanding regular season with 103 wins, it was not enough to satisfy Steinbrenner. The Yankees owner chose not to bring Howser back for the 1981 season.

Howser quickly latched on with the Royals and brought them the franchise's first World Series title in 1985 after overcoming deficits in both the ALCS and the Fall Classic.

"Dick was an exquisite man," said Jones. "He had faith in his players. He let his players go out and play. He was quiet, but when his opinion needs to be voiced, he could put some fire under you. He had a mixture of veterans and kids. The veterans were George Brett, Larry Gura, Frank White, and Hal McRae. They solidified the team. They took charge on the field. In that ballpark, for the longest time, nobody could play on that turf. It was tough to win at Royals Stadium."

---

28   Biancalana. Buddy. Wikipedia, *The Free Encyclopedia.* "Buddy Biancalana." 1 July 2024, https://en.wikipedia.org/wiki/Buddy_Biancalana

Jones spent the past two years as a coach with the Royals, but when the Marlins came calling with a chance to manage at the minor league level, he took the offer.

"I love the authority," he said. "There is more responsibility. I'm responsible for a bunch of kids eager to learn, and I enjoy it. To get to the big leagues, lots of players have skill, but it takes dedication to get there. Dedication and discipline—you've got to have heart, and you have to be a goal-setter. You have to be hungry."

Settling in for the start of the game, I joined George Levering at the top row of the third-base bleachers behind the Elmira dugout. Levering was quick to show his support for the Pioneers when left fielder Billy McMilllon dug into the batter's box. "Come on, Billy!" he shouted. He then turned toward me and politely informed me, "This team isn't hitting." The stat sheet revealed that the Pioneers were hitting a paltry .183 after six games, but McMillon was determined to do something about it as he opened the game with a double down the left field line.

"Thatta boy, Billy!" shouted Levering.

Two batters later, Erik Strickland came to the plate, and Levering informed me that he was a good hitter. Strickland, a left-handed batter, was six-foot-three and 195 pounds of raw muscle. He was a student at the University of Nebraska, where he played on the Cornhuskers basketball team. Through six games, he was the offensive bright spot, having begun the season by hitting .350. In his first at bat tonight, he reached base on an error. When Ron Brown followed him with a single, McMillon scored to put Elmira ahead 1-0.

When a foul ball sailed over our heads, Levering and I quickly turned to watch its flight. The ball flew out of the park, across the street, and into a grass parking lot, where a group of youngsters gave chase for the ball.

"One night," recalled Levering, "I was sitting here, and there was a car with a sunroof. A foul ball came over here and smashed the roof. There was glass everywhere."

Geneva tied the game in the bottom of the first inning. Demetrius Dowler scored when Gabe Duross hit a routine ground ball that was booted by Elmira second baseman Matt Martinez. When this happened, a nearby fan started yelling at Martinez for his miscue, and Levering was not impressed.

"The thing I don't like," said Levering, "was when that second baseman made that error, this guy starts riding him. He (Martinez) doesn't need that."

The Cubs added three more runs in the fourth inning to take a 4-1 lead. As the game played out through the evening, Levering and I covered several topics while both of us kept a running account of the game in our scorebooks. Levering talked about his grandchildren, Penn State football and old ballparks.

"I've been to major league ballparks all over," he said. "Yankee Stadium, Wrigley Field, Sportsman Park, Ebbets Field, the Polo Grounds. When my wife and I went on our honeymoon, I took her to a doubleheader in 1948 at Ebbets Field between the Giants and the Dodgers."

On this night, Geneva held on for a 6-4 win in a contest that saw a total of eight pitchers make an appearance. If Levering entered the ballpark concerned about Elmira's hitting, he could leave with added issues about the shaky fielding after watching the Pioneers commit a total of four errors.

Nobody in the visiting clubhouse seemed to be in a great hurry to vacate the cinder block confines following the game. I found Jones in an office to the side of the clubhouse, a tiny room that appeared to have received a fresh coat of blue paint in preparation for the season. The only furniture in the room was a desk and chair, and the space would not have allowed for anything more. On top of the desk was a briefcase belonging to Jones. His door stayed open as players walked by in the adjacent clubhouse. One of the players, Sergio Sanchez, was called into the office by Jones, who instead of talking baseball with his young player, Jone wanted to talk about food. He handed Sanchez some money and asked him to buy a whole pizza from the nearby concession stand that was still open following the game. When Jones told Sanchez to use the money to buy some food for himself as well, the young player showed a wide grin.

"It's not that big of an adjustment," Jones said when comparing a take-out pizza with the postgame spread in the big leagues. "A lot of the time, you eat at the major league level just because it's there, not that you like it."

In time, the Pioneers began filing out of the dank clubhouse and across the parking lot to board the bus that would take them on a two-hour ride to the Southern Tier of New York State, where the same two ball clubs would play tomorrow night at Dunn Field in Elmira.

Levering, meanwhile, would drive home as well, adding more miles to his 1993 Oldsmobile. He planned to match the total road trips he took a year ago and may have even added a few more.

"A guy called me the other day and left a message asking me to play golf," he said. "I only have eight days out of the next sixty-four open."

Finding an available date on the links did not seem likely to occur for this busy traveler and avid fan of the Elmira ball club.

Lynn Jones, Elmira Manager, offers advice to a player.

*Lynn Jones, Elmira Manager, hits infield practice
at McDonough Park, Geneva, NY.*

*Lynn Jones, Elmira Manager, converses with his team
prior to a game at McDonough Park, Geneva, NY.*

*Andy Pratt, Elmira Catcher, makes an equipment
adjustment at McDonough Park, Geneva, NY.*

George Levering, Elmira Pioneers fan, watches a game at McDonough Park in Geneva, NY.

The author (right) and George Levering watch the Elmira Pioneers play the Geneva Cubs.

*Elmira Pioneers players stretch before a game
at McDonough Park in Geneva, NY.*

CHAPTER FOUR:

FAMILIAR FACES IN AUBURN

June 25, 1993—Auburn, New York

Two nights later, I was back in Auburn to watch the Astros host the Geneva Cubs. When entering town, I picked up a copy of the *Auburn Citizen* newspaper and read an article written by Ed Plaisted, the *Citizen* sports editor. The headline to the story read, "Billy the Kid: Fastest Arm on the Astros' Staff?" Plaisted was writing about his introduction to Billy Wagner, the $600,000 "Bonus Baby" selected by the Houston Astros in the first round of the recent June 1993 amateur draft.

Wagner, according to Plaisted, was a left-handed pitcher who stood at five-foot-ten and weighed 180 pounds. Plaisted poked humor within his article about Wagner considering Auburn to be "such a big city." He was a native of Tannersville, Virginia, which included 239 residents.

Plaisted stated that Wagner was not drafted by a major league team when he was in high school, so he attended Ferrum College, a Division III school located in rural Ferrum, Virginia. Plaisted reported that Wagner was 17-3 at Ferrum and set a Division III record while averaging 19.3 strikeouts per game. He was also a defensive back on the school's football team.

Wagner's comments within the article revealed the characteristics of a humble individual. "Well, I've been clocked a few times at ninety-eight miles per hour," he told Plaisted. "But most of the time, I'm not that fast. Mostly around ninety-four to ninety-five miles per hour."

Plaisted told a story about Wagner originally being right-handed but that he broke his right arm twice as a five-year-old and then started doing everything left-handed.

The Auburn manager Manny Acta told Plaisted that Wagner was not yet on the team's twenty-five-man roster, but when he was, Wagner would likely be used as a starter.

"Our scouts tell me that he has great heat," Acta was quoted as saying within Plaisted's article.

Upon my entry to Falcon Park, I quickly saw familiar faces. There was the youthful general manager, Derek Duin, at his office just inside the main gate to the ballpark. Duin went out of his way to greet me with a program and stat sheets for tonight's game. A press pass, he noted, would not be necessary to do interviews. Duin did not have too much to smile about after a week of play, as Falcon Park was drawing just 1,249 per game.

Bobby Cross was right where I left him on opening night, sitting in the first-base bleachers and watching batting practice.

On my way to the field, someone called me from the grandstand, and when I looked up, it was Mike Shields and Shawn McAnally, the umpiring crew that I met during opening night here at Falcon Park. I turned back and went up to the bleachers to talk to both umpires and learned that they had traveled to Watertown, Utica, Pittsfield, and Oneonta to umpire ball games since I had last seen them on opening night. Shields did not stay long to talk, instead making his way to the locker room to begin rubbing balls with mud while McAnally stayed in the stands to take in batting practice.

"Historically, the base umpire is supposed to come out and look for fraternization," said McAnally. "At one point or another, teams were fraternizing before games, and it wasn't looked highly upon."

McAnally updated me about his travels thus far in this young season, his second tour of duty of the New York–Pennsylvania League. In Pittsfield, he told me about the sun setting directly behind the center-field fence at Wahconah Park, an issue that would occasionally cause the home plate umpire to stop the game for a sun delay. "The pitcher's motion comes through the sun," said McAnally. "There have been times where they stop the game for about fifteen minutes while the sun goes down."

When I asked McAnally about his favorite park, he did not hesitate when telling me the answer was Dunn Field in Elmira.

"The umpire's locker room in Elmira is amazing," he said. "You have field access from there. They have new dugouts, new clubhouses. They've done a good job. In terms of the whole facility, it's probably the best park."

As for tonight's game, McAnally realized he forgot to come to Falcon Park with an important piece of equipment.

"I forgot," he said, "we were going to get some bug spray. This place is bad for bugs."

During our conversation, McAnally was interrupted by the Falcon Park public address announcer, who had come to ask the names and hometowns of both umpires working tonight's game.

"It's going to be a big one tonight—2,500 to 3,000," the announcer told McAnally. "It's Tops (Supermarket) Night—free tickets."

The thought of a larger crowd than normal was appealing to McAnally. And while three thousand fans may not seem like a lot of people, in Class A baseball, it was considered a rather good gate.

"With larger crowds, the adrenaline flows a little more," said McAnally. "Everybody wants to see a big crowd in the park."

It was now 6:27 p.m., and McAnally, dressed sharply, wearing trousers and a golf shirt with a pair of Oakley sunglasses hanging around his neck, rose from his seat behind home plate. Fans were already in the ballpark at this time, and McAnally could fit right in with the crowd. McAnally made his way out of the bleachers and toward the tiny umpire's locker room behind the home plate grand-stand to join his partner Shields. When he returned to the field, few in attendance would realize he was the same person sitting conspicu-ously a half hour earlier while watching pregame activities on the field.

I also caught up with Nate Peterson, the Aussie who the Astros wanted to convert into a catcher. The experiment went on hold to-night as Peterson found himself playing left field while batting fifth. He was struggling with the bat in this early season, hitting just .231 with no home runs and only two runs batted in entering tonight's game.

"I'm still working on catching," said Peterson, "but the out-field is my original position. I'm just happy to be playing. I'll play anywhere."

Tim Kester was making his professional debut tonight as the starting pitcher for the Astros. The six-foot-four right-hander was in trouble right away when he gave up a leadoff single to Demetrius Dowler, who advanced to second when Douglas Alongi reached base on an error by second baseman Marsalis Basey. Dowler and Alongi later scored, both coming home on separate wild pitches by Kester, and just like that, the Cubs were ahead 2-0. Kester's first inning as a professional read as follows: two runs, one hit, two strikeouts, one walk, two wild pitches, and one Astro error.

With the shaky start behind him, Kester was almost flawless the rest of the way, throwing six more innings without allowing a run. On the night, Kester gave up just three hits while striking out ten and walking three over seven total innings. When Basey redeemed himself for the first inning error by hitting a solo homer in the third inning, the game was tied 2-2. In the fourth inning, Peterson led off with a double and scored what would prove to be the winning run on a fielder's choice by Chad White. Kester and the Auburn bullpen would hold the lead for the rest of the way in a 3-2 win.

"He's a starter for now," said Tad Slowick, the Auburn pitching coach, when discussing Kester's outing after the game. "He could be effective. He has a lot of confidence. It was a gritty performance. That's what it is about as a starter. He kept us in the game, and he showed character."

"My velocity increased as the innings went on," said Kester.

Kester felt right at home being in Upstate New York. He played college baseball at Florida International but was born in Batavia, just an hour away from Auburn.

"My dad is a veterinarian," said Kester. "He worked with the horses at Batavia Downs and now he's at Pompano Park (in Florida)."

When the Astros would visit Batavia on August 2, Kester may have to leave a few tickets at the front gate.

"I have aunts and uncles, and when I go to Batavia, they'll probably be there," he said.

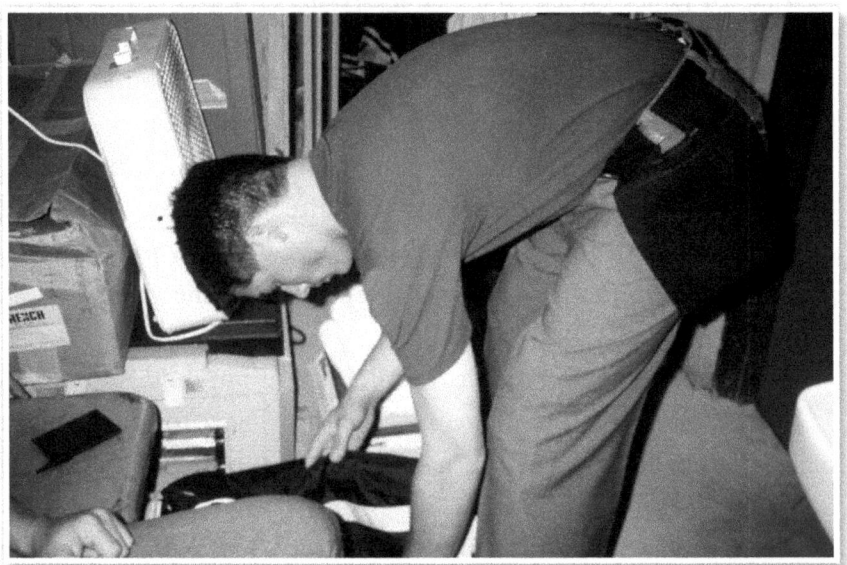

Umpire Shawn McAnally prepares for a game behind the plate in the Falcon Park locker room.

The Grounds Crew lines the field at Falcon Park in Auburn, NY.

*Auburn Manager Manny Acta watches Tim Kester
warm up before a game on June 25, 1993.*

Umpire Shawn McAnally calls a strike on Geneva's Gabe Duross.

*Fans watch the action from the home plate
grandstand at Falcon Park in Auburn, NY.*

CHAPTER FIVE:

"PASS THE PEANUTS, PLEASE!"

June 27, 1993—Batavia, New York

Halfway between Rochester and Buffalo, New York, located just off the New York State Thruway, was the city of Batavia. When approaching the Thruway exit for Batavia coming from the east, a sign on a large field read, "Batavia Turf Farms—Instant Lawns." Here on the north side of the Thruway, acres of lush green grass grew before being cut up, rolled, and shipped off to residential and commercial sites for the purpose of exactly what the sign said: instant lawns. Batavia was on the south side of the Thruway, and home to a Veteran's Administration Hospital, a State School of the Blind, Notre Dame High School, Pontillo's Pizzeria, and Dwyer Park, home of the Batavia Clippers.

Notre Dame High School has been educating students in the region since 1951, Pontillo's had been making one of the best slices of pizza in the area since opening its doors in Batavia in 1947, and the Batavia entry in the New York–Pennsylvania League was a charter member since the league began in 1939 and was known as the Pennsylvania-Ontario-New York League. The other charter members that year were

Olean, Niagara Falls, Jamestown, Bradford, and Hamilton, Ontario, Canada.[29] During that inaugural season, Ed Dwyer was president of the Batavia Jaycees and would later become a longtime president of the ball club. Through the years, the team became community-owned, and eventually, the ballpark was named in honor of Dwyer and his work that was devoted to baseball and the city of Batavia.

I found Dwyer Stadium at the corner of Banks and Denio Streets, a small ballpark with a roof-covered grandstand that backed right up to the residential streets. Inside the park, it was easy to observe that the ballpark needed repair, maybe not as desperately as Falcon Park in Auburn, but a close second. The stadium itself was part of a recreational complex that included youth baseball fields, tennis courts, and a pool, all situated beyond the walls of the outfield fence and within view from the ballpark. The pool, located beyond the right-field fence, sat empty on that summer evening, just like the one at Hyde Park in Niagara Falls.

The Clippers were an affiliate of the Philadelphia Phillies, and as a community-owned franchise, were governed by a board of directors. The president was Laurence G. Roth, a local medical doctor, but the daily operations were in the hands of general manager Brad Rogers, currently in his ninth season. Rogers, unlike other general managers in Class A baseball, performed his role on a part-time basis. His full-time job was at Batavia High School, where he was employed as a science and health teacher, a position he had held now for thirty years. Looking back, he never expected to be in this role with the ball club when he first took the job.

"I'm the oddball," said Rogers. "The position is full-time. I always thought they'd go out and look for someone to do this. They don't want me to leave right away."

29   New York-Penn League. Wikipedia, The *Free Encyclopedia*. June 2024, https://en.wikipedia.org/wiki/New_York%E2%80%93Penn_League

Rogers could accomplish both jobs by carefully balancing his time and taking advantage of school vacations during the baseball off-season. He told me that he spent time during the Christmas and winter breaks from school preparing for the start of the season. He received help during those weeks when his daughter Julia, a schoolteacher in Olean, New York, returned home to lend a hand. An even closer look at the front office showed that baseball was indeed a family affair. Rogers had two sons, Paul and Kevin, who worked as the bat boys; another daughter, Kathleen, worked in the front office; a niece, Maureen Hevron, took tickets at the main gate; and a nephew, Pat Tehan, sat in the press box and operated the scoreboard.

"It's done intentionally," said Rogers of the family connections. "I don't have to worry about work habits. I know them, and it makes it easy. Plus, they know there's a job to be done, and they do it."

In addition to family support, Rogers could also count on support from the community. "We have twenty-three volunteer directors," said Rogers. "That's fantastic. Our board of directors built the offices and the clubhouses."

Outside the home-plate grandstand was the Batavia Baseball Wall of Fame, and the list was impressive: Steve Blass, Doc Ellis, Cito Gaston, Kelly Gruber, and Manny Sanguillen highlighted a list of former players and managers who had come through Batavia.

The 1993 edition of the Batavia franchise was off to a 4-5 start and looking to even up the record as the visiting Welland Pirates were in town for a home-and-home series, the Clippers playing at Welland tomorrow night. The Pirates were out on the field taking batting practice when I entered the ballpark, and the elderly man on the mound throwing batting practice was the sixty-five-year-old Rocky Bridges, the roving infield instructor in the Pittsburgh organization and a minor league baseball legend in various circles.

Bridges played eleven years in the majors, breaking in with the Brooklyn Dodgers, and compiled a .247 career batting average during a seven-year career. His best season was in 1955 when he batted

.286 for the Cincinnati Reds. Bridges never played on a World Series team, but he did make the American League All-Star team in 1958 while playing for the Washington Senators.[30] The American League won the game 4-3, but Bridges watched the entire contest from the dugout, the manager of the team, Casey Stengel, electing not to insert him in the lineup.

"It was a break for the AL that he (Stengel) didn't play me," said Bridges, who claimed he probably would have messed things up. "It was a thrill, because Casey was running the club. Casey had a way of doing things. He loved baseball."

Today, Bridges walked around the ball field with a distinct limp that was the result of an injury that occurred years ago during the 1964 season while managing at San Jose in the Class A California League. Bridges was throwing batting practice, just like he was today, the only difference being that today he had a protective "L" screen in front of him. In San Jose, however, he threw from the mound with no protection. When a batter hit a line drive back toward him, he had nowhere to turn, and the ball struck him on the left knee and caused an arthritic condition that had left him limping ever since.

After he threw batting practice to the young Pirates hopefuls, Bridges walked to a vending machine down by the bleachers in right field. He grabbed a soda and sat with me to talk baseball while chewing on a wad of tobacco, a practice that was prohibited for the same minor league players that he was currently tutoring.

"I have no squawks about baseball," Bridges said, reflecting on his career. "It's still the number one game. Pittsburgh has been an excellent organization. I haven't run into an organization where there have been too many people I haven't liked. You always have some bum years, but if you get through OK, wake up and smell the roses and hear the music, it's a good day."

---

30   Bridges, Rocky. Wikipedia, *The Free Encyclopedia.* "Rocky Bridges." 8 April 2024,
     https://en.wikipedia.org/wiki/Rocky_Bridges

Amazingly, Bridges had been in the game for forty-eight consecutive seasons. He signed his first contract back in 1946, but didn't play that season, having spent it instead in the US Army. The following year, he broke his leg in spring training and played in only thirty games after his recovery. As for his major league debut, it did not happen until the 1951 season with the Brooklyn Dodgers when he played in sixty-three games and batted .254. His career lasted eleven years, and it was well traveled. In 1957, he played for two teams, Cincinnati and Washington. But in 1960, he did one better, playing for Detroit, Cleveland, and St. Louis. In the end, he was a career .247 hitter with sixteen total home runs.[31]

"I was lucky," said Bridges of his career. "I played when older ballparks were in existence. Ebbets Field had a mystique. It was close to everything. The fans were vocal, and they knew their baseball."

Following his playing career, Bridges had done most of his managing and coaching in the minor leagues. His tour of duty had not been without some unique situations. In Phoenix, for instance, while managing the Class AAA Giants of the Pacific Coast League, Bridges took up residence in the clubhouse during the 1982 season.

"It was a good clubhouse," said Bridges. "It had air conditioning and a TV. If it wasn't air conditioned, I wouldn't have done it. Not in Phoenix. All those years, I rented a motel room and had to check out with my clothes. I was spending money for nothing. The room at the clubhouse had a folding bed, and I always ate out."

If living in a clubhouse was different, Bridges was not alone. During that 1982 season, Bridges recalled manager Rene Lacheman taking up residence in the Spokane clubhouse while Moose Stubing did the same thing in Salt Lake City.

It had not been since 1989 when Bridges managed a team, and that was at Salem, Virginia, the Pittsburgh affiliate in the Class A

---

31   Bridges, Rocky. Wikipedia, *The Free Encyclopedia.* "Rocky Bridges." 8 April 2024, https://en.wikipedia.org/wiki/Rocky_Bridges

Carolina League. Now that he was a roving instructor, Bridges could travel with Mary, his wife of forty-three years. Today, however, she decided not to accompany him in Batavia and stayed back at the hotel in Welland.

"We see a lot of the country," said Bridges. "I see a lot of the places you read about. I'm a history fan. If you're going to be some place (with a ball club), you should enjoy it. Salem was founded in 1802. The fellas should know the city they live in. I enjoy the Revolutionary War days. Virginia is a nice state. It's nothing but history. Whenever I see a historical site, I look at it. If I'm not doing that, my wife is at an outlet store, or she goes to antique stores. I don't know why. She's married to an antique."

During the past twenty-two years, Bridges and his wife had made their off-season home in Coeur d'Alene, Idaho. According to Bridges, the town was home to the only golf course in the country with a floating green. Bridges said he lived on three acres of land and was far removed from his neighbors. "It's so far out in the woods," he said, "that I have to walk toward town to go hunting."

In the Pirate organization, Bridges was appreciated by players as well as managers.

"The Pittsburgh Pirates have done a lot of nice things," said Welland manager Larry Smith. "The nicest thing they've done is give me six weeks with Rocky Bridges. He is a great baseball mind. If you listen, you can absorb so much. He has a way of instructing that keeps things simple and to the point. It makes good sense. The players love him. I've never known anybody who didn't. I don't believe in the old school. Baseball is a game. It has been that way for over 110 years. Whatever school he is from, it's a good one."

"He has helped me a lot," said Welland second baseman Richard Luna. "He talked about the pivot, to come across the bag and toward first base. I was just standing and making the pivot toward the runner. He's straightforward. He tells you how it is. If you don't like it, oh well."

The press box at Dwyer Stadium was a shoe box, a small wooden booth able to seat not more than six people at best. Prior to the game, at the far end of the booth, sat a middle-aged man who was thumbing through an ample collection of compact discs while sitting on a stool. Wayne Fuller was preparing for yet another night of his multifaceted job with the Clippers. He was the public address announcer, official scorer, and music director. His position with the ball club was one of three jobs he was currently holding. During the week, he worked for Trailways Bus Company in nearby Rochester, and on Saturday and Sunday mornings, he was a disc jockey at WTLB Radio in Batavia.

Before the game began, Fuller played a song from the group the Pretenders and appeared overly pleased with this selection while it played through the ballpark speakers. "It's the theme song from the *Rush Limbaugh Show*," Fuller informed Pat Tehan, the scoreboard operator who was sitting nearby.

As the game progressed, Fuller barely had time to take a break. In between innings, he read lucky numbers over the public address system and often talked to a voice from the front office coming through an intercom. The requests came often and were usually a distraction. In the third inning, the voice over the intercom was heard again: "Wayne, can you announce a happy birthday to Katie Mussel, who is celebrating her sweet sixteenth?" Fuller obliged once again and made the announcement.

In the bottom of the fourth inning with Welland leading 2-1 following a two-run double by Aaron Cannaday, Fuller announced, "The owner of the car with license plate BA 224, you have the dirtiest car in the parking lot. See Brad Rogers to get your free car-wash coupon from Country Falls Car Wash."

The press box was not only cramped, but the vantage point of the field was also obstructed, because the open window to the booth was behind a wire fence. Sitting directly above the home-plate grandstand, I noticed that the bleachers down the foul lines were nearly empty. There couldn't be more than 800 fans in attendance tonight, and I knew it was definitely a small crowd when in the top of the fifth inning, with Batavia now leading 3-2, I could hear the Batavia shortstop Doug Angeli shout, "I got it," as he backpedaled to the grass in shallow left field to catch a fly ball.

Batavia increased the lead to 4-2, but in the seventh, the Pirates came to within one run again when Riegal Hunt hit a solo homer over the right field fence against Batavia starter Tony Fiore. Fiore found himself in more trouble when Jermaine Allensworth singled and moved to second on a wild pitch, the tying run now in scoring position. And that was when the skies opened, and a thunderstorm soaked the field quickly. The umpires wasted no time calling for a rain delay, and members of the grounds crew scrambled to cover home plate and the pitcher's mound with tarps. The rest of the in-field, however, would go unprotected. Few teams in Class A had tarps to cover the entire infield, and such was the case with Dwyer Stadium. At 8:57 p.m., the heavy rains made large puddles through-out the infield. It seemed unlikely that baseball would be played again that evening. If the game was called, the final score would be 4-2 and a win for the home team. Hunt's homer would not count, because the top of the inning would be wiped out.

At 9:04 p.m., the rain was still coming down hard, and the puddles were getting much larger on the infield dirt. Lightning then struck nearby, and the scoreboard in right field went into an electronic tailspin. The count now read five balls, three strikes, and Welland was ahead by a score of 44-20. At this point of the delay, I broke out a bag of peanuts and passed some down the line to Fuller and a writer covering the game for the *Batavia Daily News*. The writer showed up to start his coverage during the start of the rain delay, six and a half innings after the opening pitch. Now, he was scrambling to catch up on the game summary by reviewing Fuller's scorebook.

During the delay, Fuller and I continued to crack open our fair share of peanuts. Fuller was playing one CD after another, but few fans were in the ballpark. Dwyer Stadium was nearly vacant due to the downpour. Finally, at 9:45 p.m., the two umpires emerged from their locker room located down the first base line and were meeting with Batavia manager Al LeBoeuf before making the gesture toward the press box that indicated the ball game was canceled.

I wasted little time packing up my belongings and said goodbye to Fuller before climbing down the steps and into the grandstand below. Out in the parking lot, the Welland players were boarding the bus that would take them on a short ride down the New York State Thruway and across the border to Canada. As I was walking by the bus, Bridges was ready to board. We shook hands, and then he went limping onto the bus for still another ride through the bush leagues. When he was done with his stint in Welland, he informed me that he would go on to visit the Carolina Mudcats of the Class AA Southern League, the Salem Buccaneers of the Class A Carolina League, and the Augusta Pirates of the Class A South Atlantic League.

"Then it's back to Idaho," he said, "like a big turtle."

A view of Dwyer Stadium, Batavia, NY

Batting practice, Dwyer Stadium

Welland Pirates Manager Larry Smith leans on the batting cage while his players await their cuts.

A Welland Pirates player takes batting practice at Dwyer Stadium in Batavia, New York.

Rocky Bridges, Roving Infield Instructor, Pittsburgh Pirates

A Welland player prepares for batting practice.

*Pat Reed (26) and a Welland teammate have
a quick meal prior to the game.*

Batavia fans watch the action from behind home plate.

A young Batavia fan checks the autographs on his baseball.

The Dwyer Stadium Concession Stand

Fans watch the game from the Dwyer Stadium Bleachers.

John Tudor, former World Series pitcher, watches the action as a Roving Pitching Coach for the Philadelphia Phillies organization.

Pat Tehan, Dwyer Stadium Scoreboard Operator

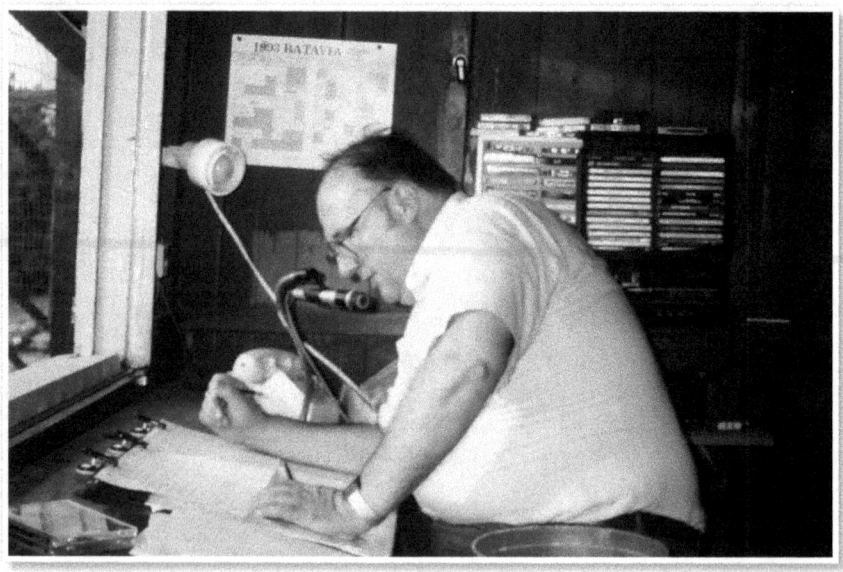

Wayne Fuller, Dwyer Stadium Public Address Announcer

CHAPTER SIX:

PITCHING GEMS IN GENEVA

June 30, 1983—Geneva, New York

Rarely did I arrive at a ballpark after the opening pitch. Coming to a ball game late, in my book, was missing batting practice. So, I was baffled when I already saw the parking lot outside McDonough Park in Geneva full and heard the crowd inside cheering at a time when I was expecting to lean on the batting cage to watch the Auburn Astros take their cuts more than an hour before the first pitch. Once inside the blue cinder block walls on Nursery Street, I quickly learned that a game was already in progress, because it was part of a doubleheader between the Cubs and Astros due to a recent rainout. An old-fashioned doubleheader at a minor league park. I was thrilled!

I made my climb up the steep wrought-iron stairs that led to the press box atop the aluminum roof which hung over the home-plate grandstand. Brian Colella, a beat writer with the *Auburn Citizen*, updated me on the half inning of play I missed by sharing the rundown of his scorebook. I arrived just in time to watch Auburn's Tim Kester surrender four runs in the second inning when the Cubs sent ten batters to the plate, the outburst triggered by Geneva shortstop Emilio Mendez and his two-run single.

I assumed that Auburn manager Manny Acta was looking to rest his bullpen, because while the Cubs were batting around the order, not one Astros reliever stood up to get loose. I was equally surprised by the fact that Kester settled down the rest of the way and never allowed another run while pitching a complete-game—seven innings in a minor league doubleheader—in a 4-2 loss.

I doubt few people took notice that Kester was settling into a groove as the game progressed, because all eyes were on Geneva starter Greg Hillman. The left-hander came within one out of pitching a complete game, giving up two runs on five hits while striking out fifteen batters in six and two-thirds innings. His only blemish was a two-run homer off the bat of Geneva's Eduardo Cedeno in the fifth inning. When Hillman worked his way into a jam in the seventh inning, Geneva manager Jerry Weinstein called upon closer Shawn Hill as Hillman's pitch count reached 105.

"He told me I did a great job and should feel happy," said Hillman about Weinstein's visit to the mound. "I knew I struck out a lot, but I didn't know until the end of the game. Anthony Locey came up to me in the dugout and said, 'Did you know you had 15 Ks?' I said, 'Golly, I knew I had a few.'"

Hillman's road to McDonough Park was preceded by two years of pitching at Tarleton State, a NAIA school, before transferring to the University of Texas, where he went unused in two seasons. During his senior season that spring, the Longhorns played fifty-six games, and Hillman pitched only nine innings and had a 1-0 record—sparse numbers indeed, but enough to get him selected in the June amateur draft. "I showed the talent in practice, most of the time, which was better competition than the other teams we played," said Hillman.

Following the first game, the grounds crew groomed the infield, and Geneva public relations director Gabe Sinicropi tried to keep the attention of the fans by announcing that June was Dairy Month in New York State. On cue, a cow then entered the field through a gate on the third-base side and proceeded to make its way down the line before stopping in front of the Auburn dugout. In honor of Dairy Month, Geneva outfielder James Young and Auburn pitcher Kendall Rhine were ready to square off in a milking contest.

"One, two, three, milk!" announced Sinicropi.

Perched on stools on opposite sides of the cow, both players began the milking process, but the cow did not cooperate. Instead, it started to kick, causing the two players and several players gathered around the cow to scatter. A few minutes later, the cow was composed, and the players tried a second time. A few squirts of milk went into the buckets, but the cow kicked a second time.

"This is the most uncooperative cow we've had at McDonough Park," announced Sinicropi.

In a third and final attempt, the owner of the cow walked it to the backstop, the cow now staring at fans seated behind a wire fence in the home-plate grandstand. The strategy proved effective, and the cow not only cooperated, but it also produced. In the end, Young was the winner when the scale revealed he squeezed one pound of milk.

"That was my first experience milking a cow," said Rhine. "He hit me on the wrist the first time. After the first couple of times, I didn't think they'd let us milk him, because he was jumping around. I didn't want to get hit again. I can see them calling Houston saying, 'He can't pitch because he got kicked by a cow.'"

In the nightcap, the Cubs threw another left-hander, Greg Twiggs, who stood at just five-foot-ten and weighed 160 pounds. Like Hillman, Twiggs also pitched at the NAIA level with Brewton Parker College in Georgia. Surprisingly, the Cubs had two players on their current roster from Brewton Parker with James Farrow, a right-handed pitcher, being the other to come out of the tiny school located in Ailey, Georgia.

Twiggs barely made it into the ranks of professional baseball, having been selected in the fifty-fourth round of the draft earlier in the month. "I just wanted to be drafted," said Twiggs, whose father played professionally in 1966–67 with the Dodgers organization. "As long as I am here, I don't care about money. I just want to play the game."

Twiggs would have a tough time matching the performance of Hillman, but through four innings, he was putting up some impressive numbers of his own by allowing no hits and striking out six. He also had the benefit of being staked to an early lead when the Cubs scored five runs off Auburn starter Bill Hartnett in the first inning, three of them coming on a home run by Gabe Duross.

In the fifth inning, Twiggs walked his second batter of the night when Trevor Froschauer reached base and advanced to second on a wild pitch. Twiggs got out of the inning, striking out the next two batters, and was now six outs away from tossing a no-hitter.

"It popped into my mind occasionally," Twiggs said afterward about the prospect of throwing a no-hitter, "but I blocked it out. I wanted to get ahead of the hitters. You don't want to think about it. I sat by myself most of the time, concentrating and watching the game."

"Everybody wants to say something," said Weinstein. "I didn't want to change my seat. It was a comfy spot."

"It was an awfully quiet bench," said Jared Snyder, the Geneva catcher, referring to the superstition that players do not want to speak about the no-hitter for the fear that they will jinx the pitcher.

"I had no idea of the no-hitter until the fifth inning," Snyder continued. "You get more conscious of what you call. Sometimes before a pitch, you begin to second-guess yourself."

In the sixth inning, the pitching gem was almost broken up when Auburn's Carlos Crispin hit a line drive to the right side of the infield that was hit hard enough for a base hit. But Geneva second baseman J. J. Biernat dove to his right and made the catch to keep the no-hitter intact.

Then, in the seventh, Auburn's Nate Peterson reached base on an error and advanced to second on a two-out walk to Froschauer.

"In that last inning, I was getting tired," Twiggs said afterward.

Unlike the first game, Weinstein was not coming out to make any pitching changes, with Twiggs one out away from going the distance and spinning the no-hitter. With two runners aboard, Twiggs finished the deal when he caught Auburn's Brent Callan looking at a third strike, his tenth strikeout of the night, recording a no-hitter in his first professional win.

So, there were Hillman and Twiggs, both winning the first games of their professional careers and in spectacular fashion. Together, they combined to pitch thirteen and two-thirds innings, allowing two runs on five hits while striking out twenty-five batters and walking six.

"It feels good, really good," said Twiggs, who said he would call his father in Florida to share the news. "He's going to probably think I'm lying."

CHAPTER SEVEN:

"I'M GLAD IT'S OVER!"

July 3, 1993—Utica, New York

Like many cities in the New York–Pennsylvania League, Utica was located near the New York State Thruway, the main ribbon of highway that stretched across the central part of the state. Some thirty miles east of Syracuse, Utica was a blue-collar city that was probably best known as the home of the FX Matt Brewery. Located near an exit to Route 12 and across the street from Faxton Hospital was Donovan Stadium, home of the Utica Blue Sox, an affiliate of the Boston Red Sox.

At first glance, there was nothing extraordinary about Donovan Stadium. The main seating area was a large aluminum bleacher with an overhead roof situated behind home plate. Smaller, broken-down wooden bleachers were situated down both foul lines. The press box was at the top of the wooden bleacher on the first-base side. I could not consider it a ballpark, and I wouldn't have called it a stadium, either. Instead, I would have described it as a collection of new and old bleachers that happened to be surrounding a baseball field. The bleacher configuration was located further from the playing field than most parks I had visited in the league, and an intimate atmosphere was lacking. Why George Levering, the Elmira fan I met earlier during a game in Geneva, had given Donovan Stadium high marks was beyond my comprehension.

Utica baseball may have been best known for being mentioned by major league pitcher Ken Brett in a Miller Lite beer commercial and for the book *Good Enough to Dream,* written by Roger Kahn, author of *The Boys of Summer.* Kahn bought the Utica franchise in 1983, assumed summer residence in Utica during the season, and wrote a book about owning a franchise in baseball's bush leagues.

I arrived at Donovan Stadium on a sweltering hot afternoon, two hours before Utica's game against the Oneonta Yankees, and found the hometown team taking batting practice. Throwing on the mound in front of the L-shaped screen was a tall, stick-like figure named Garry Roggenburk, the six-foot-six Utica pitching coach who played college basketball at the University of Dayton. Roggenburk played in the major leagues for three teams, including the expansion Seattle Pilots in 1969, a franchise that played just one season in the Emerald City before moving to Milwaukee just prior to the start of the 1970 season. Roggenburk compiled a career pitching record of 6-9 and was a Seattle teammate of Jim Bouton.[32] Roggenburk shared with me that his teammate, Bouton, was constantly writing notes into a pad while seated in the dugout, the beginnings of his tell-all book entitled *Ball Four.*

Now here was Roggenburk twenty-four years later, sweat pouring down his face while throwing pitch after pitch to the young Utica batters. A group of five hitters took their turns rotating in and out of the cage while Roggenburk labored on the mound and his gray T-shirt became drenched with sweat. The group concluded the round of batting practice with a pretend game, and the rules were simple: when a batter hit a ball that in the judgment of the other players standing around the cage was a hit, the batter stayed in the

---

32   Roggenburk, Garry. Wikipedia, *The Free Encyclopedia.* "Garry Roggenburk." 28 July 2023, https://en.wikipedia.org/wiki/Garry_Roggenburk

cage for another pitch. If it was not a hit, such as a routine ground ball or a pop fly, he was out of the cage. Roggenburk, being the pitcher, had the last say if there was any indecision among the batter and the onlooking players waiting their turns to hit.

Utica second baseman T. J. O'Donnell was among the group of hitters and was the leading hitter in the New York–Pennsylvania League, taking a .388 average into tonight's game. This was his second tour of duty in the league after playing at Elmira in 1992 when the Red Sox had their affiliate located in that Southern Tier city of New York State. For O'Donnell, the batting practice ritual led by Roggenburk added variety to the routine.

"The first ten to fifteen swings are hard work," said O'Donnell. "You try to drive the ball to different parts of the field. You hit and run, move the runner over. After we take our ten to fifteen swings, coach says, 'Let's put a little fun into it.' We see if we can beat the pitcher and see if we can get two or three hits and get a little rally going. Once in a while, he'll throw us a curveball. You might beg a little bit and say, 'That was a hit, that was a hit.' You have to put a little fun into the game. Sometimes you get too serious. Then it stops being a game and more of a job, which it is, but you've got to have fun and make it a game as well."

"They have fun with it," said Roggenburk. "Anything on the ground is not a base hit. If the ball is in the gap, and it's high, we make a judgment. You kind of make them bear down and adjust to get a line drive, to get a strike to hit. At that time of batting practice, it makes you concentrate more."

Watching the entire round of batting practice while standing behind the third-base dugout was O'Donnell's father, Tom O'Donnell, who had made the trip to Utica for the weekend from his home in Hazlet, New Jersey. The elder O'Donnell was fifty-three years old and was a sales manager for Rheox Chemical Company in Hightstown, New Jersey. The elder O'Donnell had made the four-and-a-half-hour trip to watch his son and was staying at the nearby

Howard Johnson Hotel. He said that depending on where the team was playing, he might have been able to make four or five trips that season to watch his son play.

"We talk a lot about hitting, how he feels at the plate, how comfortable he feels hitting. We talk about hopes and ambitions," said the elder O'Donnell, who had coached his son from the time he was a kid straight through American Legion ball. "Ever since he was able to walk, he has had a ball in his hand. We started with whiffle ball at three or four years old. I spent many afternoons at the high school field with as many balls as we could get, and I'd pitch to him."

Tom O'Donnell was confident that his son had a chance to climb the ranks in the Red Sox minor league ladder.

"He has a great attitude," said Tom O'Donnell. "He feels if he plays every day and gets a chance, good things will happen. He hopes to progress to Lynchburg or another Class A team (within the Boston farm system). He was with the Florida State League team (Winter Haven) through spring training, but on the last day, they dropped him down. He was not disappointed. If he is going to make it, it's going to be grit and grind. He's not flashy, he's a hardworking, nose-to-the-grindstone type of player."

Batting practice now complete, a member of the grounds crew attached the back of the batting cage to a tractor and carted it away down the right-field line and out of play near a maintenance shed. On any other day, the cage would have remained on the field so the visiting ball club could hit after the home team finished. Today, the visiting Oneonta Yankees arrived late and declined to take batting practice.

Oneonta was just an hour and a half south of Utica, nestled in the foothills of the Catskill Mountains and close to the Baseball Hall of Fame and Museum in Cooperstown. When the Yankees arrived for the game, many of them started stretching near the right-field bullpen area. Eventually, they began to gather in the first-base dugout, which was where I found their manager, Ken Dominguez, who at age thirty-eight was returning to Oneonta after being a coach there in 1990. Dominguez, a resident of Tampa, had also coached at Prince William and was a manager of the Yankees minor league entry in the Gulf Coast League.

"This was our first day we didn't take batting practice," said the five-foot-ten Dominguez about keeping the bats in the rack before the game. "We've been in a hitting slump. They're pressing too much. The way to come out of it may be to take a day off. We've been hitting every day (in batting practice). We're trying to hit our way out of it. Today, we'll try the opposite. There is not a lot of rocket science to this game. Sometimes, a day off is good. You have to pick your spots."

Dominguez sat in the far end of the dugout, staring through his sunglasses at the proceedings that took place in front of him, the Utica ball club taking infield practice. While he was willing to talk currently, he rarely took a glance away from the field. His eyes, instead, were transfixed on the Blue Sox as they went through the routines of outfielders hitting cut-off men and infielders turning the double play. The way Dominguez described it, there was a lot to learn when watching the opposition warm up prior to a game.

"When we watch opposing teams," he began, "we watch for the catcher's arm strength. We watch for the double-play pivot, and we watch how quick afoot the corner men are. You need to know if these guys are quick or slow. The catchers give you a clue as far as their accuracy is concerned. If the outfielders are throwing to the cutoff men, you look at arm strength and accuracy."

Dominguez believes that his players should share his concerns, looking for every edge they can attain in this game, but a glance around the dugout shows he does not have much company. Most of the Oneonta players are talking to each other and only a few are watching the Blue Sox go through their routines out on the field.

"The older vets will watch," said Dominguez. "I don't think they fully understand the importance of it. A craftsman studies his craft.

A journeyman takes it as a hobby. Time will separate the journeyman from the craftsman in this game."

When it was time for his own ball club to take the field, Dominguez chose to remain in the dugout while his coach Bill Schmidt grabbed a blue fungo bat to hit fly balls and ground balls to the Yankee prospects. Schmidt was a Yankee West Coast scout based out of Garden Grove, California, but during the summer months, he was a coach at Oneonta.

"Personally, I like to get my staff involved in as many things as I can," said Dominguez. "I don't like to be autonomous. The more I can give them to do, the happier they are. I want them to feel like they are an integral part."

Schmidt's routine was the same as any other ball club throughout minor and major league baseball. First, he stood on the infield grass halfway between the pitcher's mound and second base, where he hit fly balls as well as ground balls to all his outfielders. "You want to read the hops," said Schmidt. "It's higher in center field. They put a crown in."

The outfielders took the fly balls off his fungo bat and made throws to second base, third base, and home plate. Each time, they made their throws sail through the raised arms of an infielder, who strategically placed himself in various places across the infield grass while acting as the cutoff man. If the throw was off the mark, the infielder cut the ball off, pivoted, and completed the play by throwing to the bag. If the throw was on the money, the infielder let the ball continue its way to the base. The key to the play was judgment and timing. To cut the ball off or not to cut the ball off—that was the question. When the outfielders had concluded their drills, the last of the throws directed to home plate, they left the field, and Schmidt worked with the infielders.

Watching the routine with the four infielders and the catcher was an art form in that the ball moved back and forth between players and bases with sharp, crisp throws that the players seemed to make without effort. Each time I watched an infield practice at these NY-P League ballparks, I had the flashback to the summer of 1971, when as an eleven-year-old kid, I would lean on the front rail of the box seats at Silver Stadium in Rochester watching manager Joe Altobelli hit sharp grounders that his pennant-winning infielders would gobble up. Those Red Wings made athletic pivots and threw the ball like a seed. Mike Ferraro was at third base, Bob Grich at shortstop, Don Fazio at second, and Larry Johnson at first. Next to Altobelli, rotating in and out at catcher, were Johnny Oates and Jim Hutto. Over the loudspeakers, on cue, the public address announcer would blast the soundtrack of *Herb Albert and the Tijuana Brass*. The ball would make a loud pop each time it came back home to either Oates or Hutto, the ball smacking deep inside the leather pocket of their catcher's mitt. My parents did not include opera, theater, and music in my sports-oriented upbringing. For me, resting my chin on the box-seat rail and watching those players sling that ball around the infield at Silver Stadium flawlessly was my own form of poetry, music, and art all mixed, and I loved every minute of it.

Now here was Schmidt, finishing hitting ground balls to his first baseman and ready to take on the most challenging task for any coach or manager during the pregame routine: hitting high fly balls for the catcher in foul territory. As a kid at Silver Stadium, I watched this routine carefully and knew firsthand that the ball could go in any direction, and sometimes into the box seats. Once, Altobelli hit one for Oates that came down on the dugout steps away from the reach of Oates's mitt. The spin on the ball when it popped back up off the dugout step caused it to come down into the first few rows of the box seats, where it ricocheted off the bars that boxed in each section of the seats and then came right toward me and a crowd of people who lunged for the errant pop fly. I missed grabbing the ball by inches, but the adult who made the catch next to me handed it to me as a souvenir.

There at Donovan Stadium, I noticed that Schmidt had a nice knack for this skill as he hit a ball with significant hang time for the Oneonta catcher Jaime Torres. Even so, when he returned to the dugout, Schmidt was the recipient of some lighthearted ribbing from the Yankee players.

"It's an art form, and I happen to not be one of the guys," said Schmidt, his blue SSK fungo bat in hand. "There are some talented individuals who can do that. Jimmy Thrift, the Pittsfield manager last year, could do it. If you're not very good, the joke is, 'Don't blow out your back.' It's a running joke that you can blow out your back. It's from the way you toss it up."

Infield practice now concluded, Schmidt and the rest of the Oneonta players retreated to the clubhouse while the grounds crew spent the next thirty to forty-five minutes prepping the field for the opening pitch. The visiting clubhouse at Donovan Stadium was on the bottom floor of a brick building outside the fence in the right-field corner. In the more spacious top floor of the building was where the Blue Sox assumed residence. The visiting clubhouse was cramped and resembled a high-school locker room. Most of the players did not even bother using the metal lockers, instead keeping their equipment and belongings in their Yankees duffel bags. Players in the clubhouse gradually changed out of the navy-blue batting practice tops and into the road-gray uniform tops. The Yankees farmhands were mostly gathering around the center of the room for a pregame meal that was anything but elaborate. On a bench were a few jars of peanut butter and jelly along with some loaves of bread. Peanut butter and jelly sandwiches were the main course today, along with bananas and peaches to round out the meal. As for liquids, players filled up their cups with Gatorade that was being poured from a large cooler.

In the early innings, it seemed that Dominguez made the right decision to forgo batting practice as a way of resting his players to bust out of a prolonged hitting slump. The Yankees erased a 2-0 deficit with three runs in the second inning and ran the score to 4-2 when Ruben Rivera hit a solo homer off Utica starter Shawn Senior in the third. The Blue Sox, however, came right back and scored three times in the fourth inning to send Oneonta starter Jim Thomforde to an early exit. He left without making it through the fourth inning, his team trailing 5-4.

The Utica starter would not fare much better.

Senior was knocked out in the fifth inning when the Yankees tied the game at 5-5 after Kurt Bierek singled and came home on a triple by designated hitter Mike Schmitz. Senior was done for the night, having surrendered five runs on nine hits in his New York–Pennsylvania League debut after being called up from the Gulf Coast League in Florida. Senior also threw two wild pitches, committed one balk, and made one error. His parents, Joe and Bernadette Senior, had made the trip from their home in Cherry Hill, New Jersey, to watch their son make his start. Despite the shaky outing, the elder Senior, watching the game while leaning on a rail along the first-base side, offered more critique of the umpiring.

"It looked like he was getting his fastball up," said Joe Senior. "I don't think he's used to this strike zone. The league has a reputation for a small strike zone. I don't want to go behind the plate. I know it's a tight strike zone, and I don't want to see how close they were."

The shaky performances by both starting pitchers appeared to be a footnote as the game progressed to the middle innings during an evening in which it was obvious hitting would prevail over pitching. The Yankees moved out on top once again, taking a 7-5 lead in the sixth inning off Utica reliever Chad Renfroe. But Oneonta relievers Scott Standish and Joe Wharton both struggled to maintain the lead when Utica responded in the seventh. John Walker walked, O'Donnell followed with a single, and the hit parade continued when John Stratton and Dan Collier collected singles to tie the game at 7-7.

Things deteriorated for the Yankees in the eighth inning when Wharton watched his teammates commit three errors in one inning, allowing three runs to score for a 10-7 Utica lead. The costly miscue of the inning occurred when Oneonta center fielder Abdiel Cumberbatch chased down a ball in the right-center field gap off the bat of J. J. Johnson with two outs and two Utica runners on base. Cumberbatch had the ball in his glove, but it popped out, and both runners scored on the play.

Now just three outs away from sealing the victory in the ninth inning, Utica reliever Jeff Johnson opened the inning by allowing a single to Schmitz and issuing a walk to Elston Hansen, which prompted the Utica manager Dave Holt to call upon Eric Cormier, his fourth pitcher of the evening. Cormier recorded the first out of the inning when he forced Jaime Torres into an infield flyout, but he loaded the bases when Ernie Yaroshuk followed with a single. The ninth hitter in Dominguez's lineup, Silverio Novas, reached Cormier for a double to score two runs, and suddenly, the Yankees trailed 10-9 with only one out and two runners on base. That was when Cumberbatch proceeded to redeem himself for the miscue in center field by hitting a two-run single to score Yaroshuk and Novas. And just like that, Oneonta was now ahead by a score of 11-10.

Rivera struck out for the second out, and Holt then called upon his fifth pitcher of the night, Rafael Orellano. The Oneonta shortstop, Brian McLamb, greeted Orellano with a single to score Cumberbatch, and the inning ended when McLamb was thrown out trying to stretch his hit into a double. The error-plagued slugfest now plodded its way to the bottom of the ninth inning with Oneonta ahead 12-10.

Dominguez attempted to close out the Blue Sox by calling upon his fourth pitcher of the night, the six-foot-five hard-throwing right-hander Greg Resz, a native of Springfield, Missouri, and one month removed from the campus of Southwest Missouri State University. Resz entered the night having yet to allow a run as a professional ballplayer and had struck out seven batters in the five innings he had pitched to date.

Resz proceeded to retire the first batter of the inning, Collier, on a lineout to shortstop. Two more outs and the Yankees would win. But on this night, two outs seemed like a monumental task. The Blue Sox did not go down quietly. Joe Depastino reached base on a walk, and pitch-hitter Ricky Milligan followed with a single. Greg Patton then drew a walk, and Resz suddenly found himself in a bases-loaded jam.

Over in the first-base dugout, Dominguez did not flinch. The game was in Resz's hands, to win or lose.

Walker brought the Blue Sox within one run at 12-11 when he singled to drive home Depastino. And now, with the bases still loaded, up came the league's top hitter O'Donnell with one out.

The elder O'Donnell was right where I found him during batting practice, standing behind the Blue Sox dugout on the third-base side when his son hit a ground ball off Resz to McLamb at shortstop. On the crack of the bat, the ball was a tailor-made double play, which would give the Yankees the win, but McLamb could not get the ball out of his glove, and his error allowed Milligan to score from third to tie the game at 12-12.

At that point of the evening, a fan seated in the first-base bleacher section had seen enough and decided to let everyone know about it.

"I've seen better Little League games than this—six errors!" he yelled.

Resz escaped the jam when the next batter, Johnson, hit a ground ball to the third baseman Hansen, who stepped on the bag for one out and then threw to Bierek at first to complete the inning-ending double play. The game was headed to extra innings, the score tied at 12-12.

In the tenth inning, Oneonta was right back in it when Bierek opened with a walk, and one out later, advanced to second when Hansen also drew a free pass. Out of the Utica dugout came Holt to pay a visit to the mound with Orellano. As he made the slow walk across the base line, a glance at my watch revealed that the game was now pushing four hours, prompting a restless fan to yell, "Oh come on, we gotta go to church tomorrow!"

Holt opted to stay with Orellano, and his reliever responded by getting Torres to fly out for the second out. Once again, however, the bottom of the Oneonta lineup would produce when the eighth hitter, Yaroshuk, singled to score Bierek and put the Yankees in front 13-12. When the center fielder Johnson mishandled the hit by Yaroshuk, Hansen also scored on the play. The ninth hitter in the lineup, Novas, also singled off Orellano, and Yaroshuk scored to run the score to 15-12.

During the Yankees' half of the tenth inning, Resz had retreated to the bullpen located down in the right-field corner to watch the game. When Cumberbatch struck out to end the inning, here came Resz, back to the mound, not from the dugout, but from the bullpen.

"I'm more comfortable working out of the bullpen," said Resz afterward. "It's kind of away from everybody else."

Now Resz would get the opportunity most closers never got: a second chance to close the game after letting it slip away an inning earlier during his first attempt. The right-hander added more suspense to the evening when he surrendered a one-out solo homer to Nick Ortiz, and that was all Dominguez needed to see as the Oneonta skipper removed Resz in favor of a left-hander, Shawn Alazaus, with his team clinging to a 15-13 lead.

"I had enough to hang in," said Resz, "but they keep us on a strict pitch count. I get thirty-five pitches and I had thrown thirty-three."

Alazaus was also off to an impressive start this season, entering the game without having allowed a run in five innings pitched. He recorded the second out of the inning when he struck out Collier and now faced Depastino for the final out. Alazaus forced the batter to hit a ground ball to none other than the shortstop McLamb, who just an inning earlier could not get the ball out of his glove to start a game-ending double play. This time, however, he did not disappoint his teammates and fielded the ball cleanly to throw out Depastino at first to end the game as the Yankees held on for a 15-13 win.

The final line score on the night read as follows: Oneonta, fifteen runs, eighteen hits, four errors; Utica, thirteen runs, fourteen hits, four errors. The time of the game was four hours and eight minutes, and the attendance was 1,970. It was my estimate, however, that there could not have been more than four hundred fans left at Donovan Stadium when Bierek gloved the throw from McLamb for the final out.

The strategy by Dominguez to rest his players and not take batting practice obviously worked. His pitching and defense, however, were another story altogether. "I'm glad it's over," said Dominguez. "To go through a game like that and lose would have been disastrous. To win that kind of game makes you feel better."

Outside the Utica clubhouse, meanwhile, Tom O'Donnell was ready to talk more baseball with his son TJ at a local eatery called Tiny's, a restaurant that provided a free postgame meal to the Blue Sox.

"It's a buffet," said the elder O'Donnell. "It's nothing fancy. It attracts local people to see the kids. Usually, ten to twelve players will go. What will happen is we'll have something to eat and hash over the game."

O'Donnell cherished the idea of such a gathering with his son.

"I'm probably his best friend, and he's probably my best friend."

Home of the Utica Blue Sox

A view of Donovan Stadium from behind home plate

Fans watch the Blue Sox from behind a wire fence.

A view of the action from the third base side

Utica Blue Sox players watch from the dugout.

CHAPTER EIGHT:

THE AGENT

July 5, 1993—Watertown, New York

Alex Duffy Fairgrounds was home to the Watertown Indians and located off Interstate 81 across a grass parking lot on Coffin Street. One step inside the facility and I was quick to realize that it was the worst park on my summer journey thus far. The facility—I am hesitant to refer to it as a ballpark—was made up of a large, blue grandstand that was constructed for the purpose of watching events at a fair. It could best be described as rickety, and by baseball standards, bush league. Instead of preparing to watch a ball game, I was under the impression that I should be watching tractors and horses. Management attempted to spruce up the seating arrangements by placing makeshift bleachers behind each dugout. I was unimpressed with Donovan Stadium in Utica, but by comparison, Duffy Fairgrounds should have been shut down for the purpose of being unacceptable to host professional baseball games.

To complement the makeshift arrangement, the front office was in a trailer in foul ground on the third-base side. That was where I found Watertown general manager Dan O'Hara, who was seated inside the air-conditioned facility on this extremely hot and humid summer afternoon. O'Hara promptly denied my request for a press pass, informing me that there was not enough room inside the press box that sat high atop the grandstand roof. Instead, he obliged by issuing me a general admission ticket.

There were only two noticeable attractions at Duffy Fairgrounds. The dugouts were spacious, clean, and appeared to be new, and the playing field looked well-manicured. Now, back to the negative aspects: that well-manicured field was so far from the seating area that the Watertown Indians had enough room in foul territory to have two forms of batting practice taking place at the same time. In an arrangement I had yet to see anyplace else, the ball club had set up a pitching machine behind the batting cage. While players inside the cage were swinging for the fences off a live pitcher standing on the mound, players in front of the grandstand backstop were laying down bunts off pitches being fed to them by the machine.

Taking in the pregame routine was a man sitting nearby in the grandstand wearing shorts and a straw hat that read "Callaway Golf" across the front. He had a brown briefcase at his side, and I wondered if he was a scout. If so, he would have been the first scout I had met who wore shorts to a ball game. I introduced myself to thirty-two-year-old Andy Levinson, certified public accountant from Woodland Hills, California, who informed me he was in his first year working as a player agent.

Levinson told me that he quit his job on April 16 as an accountant with Boulevard Management of Encino, California, to begin his quest as an agent. He was working to represent minor league players, which meant that except for the tax work he would do for players, he wouldn't receive a percentage of a ballplayer's salary unless they reached the major leagues. Even then, Levinson said, he would not be guaranteed anything, because a player could switch agents.

"I'm almost broke, but I'll remain above water," said Levinson, who had a degree in accounting from California State University at Northridge. "I'll hook up with somebody, or I'll get funding for what I'm doing."

What Levinson was doing right then was sitting in a dilapidated grandstand in baseball's bush leagues watching the Watertown Indians take batting practice.

"Primarily, the players I represent in the draft, I wanted to come see them play," explained Levinson. "When agents are chasing down players for the draft, they fly all over to meet these players. It is unusual for an agent to travel in the minors."

Levinson informed me that the more handshakes and verbal agreements he got from players, the larger his list of clients, hence, the better his chances would be to represent a prospect. In Watertown, he was checking on players he currently represented. One of those players, Elmira catcher Mike Sims, was in the batting cage taking his cuts while we watched from the grandstand behind home plate. The other player Levinson represented was Elmira third baseman Andy Small. Levinson said that there were four other Elmira players he would have liked to represent because they were from Southern California. The contractual agreement between an agent and a minor league player was a handshake, but if that player was promoted to the major leagues, Levinson would need to get the agreement in writing.

"Once a player gets on a forty-man roster, he's subject to the Major League Baseball Players Association," said Levinson. "Then I want it (a contract) finalized."

Until that occurred—many players never see Double A ball, let alone the major leagues—there was only so much that Levinson and other agents could do for a minor league player.

"I can hook them up with a glove, shoe, or bat company," said Levinson. "It's not like I can get them more money. I can't. Once they're signed, they're all making the same: $850 a month for every player."

If a player did make a forty-man roster, the agent then took a percentage of the player's salary.

"Most guys charge between three to six percent (of the player's contract)," said Levinson. "You can't charge a commission that would take him below the major league minimum salary of $109,000."

The agent business can be risky and comes with few guarantees. Levinson had to hope that his clients made it to the majors and that they stuck with him when that day arrived. If they did not, there would be other agents waiting. Levinson said that there were more agents than there were major league players.

"The problem is, it's extremely cutthroat and competitive," he said. "A lot of agents don't bother getting involved until they get to the big leagues. Those guys will take players away from me. I know that will happen." This scenario, however, did not seem to faze Levinson. He sounded content with charting a new career path, one that was taking him to ballparks across the country. He currently represented forty minor league players who were playing this season in Class A leagues across the country, including the New York–Pennsylvania League, Gulf Coast League, Pioneer League, and Northwest League. He drove a rented Ford Escort to ballparks through the New York–Pennsylvania League, staying in hotels along the way. While at the ballparks, he checked in with players he represented and combed through the bush leagues trying to gain more clients. Soon, he would drive to New York City and fly across the country to the Pacific Northwest, where he would rent another car and begin a twelve-day journey combing through the Class A Northwest League, which had teams located in Oregon and Washington. When he was not at a ballpark, he was going through paperwork at the hotel room, making phone calls, or sitting behind the wheel of his rent-a-car, driving to the next minor league city.

"Travel is a hobby," said Levinson. "The actual driving gives me enjoyment."

Levinson had his brown briefcase with the letters "AML" engraved on top of it at his side. The briefcase contained several items that included the *Baseball American Directory*, the *Baseball America Almanac*, and the *Baseball Blue Book*. He also had several binders, and it was easy to notice that Levinson did his homework well. The binders contained rosters of high-school and college baseball teams from Southern California and other regions of the country.

"I do a lot of research," he said. "I try to follow every player from the state of California. I'm already working for the draft next year."

Levinson also carried a copy of a paperback book entitled *Dollar Sign on the Muscle—The World of Scouting*, written by author Kevin Kerrane.

"I'd like to get a lot of copies of this and give it to high school and college players that are going to be drafted," said Levinson. "A lot of kids think if they aren't offered a lot of money, they should go to college. The reality of it is there are only twenty-eight teams, multiplied by the number of guys in the first three rounds, about a hundred guys that will get the money."

Levinson agreed with the idea of getting a college education, but he did feel a player should take a shot at professional baseball whether he was offered a lot of bonus money or not.

"They all think they'll go to school, and three years later be drafted again," he said. "I think kids should go with their heart. They want to play ball, and when the reality hits them that they can't get the (signing) money, they go to college in spite of professional baseball and say, 'I'll show you in three years.' You may waste three years from a professional baseball point of view. I'm just talking about the kids that really don't want to go to school. The kids that are students, they should go to school."

In addition to combing the minors, Levinson was also a fixture at high school and college games in California. While attending games, he often sat alongside major league scouts. According to Levinson, some of the scouts were friendly, but others wanted nothing to do with agents. Scouts would give clues, he said, regarding what players they planned to draft, and by staying close to their side, Levinson believed that he could develop an eye for baseball talent.

"You watch and you develop a bit of a sense of what a major league player looks like," said Levinson. "I'd rather have ten left-handed pitchers than righties. They're in short supply. That's the first thing I'd look for, a left-hander who throws hard. Scouts don't care about statistics. The players don't understand what scouts look for in a player. They're looking for athletes. The major league teams are convinced they can teach them to hit or field."

Another contact for Levinson and his fellow agents was the position of farm director. Every major league team had one, and this was a key person in an organization responsible for players' promotions, demotions, and getting "released." Levinson called several farm directors and asked them what he considered *the* question: "Where's this guy going?"

"Some won't talk, and some won't return calls," said Levinson. "They have better things to do. The ones who do call back will hopefully give me an honest answer."

And when farm directors answered back that a player was being released, Levinson's job got tougher. "Most (ballplayers) don't want to give up," said Levinson. "My first suggestion is to remember when they were signed out of college. Usually, a lot of scouts watched. They should save their cards. A lot of these kids, when they get released, will be in a haze of anger and shock. I try to counsel and help them and make calls to scouts in the Los Angeles area."

According to Levinson, 30 to 35 percent of all major leaguers had been released at least once. Looking ahead, by the end of summer, Levinson hoped to have fifty to one hundred clients, although it could become unmanageable to have too many players. He also wanted to connect with an established agent and predicted that this could happen within the next six months. A roadblock he saw on the horizon, however, was the 1994 season, which could begin by owners imposing a lockout on players at the start of spring training.

"They're looking at potential loss of income," said Levinson of the agents. "And they don't want to be committed. Why would they want to pay me when around the corner they could be cut off? They live off the commission. They'd have no income."

Levinson would watch the game tonight and check for phone messages at his hotel room, and soon he would be off to the West Coast. While traveling on his new career path, he wanted to make sure he left a positive impression along the way.

"There are a lot of bad people, greedy, slimy," said Levinson of the sports agent business. "I've met some. I'm trying to develop a reputation as honest and less hostile."

Watertown was the first ball club I had encountered in the league which did not sell a program upon entry to the ballpark. A scorecard was sold instead, and on the cover was a picture of Duffy Fairgrounds and the Baseball Hall of Fame and Museum. A caption read, "From Watertown to Cooperstown, Watch Today's Players Become Tomorrow's Legends."

Like the makeshift seating that surrounded the field, other characteristics of Duffy Fairgrounds were second-rate as well. Two examples would be the fifteen-dollar price tag for a souvenir Watertown Indians T-shirt and soggy hot dogs, which came in a roll that crumbled.

During the game, I noticed there was a constant ringing sound coming from the folding chairs to the right side of the backstop. The noise was coming from a bell which was being rung by Bill Beaumont, an elderly man who said he brought the small bell each night to energize the fans. "It gets them alive and gets them going," he said of his bell, which he claimed was one hundred years old. Beaumont, who had been ringing his bell at Watertown games since the city received a franchise in 1983, watched the game while sitting next to John Layton, a former groundskeeper at Duffy Fairgrounds.

After allowing a run in the top of the first inning, Watertown jumped all over Elmira starter Andy Larkin in the bottom of the inning, scoring four runs on four hits and two walks. A two-run single by Elmira's Billy McMillon in the second inning brought the visitors within one run, but that would be all the scoring for the rest of the night as Watertown held on for a 4-3 win. It was a productive night for the Watertown designated hitter Steve Hodson, who had three hits in four at bats, but it would be a long ride back to the Southern Tier for Elmira's Rich Seminoff, the Pioneers' first baseman who was hitless in four at bats while striking out three times.

A young fan writes the lineup in his scorebook for a July 5 game in Watertown between the Indians and visiting Elmira Pioneers.

The seating at Duffy Fairgrounds in Watertown is a makeshift arrangement.

The home plate umpire works a game at Duffy Fairgrounds.

Elmira Pioneers players in the dugout

The Elmira Pioneers have runners at first and second.

Elmira's Billy McMillon waits his turn to bat.

*A Watertown Indians runner slides safely back
to first during a pick-off attempt.*

CHAPTER NINE:

MOTH ALERT

July 10, 1993—Elmira, New York

Today, I was off to the Southern Tier to watch the Elmira Pioneers and to look for dedicated fan George Levering, who I met earlier in the season at McDonough Park in Geneva, the city I passed through today on my way to my destination. Route 14 southbound took me alongside Seneca Lake, which stretches from Geneva at the north end to Watkins Glen at the south with rolling vineyards in between. On the west side of Route 14, the vineyards often stretched right down to the shores of the lake. When I arrived in Watkins Glen, I found a quaint town that was waking up on this Saturday morning with umbrellas popping open at tables situated on the main-street sidewalk in front of small cafes and coffee shops. The town may have been desolated in the winter, but it came alive in the summer when auto-racing enthusiasts descended to the area to watch Grand Prix racing at Watkins Glen International, a historic auto racetrack located three miles outside of the village on Route 16.

Further south of Watkins Glen was Elmira, whose most famous citizen could arguably be Mark Twain. The most famous event, however, would be June 22, 1972, when Hurricane Agnes came ripping up the East Coast and across New York State, causing the Chemung

River to break through levees and flood the city of Elmira. The flood was devastating, water rushing through downtown streets, destroying the business district, and forcing residents to evacuate to higher ground. A total of twenty-three lives were lost in the Southern Tier due to the flood, but amazingly, not one life was lost in Elmira.[33]

Twain was buried at Woodlawn Cemetery, which was also the burial ground of another famous Elmira native, Ernie Davis, who won the Heisman Trophy award in 1961 as the nation's top college football player while attending Syracuse University. In his sophomore season in 1959, Davis led the Orangemen to the national championship when he was named the Most Valuable Player in a Cotton Bowl victory over Texas. Davis was drafted by the Washington Redskins, traded to the Cleveland Browns, and never had a chance to launch an NFL career that appeared destined for greatness when he became ill with leukemia and passed away at the age of twenty-three in 1963.[34]

My travels to Elmira brought me into a residential section of the city and alongside the Chemung River, which was well below the levee and appearing harmless on this July afternoon. My journey took me to the end of Luce Street, the location of Dunn Field, home of the Elmira Pioneers. Dunn Field was an impressive site for a Class A ballpark, a tall structure made of steel and brick through funding by WPA monies in 1939. From the outside, its size could have easily made it pass as a Double A ballpark, and while the park may have been old, it appeared in good condition. Teal-and orange-colored awnings overhung the three entrances outside the stadium with a sign above one of them that read "Dunn Field Municipal Stadium."[35]

Once inside the park, I was quickly impressed with the lush green turf that looked to be the best manicured field in the league

33 Elmira, New York. Wikipedia, *The Free Encyclopedia*. "Elmira, New York." 28 July 2024, https://en.wikipedia.org/wiki/Elmira,_New_York

34 Davis, Ernie. Wikipedia, *The Free Encyclopedia*. "Ernie Davis." 26 July 2024, https://en.wikipedia.org/wiki/Ernie_Davis

35 Dunn Field (Elmira). Wikipedia, *The Free Encyclopedia*. "Dunn Field (Elmira)." 1 August 2024, https://en.wikipedia.org/wiki/Dunn_Field_(Elmira)

that I had seen this season. Hardly a brown or bare spot could be found throughout the infield and outfield grass. The stadium had new dugouts that connected to new clubhouses for both the home and visiting teams, which left the old Elmira clubhouse vacant and available for the umpire crews. Umpire Shawn McAnally had told me that the umpire quarters at Dunn Field were the most spacious in the entire league, and to make matters even better, the locker room was accessible for the men in blue through a gate that opened under the screen behind home plate.

The outfield fence might have been one of the most attractive features at Dunn Field, a tall wooden structure with colored advertisements stretching from the left-field foul pole to the right-field line. The capacity at Dunn Field was 5,100, second in the league in size to East Field in Glens Falls. The only downside to the park at a quick glance appeared to be some seats that needed a new coat of paint. The recent renovation project, which also included a new front office, came with a price tag of $700,000.

When the stadium was built in 1939, the cost was $104,000. The ballpark sat on land that was owned at the time by Edward Dunn, and the stadium was named after the Elmira businessperson. Over the years, Elmira has had working agreements with the Brooklyn Dodgers, St. Louis Browns, and Washington Senators. The longest partnership, however, was with the Boston Red Sox, an affiliation that started in 1972 and just ended a year ago in 1992. As the city now began its 105th season of minor league baseball and its fifty-fourth season at Dunn Field, the major league affiliate was the expansion, Florida Marlins. The ballpark looked great as it began this new affiliation.

Through the years, Dunn Field had seen its cast of players come through on their journey to the major leagues: Jim Palmer, Curt Schilling, and Wade Boggs. Before Don Zimmer went to the majors to play for the Brooklyn Dodgers, he married his wife at Dunn Field at home plate in 1951. Earl Weaver managed here in 1962 when the Pioneers were in the Double A Eastern League, and six years later he was in Baltimore managing the Orioles. Walter "Rabbit" Maranville passed through Elmira on his way to a twenty-three-year major league career. Maranville played for two different teams in the World Series, playing shortstop for the Boston Braves in 1914 and the St. Louis Cardinals in 1928[36]. He would be selected to the Baseball Hall of Fame, as would another Elmira alum, Johnny "Big Cat" Mize, who played fifteen years in the majors while compiling a .312 batting average and collecting five World Series rings with the New York Yankees from 1949 to '53.[37]

Clyde Smoll was the president and general manager of the Pioneers, and I found him walking outside his office while carrying a tin can containing some nails and screws. He seemed preoccupied when I inquired with him about acquiring press credentials for the evening, at first bristling over the matter and then turning silent while he walked around his office area. Finally, he broke his silence and told me that I could get a general admission ticket from his wife, "When you come back into the stadium when the gates open." I continued the conversation with him, and he eventually changed his mind, granting me a press pass that sent me inside the home plate grandstand, where I found a seat to watch batting practice instead of standing outside the park waiting with the fans for the gates to open.

After batting practice, I made my way toward the press box located on the grandstand roof, where I introduced myself to public address announcer Marc Sanders, whom I had seen the night before in the press box at McDonough Park in Geneva. Sanders was there to announce the Pioneers ball game against the Cubs back to the listening radio audience in the Southern Tier. The Jamestown

36   Maranville, Walter. Wikipedia, *The Free Encyclopedia.* "Walter Maranville." 20 July 2024, https://en.wikipedia.org/wiki/Rabbit_Maranville

37   Mize, Johnny. Wikipedia, *The Free Encyclopedia.* "Johnny Mize." 26 June 2024, https://en.wikipedia.org/wiki/Johnny_Mize

Expos were in town tonight, and Sanders informed me that a visiting radio announcer would not be joining the team. And on that note, he swung open a huge glass window at the front of the booth and invited me to assume residence for the night in the visiting radio booth. When Sanders opened that window, I was provided a spectacular view of the field below, along with the Chemung River that was flowing slowly beyond the wall in left field. The downside to the spacious booth with the panoramic view was the presence of many dead moths in a room that was scorching hot. The moths were everywhere, sprawled all over the ledge and on the floor, at least one hundred of them or more. There were so many moths, in fact, that I had to scrape a bunch of them off the ledge in front of my chair to make space for my scorebook, journal, and notepad.

The view of the field from my moth-infested perch confirmed my earlier assessment that the grass turf at Dunn Field was in lush condition. I also admired the height of the outfield fence, at least fifteen feet high and with colorful advertisements. There were amenities at Dunn Field that were not common in other Class A ballparks: access to the clubhouses from both dugouts, padding on the fencing behind home plate, and a rectangular batting cage adjacent to the Elmira bullpen in the right-field corner.

The Pioneers were on the scoreboard early tonight, scoring three runs in the first inning, two of them coming off a home run by Ron Brown. His two-run homer went over the fence in left field, sending a group of youngsters who were watching the game from atop the levee scurrying for the ball.

It only took a few innings for me to realize that Smoll was unlike most modern-day operators of minor league ball clubs. There was no circus atmosphere at Dunn Field with goofy gimmicks in between every half inning. The only promotion I saw took place in the sixth inning when front office staffers brought out a wooden cutout of Little Caesar, the mascot for the pizza chain noted for its five-dollar pizzas. The mouth of the wooden Caesar was cut out, and the gimmick was for a fan to throw a yellow baseball through the opening to win a prize. The attempt was not even close, the wooden cutout was taken away, and it was back to baseball for the rest of the night.

The Elmira and Jamestown ball clubs had been slow out of the gate this season, the Pioneers entering the game at 8-12 and in last place in the Pinckney Division while the Expos came to town at 7-14, cellar dwellers in the Stedler Division.

Jamestown came back to tie the game at 3-3 in the second inning when Jon Saffer hit a two-run single, but the rest of the night would belong to Elmira as the Pioneer hitters feasted on Jamestown pitching much the same way those pesky moths were bothersome to anyone in the park who entered without wearing bug spray. Those moths converged on Dunn Field in such large numbers that when I looked at the light towers, the convention of bugs gathered there gave the appearance of a snowfall in July.

When the evening was over, the Pioneers had collected fifteen hits in a 11-4 win, marking the team's fourth straight win and bringing the ball club within three games of the .500 mark. Pitching was not the only issue for Jamestown as the Expos committed a total of four errors. I would be back again tomorrow to watch the same teams go at it again. On my way out of town, I realized that it was not just the lights of Dunn Field that attracted the moth invasion. Driving down Luce Street past a Pizza Hut, I saw a bevy of moths fluttering around the light of the restaurant sign. I had seen enough, and before I retreated to the confines of my tent at nearby Newtown Battlefield State Park, I stopped at a local supermarket to purchase a bottle of bug lotion.

July 11, Elmira, New York

When I opened the Sunday edition of the *Elmira Star Gazette* this morning, one of the story headlines read "Moths Invade Tiers."

Kelly Quinn, staff writer for the newspaper, opened with a lead sentence in her story by posing the following question: "Snow in July?" Quinn went on to inform her readers that the elm spanworm moth was taking this area by storm. In the article, Joy Thomas of Cornell Cooperative Extension said the moths would be around this area for the next few weeks and that they were presently mating and laying eggs. Ron Case, an employee of the local Atlantic Service Station on the corner of Main and Second Streets, was quoted in the article as well, stating, "They're all over. At night, it looks like a blizzard. I've never seen it like this before." Quinn quoted Mark Vincent when he said he was driving down Water Street the other day "and saw a bird running around in the middle of the road. It turns out a moth was chasing him around."

Later in the day, I arrived at Dunn Field around 4:00 p.m., this time without any conflict with Clyde Smoll. The Pioneers had just finished stretching and were heading toward the right-field foul line after running a series of sprints. The heat was brutal once again. During my ride to the ballpark, a time and temperature sign in front of an Elmira bank showed a reading of eighty-five degrees.

Out on the field, Elmira manager Lynn Jones had a fungo bat in his hand and was ready to lead his infielders through a drill designed to defend against the bunt. He had stationed all his pitchers in a line in foul ground near first base. One by one, they awaited a turn on the mound. Down at the third base coaching box was the fifty-seven-year-old Tony Taylor, a nineteen-year major league veteran, who was currently employed as Florida's roving infield instructor. All the outfielders, meanwhile, were wearing helmets and waiting their turn to run the bases.

The drill began when the pitcher threw home, and Jones laid down a bunt by hitting a ball that he had in his hand. Almost every time Jones laid down the bunt, the catcher called off the pitcher to field the ball, and almost every time, he threw to first base to get the sure out. When pitcher Bryan Ward delivered, he fielded the ball and opted to throw to third to get the runner. Ward, wearing number seventy-one on his black mesh practice jersey, tripped over his own feet and fell to the ground, the play going completely awry. At first, the other pitchers chuckled over his defensive miscue, but the mood quickly became solemn when Ward did not get up. An Elmira player then sprinted to the clubhouse to get trainer Steve Tolly, who came out to tend to Ward, who hurt his left ankle. Ward finally stood up and was helped off the field.

Jones liked to banter with his players, attempting to keep them loose, yet focused at the same time. When throwing batting practice, Jones was at his best. He had friendly ribbing with Rich Seminoff, his 22-year-old, six-foot-four, 220-pound first baseman.

When Seminoff came to the plate to take his cuts, Jones started the commentary. "Drive it," he instructed in the middle of his delivery. And Seminoff did, sending the ball on a rope over the 386-foot sign in center field.

"Must have been the ball," Jones quipped.

Seminoff was not fazed by the ribbing from his manager. He continued to hit line drives, most of them to the gap in right-center field, and still others out of the ballpark. In response to Seminoff's impressive display of hitting.

Jones asked nobody in particular, "What time is it?"

Jones did not really want the time of day, but instead was using an old baseball joke by referring to Seminoff as a "five o'clock hitter," a player who collected all his big hits during batting practice, two hours before game time.

Rob Moen, the Elmira right fielder, was standing behind the cage listening to all those barbs thrown by Jones while waiting his turn to bat. He had a few moments during the lull between his at-bats to weigh in on the bug issue with me. "Those gnats are a pain," he said. "They don't bite you; they just stay by your head. This is the worst park in terms of bugs. It's because of the river right there. I haven't seen moths like that, and so many! Not just here, but all over town, at every light you come to."

When Moen was done hitting, Seminoff was back in the cage, and Jones was back at it again. He threw a pitch right down the middle of the plate that Seminoff let go.

"Striiike!" yelled Jones.

"Gnats," muttered Seminoff.

"What?" asked Jones.

"It was," said Seminoff. "I wouldn't miss turning on your stuff."

The comment forced Jones to raise the bar. The Elmira manager was teaching his young hitters to hit line drives, not just home runs. So now, he posed a challenge to Seminoff when he told him, "You hit a one-hopper to the fence, and I buy you a Coke."

Seminoff quickly responded with the bat by blasting a shot over the outfield fence and off the netting that protected the electronic scoreboard in right-center field.

"That ain't no one-hopper," shouted Jones.

A few pitches later, Seminoff hit a ball hard and, on a line, the ball descended past the right side of the infield. When it hit the outfield grass, the ball quickly rose and slammed into the right-field fence.

A one-hopper, indeed!

"I owe you a Coke," Jones yelled to Seminoff.

I caught up with Jones ten minutes later at his office inside the Elmira clubhouse, a spacious facility for the players, manager, and coaches. Jones's office had carpeting and a refrigerator. He leaned over and grabbed the Coke that would go to Seminoff when he paid a visit after delivering the one-hopper off the fence. Over in the corner stood Jones's golf bag, but he said he simply did not have the time to play. Jones was reclining in his chair without a shirt and using a towel to wipe sweat off his chest when he quickly flicked the towel to swat a moth that was flying nearby: a direct hit, causing the moth to drop to the carpet.

"It was the attack of the mayflies, and now it's the white moths," said Jones. "It's annoying at times, but not that bad on the field. As soon as you open the door from the dugout to the clubhouse, they come in and they cover the walls. In Kansas City, we had big brown moths that were five times as big."

When I got up from my chair, I noticed that the moth he hit with the towel was moving around on the carpet.

"It's still alive," I informed Jones.

Jones leaned forward with towel in hand, assessed the situation, and flicked his wrist with the towel once again, delivering a blow to the wounded moth.

"Not anymore," he said.

Tonight, instead of watching the game from the moth-invested perch inside the press box, I found a seat in the reserved section next to superfan George Levering. I was also joined by David Mule, a young freelance writer from New Jersey whom I had met earlier this season on June 20 in front of Sal Maglie Stadium in Niagara Falls. Mule told me that he was living in Jamestown for the entire season and was traveling with the ball club on the team bus while planning to draft a book about a season with the Expos.

I was confused about Mule's approach to his work. When we were watching the game back at Niagara Falls, I recalled him root-ing for Jamestown's Angelo Thompson when the hitter dug into the batter's box, conduct that contradicted the baseball etiquette of no cheering in the press box. Tonight, Mule and I talked briefly, the freelance writer leaving Levering and me to go sit with a fan he spot-ted wearing a Columbia University T-shirt. Mule had told me in a prior conversation that he was interested in attending Columbia's School of Journalism for his graduate studies.

Mule's bus rides with the Jamestown ball club may have seemed longer as the summer progressed, because after leading 7-1 through six and a half innings, the Expos found a way to squander the lead in the seventh when the Pioneers sent nine batters to the plate and scored five runs to trail 7-5. In the eighth, the Pioneers tied the game when Seminoff chose not to hit a one-hopper off the fence, opting instead to drive the ball over the center-field fence for a two-run homer. In the tenth, the Pioneers scored a run to win the game 8-7, their fifth in a row. The loss, meanwhile, sent the Expos reeling in this young season with a 7-16 record.

After the game, I departed the parking lot and drove down Luce Street on my way out of town, where the moths were still fluttering, one streetlight after another.

The pup tent provided the author his accommodation
at Newtown Battlefield State Park near Elmira, NY.

The exterior of Dunn Field in Elmira, NY

Charlene Smoll, wife of team owner Clyde Smoll, sells tickets.

A vendor sells programs inside Dunn Field.

*Elmira's Andy Prater waits his turn to
hit during batting practice.*

Batting practice at Dunn Field.

*Elmira Manager Lynn Jones provides
defensive drills for his players.*

A member of the Dunn Field Grounds Crew prior to the game

Elmira players help clear the field after batting practice.

Elmira Pioneers players converse with fans before the game.

*The walkway to the press box atop the
Dunn Field grandstand roof.*

A view of Dunn Field from the rooftop press box

A cluster of dead moths are to the right of the author's journal in the Dunn Field press box.

The view of the ballgame is free from atop the Chemung River levee adjacent to Dunn Field.

CHAPTER TEN:

BACK TO THE PENINSULA

July 16, 1993—St. Catharines, Ontario, Canada

A return trip to the Ontario Province Peninsula came with good timing. The NY-P League standings on this date showed St. Catharines and Niagara Falls battling for first place in the Stedler Division, the Rapids (18-9) leading the Blue Jays (18-10) by just a half-game, entering a two-game set here at Community Park on a Friday and Saturday night.

Once again, one of the first Blue Jays players I saw upon my entry to the clubhouse was the left-handed reliever, Chad Brown. The Blue Jays had just returned to town at 5:00 a.m. from a road trip to Oneonta, where they were at the short end of a 12-1 game last night despite outhitting the Yankees 12-11.

"People don't know what it's like to do that," said Brown, "to get in at 5:00 a.m. and then be back out here in the afternoon."

Unlike my last visit here when the game was canceled due to a downpour, the sun was shining brightly, and the mood seemed upbeat. Inside the front gate, a musician named Jim—he did not use his last name—was playing his guitar. Concession workers, meanwhile, were cooking hamburgers and hot dogs on a large charcoal grill. "They taste better grilled," the general manager Ellen Harrigan

Charles would tell me. A few Blue Jays pitchers in game uniform were stationed at entrances handing out free giveaways to the fans entering the ballpark, a public relations strategy that Harrigan Charles implemented to enhance the fan-friendly atmosphere.

"The ticket takers were having a tough time handing out prizes *and* taking tickets," she said. "Plus, it gives fans a chance to meet the St. Catharines Blue Jays on an individual basis. Every game, you'll see two of them at the gate."

Getting the assignment at the gates for tonight's contest were Jay Maldonado and Harry Muir, the latter being the only Canadian on the St. Catharines roster. Muir was a resident of nearby London, Ontario.

Another promotional gimmick was taking place nearby, where Brown was standing behind a table near the Blue Jays clubhouse. Behind Brown stood a portable blue curtain used as a backdrop with the words "Maclean Hunter Cable TV" written on a sign that was attached to the portable stage. The prop that was attracting the fans to this setting was the 1992 World Series trophy that was won by the parent Toronto Blue Jays against the Atlanta Braves. Fans could pay five dollars and stand next to Brown for a picture with him and the Series trophy. While the idea of using the proceeds for the Community Park Playground Project sounded worthy, the photo opportunity seemed a bit tacky considering that the St. Catharines ballplayers had nothing to do with winning baseball's biggest prize at the major league level.

Despite the public relations gimmick, I decided to take a photo of the trophy without paying the five-dollar fee. Within seconds, I was confronted by a gentleman wearing dress slacks with a white shirt, tie, and sunglasses.

"Excuse me, sir; I'm in charge of that trophy," I was told by the man, leading me to think for a second that I committed an Ontario provincial crime. The man introduced himself as Steve Ramsden of Toronto, a twenty-year-old employee in the Toronto Blue Jays public relations department. Ramsden, it turned out, initially thought that I was a writer/photographer for a local newspaper. When he found out otherwise, he proceeded to tell his story, nonetheless.

"I've brought the trophy to all of our minor league teams," said Ramsden. "Its worth is incredible. It's the pride of all of Canada."

Ramsden's tour of duty with the prized possession of major league baseball began in Dunedin, Florida, where the Blue Jays had a Class A ball club in the Florida State League. Next, he traveled to other Blue Jays minor league outposts in Knoxville, Hagerstown (Maryland), and Syracuse. Following his stay in St. Catharines, he was heading west to the port of entry in the Blue Jays organization, Medicine Hat, Alberta, Canada. He would then turn around and head back to Toronto, hopefully with the fifty-pound trophy, its ebony base and fourteen-karat gold plate completely intact.

"It's locked in a vault, sometimes at a hotel, sometimes at a bank," explained Ramsden while giving the trophy similar attention to another Canada treasure, hockey's Stanley Cup. "It changes from each location. Sometimes it's nerve-racking. The normal precautions are taken, and you use a lot of common sense."

For all the high security that Ramsden was emphasizing, I found it humorous that I knew where the trophy was the following day without even looking for it. Across the street from Community Park and the Merritton Lawn Bowling Club was the St. Catharines Blue Jays Souvenir Store and Team Office. I visited the store to talk with Harrigan Charles for a few minutes. When she invited me behind the counter and into her office, there stood a tall, black case with a sticker attached, revealing a Toronto SkyDome address. Harrigan Charles confirmed my notion that the black case—not locked in a bank vault—standing next to her desk contained the World Series trophy.

In all the years of watching professional baseball, beginning in the mid-1960s at Red Wing Stadium in Rochester and including the two seasons as a public address announcer for the Redwood Pioneers of the Class A California League, I could not ever recall witnessing a bench-clearing brawl.

Tonight, the drought almost ended.

In the top of the first inning with the Rapids' Glen Barker on first base following a walk, he attempted to steal second base. Halfway down the base path, he suddenly had second thoughts and was trapped in a rundown. Barker tried to escape the jam he found himself in by knocking the Blue Jays second baseman Robert Mummau to the ground. The Blue Jays infielder held onto the ball for the out, and when he rose to his feet, he gave Barker a shove of his own. The dugouts and bullpens were emptied within seconds, but as it turned out, the cluster of players on the infield dirt resulted in nothing more than a social gathering.

"He came flagrantly at me," Mummau would say later. "I guess he was mad. He got picked off, so he retaliated."

When the dust settled, Barker, the New York–Pennsylvania League's stolen base leader, was ejected, and Mummau remained in the game. Speed, however, could be found throughout manager Larry Parrish's entire lineup. The team did not know what a red light looked like and had swiped seventy-six bases through the first twenty-seven games while being caught thirty times. The Rapids had the league's stolen-base total in the bag, and it was not even August. The Geneva Cubs were second in the league in thefts, a distant twenty-two stolen bases behind the fleet-footed Rapids.

The press box was filled tonight, so I opted to watch the ball game from the second-to-last row of the aluminum bleachers of the home-plate grandstand, a prime view of the adjacent Merritton Middle School, a building so close to the field that I wondered how often the windows were in danger of foul balls. I was soon joined by Harrigan Charles, the enthusiastic thirty-year-old general manager whom I had last seen on June 19 when she was soaking wet during a rain delay against the Batavia Clippers. The redheaded general manager of the Baby Jays—as they refer to the team here in St.

Catharines—was born in Derry, Northern Ireland, and moved to Toronto when she was two. She informed me that her father was a shirt-cutter in Northern Ireland before switching his career in Canada when he became a police officer with the Metro Toronto Police Department. Harrigan Charles told me that she, too, wanted to become a police officer, but when she reached the age of eighteen, her father advised her to wait three more years before applying. In the meantime, she was looking for a secretarial position and found one with the Toronto Blue Jays.

"It wasn't baseball (I was looking for), I was just looking for a secretary position," recalled Harrigan Charles. "I wanted to be a police officer but was looking for a secretarial position until I was twenty-one."

When she turned twenty-one, she did apply with the Metro Police and received an interview. At the same time, though, the Blue Jays made her an offer, an assignment to Dunedin, Florida, the team's spring-training home. She could not refuse the offer, and her career in law enforcement was put on hold once again.

"I thought I liked baseball," she said. "It was an interesting game, and I wanted to give it a few years and try it out."

She stayed with the organization and eventually was offered the assistant general manager position with St. Catharines, a ball club that was owned by the parent Blue Jays, in 1988. After two years as the assistant general manager, she was preparing for a maternity leave in March of 1990 when the general manager Steve Stunt resigned from his position.

"When my child was five weeks old, I got the job and went back to work," she said. "I love it. I enjoy working one-on-one with ballplayers and fans. I enjoy the people part of the job."

She was the only female general manager in the New York–Pennsylvania League and said she had heard her share of inappropriate comments. "I've learned to work with men better than women," she said. "I have a strong dominant personality. They (men) don't intimidate me."

In the top of the second inning, an adult fan climbed the bleacher steps wearing a look of discontent as he approached the general manager, who listened to the issue and left the fan smiling as he walked away.

"He wanted a Junior Jays card for his kid, and we don't have them at the park," explained Harrigan Charles. "I'll give him three cards tonight. That'll bring him back, and he'll probably buy something at the concession stand. He's a happy camper. Concession sales are a great source of revenue. We want clean family entertainment. We're not going to have races in the outfield. They did that in Hamilton. We sell all thirty-nine nights as an event, and every program has a prize in it called Search and Win. You look for the circle, and it could be a free hot dog, sunglasses, Coke, or pizza tickets."

St. Catharines took a 3-0 lead after the first inning, but the Rapids sent nine batters to the plate in the second inning against Blue Jays starter Doug Meiners to take a 5-3 lead. As the game continued, Harrigan Charles spun one story after another. She stared out at the field, saying that she was disappointed with the grass of late, even though the turf looked lush, and maybe even better than the surface at Dunn Field in Elmira. "I look at the field and we're embarrassed, because we have three bald patches," she said. "A recycling plant across the street from the park was on fire and burnt for fourteen hours. Firefighters put so much water on it that three days later, it affected our irrigation equipment. Our irrigation system produced little water and had little strength. The patches will be fine in a week."

When the topic turned to her future in baseball, Harrigan Charles talked about the dream of returning to the major leagues.

"I'd like to be a farm director," she said, "but I don't know if I'll ever see that day: a woman as a farm director. You've got to have deep baseball knowledge, more than paper knowledge. I need to grow personally with baseball knowledge. I never played, and a lot of things I'm learning every day. I read the rule book and the *Baseball Blue*

Book almost every night. I won't use the fact that I'm a woman to my advantage."

St. Catharines battled back in the fourth inning and would eventually take the lead, 6-5, when Adam Melhuse hit a two-run homer over the 400-foot sign in center field against Niagara Falls pitcher Mike Richardson. But the lead didn't last long. The Rapids' Robert Dickerson scored on a single by Del Marine, and the game was tied 6-6 in the fifth inning.

During the seventh inning stretch, the baseball tradition of singing "Take Me Out to the Ball game" didn't happen. Instead, the crowd of 1,578 followed the lead of young female usherettes who were stationed at various points in ballpark doing a series of stretches while singing, "OK, OK...Blue Jays, Blue Jays...let's...play...ball!"

The game remained tied at 6-6 through nine innings, and with Harrigan Charles now tending to responsibilities elsewhere in the ballpark, a middle-aged gentleman sitting nearby named Larry Newhouse was quick to fill the social void for me. Newhouse, I learned, was a season-ticket holder, who, like George Levering in Elmira, would follow his beloved Blue Jays on the road. Last year, he went to fifty-seven games, home and away, and tonight he was attending the game with his wife Mary and his two school-aged children. Most recently, he had returned from a trip to Hagerstown, Maryland, where the Blue Jays had a farm club in the full season Class A South Atlantic League.

"I want to go to Fenway Park, I want to go to Wrigley Field," he said. "I could take a whole summer off and not come back."

Jeff Cheek, the son of the Toronto Blue Jays radio play-by-play announcer Tom Cheek, entered the game in the tenth inning and would run into trouble in the eleventh when he gave up a leadoff single to Dalvis Martinez. Parrish wasted little time jumping on this opportunity and was ready to employ his running game when he sent in a pinch runner, Malvin DeJesus, who was successful in his attempt to steal second base. Corey Broome followed with a walk, and a weak single by Shawn Brown would score DeJesus. Broome would also score in the inning, and when Niagara Falls reliever Joshua Neese retired the Blue Jays in order in the bottom half of the inning, the Rapids came away with an 8-6 win to extend their lead to one and a half games over St. Catharines in the Stedler Division.

July 17, 1993—St. Catharines, Ontario, Canada

My place of residence in between the two-game series was a Eureka dome tent I had pitched at the Four Mile Creek Campsite outside Youngstown, New York, and just minutes from where the Niagara River dumped into Lake Ontario. At 1:27 p.m. today, I felt like I was losing two close friends while sitting on a lawn chair at my campsite. The batteries inside my General Electric transistor radio were dying, and the voices of Toronto Blue Jays announcers Tom Cheek and Jerry Howarth were fading quickly on a Saturday afternoon. Their play-by-play account of the Toronto–Kansas City game was then history, and I would be suffering from baseball withdrawal for about three hours before heading back across the Canadian border at the Lewiston-Queenstown Bridge for the return trip to Community Park and another game between the Baby Jays and the Rapids. I had plenty to do to keep myself occupied. Updating my journal of my baseball travels and cooking hamburgers on my portable grill were at the top of the list.

When I arrived a few hours later at Community Park, the Blue Jays were taking batting practice and were suddenly distracted when five parachuters landed in the recreation park just beyond the left-field fence. Blue Jays manager J. J. Cannon was watching this scene unfold in front of him when one of the parachuters nearly hit the light tower behind the left-field fence but managed to just avoid it for a successful landing.

Cannon appeared impressed.

"That's pretty smooth," the Blue Jay skipper commented.

Cannon sent Edwin Hurtardo, a twenty-three-year-old Venezuelan with a 3-1 record, to the mound for the home team. Over the course of seven innings, he would throw seventy-four pitches and the Blue Jays would lead 2-0.

It was not enough, however.

Parrish went to his bench again after using fourteen players the previous night. In the eighth inning, he inserted DeJesus as a pinch hitter, and he produced a leadoff walk. Broome came to the plate and delivered the key blow, a two-run homer to right field, and just like that, with one swing of the bat, the game was tied 2-2.

Hurtardo finished the inning, but he gave way to Dilson Torres to open the ninth. Torres struck out Shawn Brown and then gave up a double to Dickerson, who would advance to third on a groundout by Tyrone Dixon. Torres appeared to be out of the jam when the next batter, Eric Danapilis, hit a routine fly ball to shallow center field. Blue Jays center fielder Rafael Debrand came in on the ball, but at the last second seemed distracted by the oncoming right fielder Emmanuel Hayes, causing him to drop the ball. Dickerson scored on the miscue, and the Rapids hung on in the bottom of the ninth for the 3-2 win and a sweep of the two-game set.

All told, Parrish wore out his pencil by making seven lineup changes over the course of the last two innings. In all, he used seventeen players tonight, and his Rapids (20-9) would make the short commute back across the border to Niagara Falls, New York, with a two-and-a-half-game lead over the Blue Jays (18-12).

July 18, 1993—Welland, Ontario, Canada

I ended my three-game weekend road trip on the Ontario Peninsula at Welland Stadium to watch two ball clubs in a different sort of race. The hometown Pirates and the visiting Erie Sailors were both battling to avoid the basement. Unexpectedly, I ran into George Levering when entering the ballpark, which confused me, considering that the Elmira Pioneers were not in town. When I inquired, Levering informed me that he was embarking on a two-city doubleheader: the afternoon contest between the Sailors and Pirates and a nightcap at nearby St. Catharines between the Blue Jays and his beloved Elmira Pioneers.

Unlike my first visit to Welland, this time I chose to watch the game from the press box instead of the stadium seating. The press box there was one of the best in the league: long, spacious, and comfortable, and it featured attractive knotty pine walls. I was keeping score of the game from my perch in the booth when Brian Sloan, the twenty-seven-year-old general manager of the Welland ball club, came by to introduce himself.

"I enjoy Sunday afternoon baseball games, and it's nice for our staff," said Sloan. A look across the league schedule showed Sloan as one of the only operators in the league who offered afternoon baseball.

"This is how it should be played," said Sloan. "I called and asked the other general managers if it was OK with them for travel arrangements."

If Sloan came off as traditional with the concept of day baseball, he was the opposite when it came to promotions. Looking down at the seating section below me, it looked like Halloween in July with vendors wearing costumes that included Dracula and a court jester.

"Our target is kids, and they get bored," Sloan said, justifying the carnival atmosphere. "I try to do things like a Walt Disney theme. People like that. Wearing a costume draws attention."

Sloan's entry into professional baseball was just as intriguing as his ideas on how to promote it. A native of Montreal, he attended the University of Western Ontario in London, where he graduated in 1988 with a degree in psychology and intentions to become involved with social work. Things never happened that way, however, as his first job out of college consisted of a seven-month stint selling life insurance.

"I learned that I didn't mind selling things, but I have to like what I sell," he said.

Selling life insurance was not at the top of his list, so Sloan began to plan his next move. Back home in Montreal and recovering from shoulder surgery, he saw an advertisement in the newspaper for a seminar on sports administration at Concordia University.

"I went to the seminar and said to myself, 'This is what I'd like to get into,'" remembered Sloan.

At first, he had hopes of rising right to the top with the idea of landing a job in the major leagues without spending time beating the bushes of the minor leagues. During the summer of 1990, he packed up his Honda CRX and left a friend's house, coincidentally from right here in Welland. He would embark on a journey that took him on a twelve-thousand-mile round-trip tour of the United States with stops at many major league front offices along the way. Sloan knocked on the administrative doors of the Chicago Cubs, Los Angeles Dodgers, San Francisco Giants, Oakland A's, Cincinnati Reds, and Detroit Tigers. The only minor league stops were in Louisville and nearby London, Ontario. Despite his efforts, not a single offer came his way. The best advice he received along the way was to go to a place where all the general managers, major league and minor league, would come together at once: the annual baseball winter meetings.

Sloan went back to Los Angeles in December of 1990—this time by airplane—to attend the annual baseball winter meetings, and opportunities came his way.

"I had twelve interviews and three offers," he said.

The St. Petersburg Cardinals offered a position in concessions while the Kane County (Illinois) Cougars offered an internship. He was most interested in going to St. Petersburg but opted not to because the Persian Gulf War was about to take place. He ended up taking a position as a sales representative in Welland, right where his twelve-thousand-mile journey began.

"I didn't stop at the park in Welland," he said. "I was thinking major league all the way. My first year in Welland, I worked for $650 per month. I had talked to Dave Dombrowski when he was with Montreal. He said, 'Try to get your foot in the door at any level; do your best, and it'll get noticed."

Sloan was noticed, arriving at the ballpark at 9:30 a.m. following night games to clean the grandstands. Following his second season in Welland, he was quickly promoted to the position of general manager. While the title may have sounded and seemed glamorous, it did not come without headaches. Sloan may have been putting in the long hours, but it did not guarantee big crowds. And attracting fans to watch Welland Pirates baseball had not been an easy task. Last season, nine other ball clubs in the fourteen-team New York–Pennsylvania League drew more fans than the 38,209 that came through the turnstiles at Welland Stadium.

"It's a saturated market," said Sloan. "Given the choice of watching the Blue Jays on TV and having a cold beer in the comfort of your living room, they would rather choose that than come watch the Welland Pirates."

Sloan also had competition from three other nearby teams, as the Niagara Falls Rapids, St. Catharines Blue Jays, and Buffalo Bisons (Class AAA International League) were all located within forty minutes of Welland Stadium. He noticed that the Bisons were pushing into the Southern Ontario Peninsula trying to promote Triple-A baseball for the purpose of expanding a fan base following Buffalo's denial as an expansion entry in the National League. Sloan viewed the Bisons' marketing tactics as infringement on the Welland fan base.

"They're coming in here trying to sell groups," said Sloan. "Ethically, they can't do that."

Today, Sloan also had another competitive factor to consider, and it was not a baseball team. The Ethnic Festival was underway in nearby Port Colborne, and Sloan was certain it would impact the attendance at Welland Stadium. The more I listened to Sloan talk, the more he seemed frustrated with the obstacles that stood in his way to draw a respectable gate.

"I just had a lady ask me, 'Is this a semipro team?'" said Sloan. "That's not an uncommon question."

While Sloan and I continued to talk inside the press box, the game in front of us moved along at a steady pace, with Erie leading 1-0 through five innings, the lone run coming in the fourth when Michael Hill scored on a single by Brian Clark Blair. Sloan introduced me to his younger brother, twenty-five-year-old Steve, who worked for the ball club in the position of director of concessions.

"Right now, I love baseball," said Brian Sloan, who held a marketing degree from Concordia University. "After the season, I'm not sure what I want to do. When you're in minor league baseball, you're doing everything: sales, accounting. There is nothing in the business part that you don't get to do."

In a game that was a pitcher's duel between Erie's Bert Gerhart and Welland's Jason Phillips for five innings, batting practice suddenly broke out in the top of the sixth. The Sailors knocked Phillips out of the game with a four-run inning to grab a 5-1 lead. Erie added two more runs in the seventh and capped a sixteen-hit attack with four more runs in the eighth off a grand slam by Wes Shook. It was Shook's seventh homer of the season, ranking him third in the league and three behind Utica's Dan Collier, who led the circuit with ten. Welland's Mitch House led off the bottom of the ninth with a solo homer, but the Pirates then went down quietly, losing to the Sailors by a score of 11-2.

The Sailors and Pirates now had identical 13-17 records and trailed Niagara Falls by seven and a half games in the Stedler Division. Jamestown, still struggling at 11-18, was in last place in the division, nine games behind the Rapids.

*Ellen Harrigan Charles, St. Catharines
Blue Jays General Manager*

*Ellen Harrigan Charles, St. Catharines
Blue Jays General Manager*

Alonso Beltran, St. Catharines Blue Jays starting pitcher

Alonso Beltran, St. Catharines Blue Jays starting pitcher

Helmets in the Blue Jays dugout ready for gametime

*The 1992 World Series Trophy won by the Toronto
Blue Jays is on display in St. Catharines.*

Young fans converse with a Blue Jays player prior to a game.

A Blue Jays player hands out a giveaway at the gate

Dugouts empty and tempers rise among
Blue Jays and Rapids players

CHAPTER ELEVEN:

THINK OF OUR CHILDREN: KEEP BASEBALL IN AUBURN

August 1, 1993—Auburn, New York

As the dog days of summer approached, I returned to the ball-park where my summer journey began: decrepit Falcon Park, the home of the Auburn Astros. I found the Astros to be in as rough a condition as the park that they call home, limping along at 16-26, a full nine games behind Watertown in the Pinckney Division. The season, now beyond the halfway point, included tight races for first place in all three divisions through the month of July.

Stedler Division

	W	L	GB
Niagara Falls	25	17	---
St. Catharines	25	18	1.5
Batavia	21	22	4.5
Welland	21	23	5
Jamestown	17	25	8

McNamara Division

	W	L	GB
Oneonta	24	19	---
Utica	22	20	1.5
Glens Falls	22	22	2.5
Pittsfield	20	21	3

Pinckney Division

	W	L	GB
Watertown	25	17	---
Geneva	24	19	1.5
Elmira	17	25	8
Auburn	16	26	9

The Batavia Clippers were in town for a Sunday night game at Falcon Park, and Leo Pinckney, an elderly man who was a former sportswriter and editor at the *Auburn Citizen* from 1938 to '83, threw out the first pitch of the game. Pinckney was considered a baseball legend in Auburn as he could recite the details of Auburn professional baseball in one sitting. As he was a former president of the New York–Pennsylvania League, the division Auburn played in was named in his honor. Pinckney still dabbled in the game, working as a part-time scout for the Florida Marlins.

I noticed a different tone in the ballpark tonight when compared to my visit there on opening night in June. Several signs were hung throughout the ballpark, all of them with the same message to keep baseball in Auburn. The sign above the railing at the top of the home plate grandstand read, "Think of Our Children: Keep Baseball in Auburn."

Entering tonight's game, Batavia was trying to snap out of a mid-season slump. The ball club was 16-12 in mid-July, but the Clippers had dipped below the .500 mark. Tonight, they'd try to even the record at 22-22 when Silvio Censale (4-2, 2.38 ERA) took the mound against Auburn right hander Mike Diorio (3-2, 5.16). Diiorio was one of only two Auburn pitchers with a record above the .500 mark, Thomas Czanstkowski (4-1) being the other. A glance at the stat sheet revealed that the Astros had a team ERA of 4.23, and an even closer look showed that Tim Kester still had only one victory, in a game that I attended on June 25, a 3-2 win over the Geneva Cubs.

The Astros' pitching woes continued right away when Batavia sent nine batters to the plate in the first inning, the Clippers collecting five hits and scoring four runs against Diorio. During this early outburst, Diorio would have to endure as Auburn manager Manny Acta never signaled activity in the bullpen.

The frustration on the part of the Astros was evident in the bottom half of the inning when John Vindivich struck out to end the inning while stranding two base runners. Vindivich then threw his helmet in disgust and proceeded to walk to his position in the outfield.

The evening did not get any better for the Astros as the game progressed.

Batavia added another run in the third inning for a 5-0 lead and the Auburn bats were silent through six innings, the Astros managing just two hits through six and two-thirds innings against Censale when he exited in the seventh. Censale would have stayed in the game, but with a 1-2 count on Auburn second baseman Eduardo Cedeno, Censale suddenly lifted his arm in the air and grimaced in pain while standing on the mound, which led Batavia trainer Brent

Lieby and manager Al LeBoeuf to sprint to the mound to assess the problem.

"He threw a fastball, then a slider, and felt something stretch," said LeBoeuf after the game. "He flexed it a few times, and I knew something was wrong. When my guys are out there, I care about their welfare. When I see something wrong, right away, you think the worst."

I spent a portion of tonight's game talking with Pinckney in the concourse area behind the first-base grandstand. He was a tall, distinguished-looking man with silver hair, and he moved throughout the ballpark talking with people along the way. It seemed like Pinckney knew everyone and everyone knew him. Pinckney pulled out of his wallet a faded yellow laminated press pass he used when he was the official scorer at Falcon Park in 1938 at a time when the team was a member of what was known as the Can-Am League.

"This is the worst park in the league," said Pinckney, assessing the sixty-nine-year-old ballpark. "They need to tear it all down. It's in bad shape. No visiting teams dress here. There was a nine-foot drop-off in center field, and they've filled it in over the years."

According to Pinckney, if the city council did vote for a new stadium—it was turned down 3-2 in a recent vote, and a 4-1 tally was needed for approval—Pinckney believed that a new playing field should come with the new ballpark as well.

Pinckney's fondest memory at the ballpark went back to 1966 when Auburn was affiliated with the New York Mets. The team won the league championship that season with a roster that included several players who would go on to play with the New York Mets: Jerry Koosman, Tug McGraw, Cleon Jones, Ken Boswell, and Jim McAndrew, five players who were members of the World Series Champion Miracle Mets in 1969. Among the alumni, Pinckney befriended Koosman more than any other player and would arrange for the major leaguer to come back to Auburn on more than one occasion to speak at banquets.

Pinckney also spoke highly of the 1972 season when the first female umpire in professional baseball, Bernice Gera, worked the bases involving an Auburn game at McDonough Park in Geneva.

"She worked the bases and threw out Auburn manager Nolan Campbell over a dispute at second base," recalled Pinckney. "In between games of the doubleheader, she quit and left the park with her husband."

Pinckney also had ties with another baseball first, when in 1974, the youngest player ever to participate in professional baseball did so with the Auburn Phillies. Jorge Lebron was only fourteen years old when he came to Upstate New York from Puerto Rico to play shortstop at Falcon Park.[38]

"We had to play some games early, at 5:00 p.m., because of the child labor laws," said Pinckney. "Lebron wasn't supposed to play past 9:00 p.m. They went before a judge and straightened it out. He was here two years, then he went up to a long season Class A team and fizzled out."

As a result, it was very likely that Lebron held two baseball records.

"He's the youngest player to retire, at age seventeen," said Pinckney, "I heard he's teaching school now in Puerto Rico."

Later in the game, I settled into the bleachers behind the third-base dugout, the same location where I took a fall through the gaps in the seats and spilled my soft drink on my hamburger on opening night. While enjoying the game unfold in front of me on this August evening, I noticed an elderly gentleman and a younger woman who were sitting with each other a few rows behind me. They seemed focused on the game, the woman wearing a T-shirt which had a picture of Tiger Stadium on the front. I soon introduced myself and met the

---

38   Lebron, Jorge. *thisdayinbaseball.com*. 10 August 1974, https://thisdayinbaseball. com/1974-jorge-lebron-the-youngest-professional-player-ever-makes-his-debut-for-the-phillies-farm-club-auburn-the-fourteen-year-old-shortstop-plays-three-games-before-return/

sixty-five-year-old Franklin Fry and his thirty-five-year-old daughter Christine. The father-daughter team had been coming to Falcon Park since Christine Fry was a young child, the elder Fry being a patron of the ballpark for fifty-five years. It all started, I learned, when Franklin Fry's parents began taking summer vacations at their cottage on Skaneateles Lake while visiting the area from their home in Akron, Ohio. When Fry grew older and married, he had four daughters and one son. Among the five children, Christine emerged as the biggest baseball fan. She and her dad came to Falcon Park every summer while still vacationing at Skaneateles Lake.

"Coming here as a kid, I made a lot of racket," said Christine Fry. "I would go around and bug the opposing pitchers in the bullpen. Dad always took us to minor league games, and I'm forever grateful."

Today, Christine Fry resided in Boston and was pursuing a master's degree in occupational therapy. She held season tickets in the bleachers at Fenway Park but claimed that the major league diet had not spoiled her desire for minor league baseball, having seen games in more than thirty minor league ballparks across the country. A few years ago, she and a friend made a trip to the Appalachian League, where she saw games in Bristol (Virginia), Johnson City (Tennessee), Elizabethtown (Tennessee), Bluefield (West Virginia), and Princeton (West Virginia).

"I had a desire to see that league," she said. "And I had a fear that some of those parks wouldn't last. We have the Grim Reaper Tour: you look at the ballparks in peril, and that's where you go."

Fry reported that she had also seen games in Rochester, Buffalo, Syracuse, Toledo, Scranton/Wilkes Barre, New Britain, London, Albany, York, and Reading. In the New York–Pennsylvania League, she had attended games in Geneva, Batavia, Oneonta, Pittsfield, and Elmira. She was also a member of the Tiger Stadium Fan Club and the Society for American Baseball Research, whose members conducted historical and statistical baseball research. One of her personal projects was to prevent the destruction of Tiger Stadium in Detroit, a ballpark that she considered her favorite.

"When the Tigers come to Fenway Park, I'll hand out fliers reminding fans to save that park," she said. "It's my favorite because of the upper deck and closeness of the seats, and the fact that it's enclosed. I saw the most exciting game of my life there. The new ballpark in Chicago, I don't call it Comiskey Park, because it's gone. The first row in the upper deck in the new ballpark is farther away than the last row of the upper deck in Tiger Stadium."

Franklin Fry said he was at Falcon Park tonight because it was obvious the old ballpark was on the way out. Instead of looking forward to the prospects of a new park, he seemed more concerned about missing the current structure. "It's tragic," he said. "That's why we had to get over here. I'd be much less inclined to come to a new park. It won't have the particular character and flavor. And it won't have the memories of me coming here as a kid with my dad, and now bringing my own kid."

The game had now entered the ninth inning with the Astros behind 7-0. Auburn was just two outs away from defeat when the second baseman Cedeno came to the plate. Although he had struck out twice and grounded out, he also accounted for one of only two hits Auburn had mustered against Batavia's Censale and reliever Scott Barstad.

"I'm tracking Cedeno and (Carlos) Crispin because of their infield play," said Christine Fry, sounding more like a professional scout than avid fan. "And they're speedy. It's fun seeing them this low and then watching them make the major leagues."

Auburn managed to load the bases on two walks and a Batavia error, but with two outs, Barstad closed the door on the Astros when he forced Nate Peterson to fly out to right fielder Joey Madden, preserving the two-hit shutout and a 7-0 win for the Clippers.

I bid farewell to Franklin and Christine Fry as I exited Falcon Park and was surprised when my car radio picked up the play-by-play account of the Lynchburg Red Sox game against the Kinston Indians on WLLL Radio 930 AM out of Lynchburg and the faraway Smoky Mountains.

CHAPTER TWELVE:

WARM UP THE BUS

August 2, 1993—Geneva, New York

The pregame routine in professional baseball—major league or minor league—works like clockwork: batting practice for the home team followed by the visiting team; infield practice for the home team followed by the visiting team. Then, with thirty minutes to go, the grounds crew takes over the field and goes through a routine of its own: dragging the field, lining the bases, matting down the pitcher's mound and batter's box, and putting on the finishing touches by spraying down the infield dirt to prevent the dust from blowing.

So, when the Geneva Cubs finished batting practice on this Monday evening at McDonough Park, it looked strange to see the batting cage sitting vacant at home plate. The visiting Glens Falls Redbirds neglected to take their hacks and instead were gathered in a large circle in the left-field corner, conducting a series of stretching exercises followed by sprints from the foul line to center field.

"It took an hour and thirty-five minutes to get here from Syracuse," explained Glens Falls manager Steve Turco. "We took a different route, hit traffic, and got here forty minutes late."

What needed more explanation was why the Redbirds were staying in Syracuse in the first place. The Redbirds played here in

Geneva last night, won the game 2-0, and traveled to Syracuse even though they had another game here tonight.

Turco explained that tomorrow would be an off day before heading west to Erie. Instead of driving four and a half hours back to Glens Falls for a day off, he wanted the team to stay put and decided that Syracuse would have more to offer than Geneva.

"We may even go to a Syracuse Chiefs game on the day off," said Turco.

The way things were going lately for Glens Falls, it wouldn't matter where the Redbirds spent their off day. The Redbirds were the hottest team in the league, having turned around their season in a matter of just two weeks by winning eight in a row and twelve of their last fifteen. On July 18, the Redbirds were sputtering at 11-19 but entered tonight's game with a mark of 23-22 and had climbed out of the McNamara Division cellar to close to within one and a half games of division-leading Oneonta.

"It has been a combination of three things," said Turco. "We're starting to get some breaks, for one. We've had solid pitching performances, both with starting and relief roles. And the defense has been outstanding throughout (the streak)."

Since Turco and the Redbirds were behind schedule, batting practice would have to be shortened. Usually, the players came to the cage in groups of five, but today, he told all his players to put on helmets at the same time. Turco cleared the infield and sent all his pitchers to the outfield to shag balls. The sixteen Redbird hitters were divided into two teams by Turco and would play a pretend game during batting practice with invisible base runners. The rules were simple: Turco was not only the pitcher, but the umpire as well, and would determine whether batted balls would be ruled as hits or outs, depending on where fair balls were hit. Foul balls, meanwhile, would be ruled as automatic outs.

As the batting practice "game" moved along, there was a feeling among the players gathered around the cage that Turco was exceptionally stingy with his calls and only now and then was willing to award base hits coming off the bats of his Redbird players. As a result, there were only a few "invisible" players moving around the base paths, and the pretend game was scoreless entering the sixth inning.

Osmel Garcia tried to get something started by laying down a bunt, but it wasn't good enough, and Turco ruled it to be an out, calling it a sacrifice bunt instead. As a result, Garcia then took his share of razzing from teammates around the cage by laying down a bunt instead of taking his cuts.

Up next, Trey Ritz delivered a hit through the hole, a single in everyone's mind, no doubt.

"Hey, Ritzie, three for three," a teammate remarked.

"Hey, five o'clock hitter," said Ritz, who was one of the few players to get a hit off Turco, having collected three hits in three at bats.

Now the game was scoreless in the seventh inning, but Joe Jumonville ended the drought by giving the infielders a 2-0 lead over the outfielders with his two-run homer to right field over the Bob Stenzel Chevrolet billboard.

Greg Almond, the Redbird catcher, had been a quick wit throughout batting practice. "Let's go, time's a-wasting," he cracked when he entered the cage but had to wait while Turco and the infielders refilled the shopping cart with baseballs. Almond was unlike his teammates because he didn't wear a batting helmet, let alone a baseball cap, an uncommon sight inside any batting cage. Some of the Redbird players started calling him "Pretty Boy" because his head of hair was fully exposed when he dug into the batter's box.

Almond, whose team was ahead 2-0, heard the barbs and snapped back with a challenge: "Losers buy winners hot dogs after the game."

"They have ten minutes left," said Turco, "and we could go thirteen innings."

After nine complete innings of the pretend game, Almond's team, comprised of the catchers and infielders, held onto the 2-0 lead, but as Turco had predicted, there would be extra at bats, and the game would play on. This meant another opportunity for the outfielders, and they delivered when Sal Bando Jr.—son of Sal Bando, captain of the Oakland A's of World Series fame in 1972, '73, and '74—hit a three-run homer to win the contest 5-2.

When the batting-practice game ended, Almond was quick to point out that his team won the game through nine innings. Few seemed interested in listening, however. They were too busy picking up baseballs and loading them back into the shopping cart on the mound. Almond, meanwhile, did not offer any assistance, walking away instead toward the dugout.

"Pick 'em up, chumps," he said.

Turco did not mind the bantering. His goal was simply to get all his position players a few cuts before the game.

"He wanted to make the most out of his time," said Almond afterward. "It helped us mentally, because every time you dig in, you get one cut."

"That was a friendly competition," said Turco. "It's something we've done in the past within this organization. It breaks up the monotony. I was even thinking of letting the pitchers hit. This is a business, but it's also a game. You want them to enjoy themselves when they come out to the park. When you play baseball, you're talking about the ability to compete. There is a little razzing going on, and even though it's just in fun, everyone wants to win."

Turco was a former Cardinals farmhand himself. He had managed St. Louis minor league affiliates in the Midwest, Florida State, and Appalachian Leagues. Two years ago, he managed this same Glens Falls franchise when it was based in Hamilton, Ontario, Canada. Last year, he was at Johnson City, Tennessee, of the Appalachian League.

I began watching the game from a vantage point in the visiting radio booth, which was left empty because the Redbirds did not broadcast road games. It was noticeably cooler tonight than it was thirteen nights earlier on July 20 when I was here to watch the Cubs and Watertown Indians in a doubleheader. My stay in the booth, however, was short-lived when George Park, the publisher of the *Finger Lakes Times*, the regional daily newspaper, entered the booth with his son and some guests.

The pitching matchup for tonight's game had Geneva's Darren Dreyer opposing Marc Ottmers of Glens Falls, a right hander who would try to run the Glens Falls winning streak to nine games. The eight-game winning streak, and the escape from the McNamara Division basement, had the Redbirds approaching each game on a more positive note.

"Right now, these kids are confident, and when they come to the ballpark, they know they're going to win," said Turco. "It's really not a question whether they're going to win. They know they're going to (win). It's not as though we have to just put our gloves on the field. They know they still have to come to work, but there is a great sense of confidence they're playing with."

"A big aspect of us being loose is the winning," said Almond. "If we had lost eight or nine in a row, it would be a different story. In the beginning, we lost a lot of games, and everyone was really tizzed. But now, since we're on a good streak, it seems like we can't do anything wrong. Everybody enjoys winning, and who wouldn't enjoy winning?"

As the game began, it had become apparent that a small contingent of local fans had come to watch a Redbird reliever named Dan Pontes, a twenty-two-year-old, six-foot-two right hander who was a graduate of Geneva High School.

Pontes went on to play college baseball at Long Island University. He had a 1-2 record and a 4.12 ERA with Glens Falls, and although he had some tenderness in his throwing arm, it was possible that Turco could go to him tonight if the need arose.

In the bottom of the second inning with the game scoreless, Geneva's James Young drew a two-out walk against Ottmers, but

Young was quickly erased when he was thrown out by Almond attempting to steal second base.

Curious that someone in Geneva knew the Glens Falls catcher by his nickname, I turned to see who it was and quickly introduced myself to the Redbirds' bus driver Walt Olszewski. The fifty-one-year-old Olszewski and I then talked in between pitches while Dreyer and Ottmers became locked in a pitcher's duel during the early innings. Dryer retired the Redbirds in order in each of the first three innings, not allowing a hit or a base runner. Ottmers, meanwhile, was equally impressive, striking out four of the first six batters he faced. In the bottom of the third, Ottmers gave up his first hit of the night, a solo homer off the bat of Geneva's Brandon Pico to put the Cubs ahead 1-0. Two batters later, Emilio Mendez flew out to center field for the second out, and the umpires quickly called for a delay in the game even though not a single raindrop was falling on McDonough Park. The reason for the delay was due to the lightning strikes that were visible in the distance beyond the center-field fence.

I headed for the parking lot to take cover in my car, but instead paid a visit to Olszewski, who was inside the Upstate Tours bus which was parked nearby. The coach bus had light-blue stripes on the side and a Glens Falls Redbirds logo on the back. Inside, there were forty-seven seats, six TV sets mounted from the ceiling throughout the bus, and one bathroom located in the back.

Olszewski began to tell me about his career as a bus driver, one that began eight years ago following twenty years in the horse-training business near Saratoga Springs, New York. In the last five years at Upstate Tours, Olszewski had primarily been transporting professional teams. He drove the Albany-Colonie Yankees of the Class AA Eastern League and the Glens Falls Red Wings of the American Hockey League. He had seen his share of baseball over the years and preferred the short-season Class A Redbirds over the Double A Yankees.

"This is better ball," he said. "They have one chance. If they blow it here, they're not going to make it. You see them playing hard. There's a different attitude in Double A: a lot of Double A guys think they're in the majors already. These Class A guys run out all ground balls and run into fences. In Double A, some of them just don't play hard."

When Olszewski drove the Albany-Colonie Yankees, the manager of the team was Buck Showalter, who in 1993 was manager of the New York Yankees. Olszewski first met Showalter late in the 1989 season at Albany.

"We got through a road trip, and I had just met him," recalled Olszewski. "He gets off the bus and asks, 'Will you be here for the playoffs?' I told him no because I had to move my daughter to Washington, DC. When I got back, he asked, 'Did you get your daughter moved OK?'"

Aside from Olszewski noting that Showalter was sincere, he also remembered him to be extremely structured.

"Showalter is very intense," said Olszewski. "He said, 'At 3:25 p.m., you go back to the hotel to bring players to the park, and at 4:15 p.m., the same thing.' Then he said, 'That's 3:15 p.m. and 4:15 p.m., not 3:16 p.m. or 3:17 p.m. You leave if they're not there.' With Buck, you like to see him go to the major leagues, but not to be a puppet to (George) Steinbrenner. He's going to do things his way."

Olszewski also respected the way Showalter managed his players, saying that he wouldn't chew out a player in front of another.

"He would do that in private," said Olszewski, "to the best of my knowledge, anyway."

Olszewski did not have fond memories, however, for all the Albany-Colonie managers. During the 1991-92 seasons, the ball club was managed by Dan Radison, a skipper who, according to Olszewski, once made him step off the bus so he could chew out his team.

"We were in Albany, ready to leave (after a home game to travel at night) and had just pulled out of the park and into a parking lot," recalled Olszewski. "He made me and the radio man, John Thomas, get off the bus. He was upset with the lack of hustle. We waited twenty minutes outside the bus, and it started to rain."

Olszewski had met a lot of players during his travels, and his favorite was the five-foot-nine Andy Stankiewicz, who played second base for Albany-Colonie during the 1989 season when Showalter was the manager.

"The first time I met him," said Olszewski, "he says, 'Hi, my name is Andy Stankiewicz. I play second base. If you need anything and I can help you, let me know.' He's a great kid. Stankiewicz has hustled as much as anyone. You want to see good things happen to him."

Good things did happen to Stankiewicz when in 1992 he was reunited with Showalter after being called up to the Yankees from Class AAA Columbus. The twenty-seven-year-old rookie made the most of his opportunity when the call came from the Bronx, and he batted .268 during the '92 season.[39]

Olszewski's traveling schedule was different than it was when he drove the Class AA Yankees. In the Eastern League, road trips would begin following the completion of the last game of a homestand, the team traveling to the next city through the night. By comparison, he transported the Redbirds by day, doing most of the driving beginning early in the morning, or in some cases in the early afternoon, depending on the team's destination. If Olszewski had things his way, he would much prefer traveling through the night instead of during the day.

"You make better time," he said. "There's less travel and less aggravation."

Through the years, Olszewski has been fortunate to have safe travels and had only broken down once. It happened on the New York State Thruway outside the city of Buffalo when the Yankees were heading to Canton/Akron.

39 Stankiewicz, Andy. Wikipedia, *The Free Encyclopedia.* "Andy Staniewicz." 10 July 2024, https://en.wikipedia.org/wiki/Andy_Stankiewicz

"I lost all my gears," recalled Olszewski. "It was still running. I went to a rest area and called the company. They called Empire Trailways, and they brought a bus and took the team to Canton/Akron while I stayed with the bus. I caught up with them later on. You can't have breakdowns. These guys are on a schedule."

The bus driver collaborated closely with the trainer of the team as well as the manager.

"I've never had a problem with the manager," said Olszewski. "They have the last word on everything. They are the boss."

Tomorrow, Olszewski would spend his day off with Turco and trainer Steve Proctor by playing a round of golf at a course in Liverpool, a suburb of Syracuse.

Olszewski has driven teams to several minor league cities, and his favorite place to watch baseball was Reading, Pennsylvania, home of the Reading Phillies of the Class AA Eastern League.

"They're family-oriented and sold out every night," said Olszewski. "For two dollars, you get a hot dog and a Coke. There aren't too many places you can do that. I love it. The best value you can get is minor league baseball."

Tonight's delay lasted less than an hour, and during the break in the action, it didn't even rain, and the expected lightning strikes never took place. When play resumed, the Cubs added to the lead at 2-0 in the fifth inning when Pico doubled to right field and scored on a single by Jared Snyder.

The Redbirds' bats came alive in the seventh inning when Jeff Berblinger led off with a double. It may have been his last at bat in a Glens Falls uniform. Turco told me before the game that his second baseman was being promoted to St. Petersburg, a long-season Class A club in the Florida State League. Berblinger had the numbers to warrant the promotion with a .305 batting average and twenty-one runs batted in.

Almond followed Berblinger with a single to put two runners aboard with nobody out. Mike Matvey then kept the rally going when he answered with a double to score Berblinger, cutting the deficit in half to 2-1. The rally ended quickly, however, when Mike Taylor and Joe Henson both grounded out to end the inning.

The local fans who came to McDonough Park tonight to watch Geneva High School product Dan Pontes would get their wish when Turco brought him into the game in the eighth inning. Pontes would not disappoint, striking out the side and keeping the Redbirds within one run entering the ninth inning.

Berblinger would get one more at bat with the Redbirds when he led off the ninth, and he delivered with a single. He was quickly erased at second base, however, on a fielder's choice when Almond grounded a ball to the shortstop Mendez. Matvey followed with a fly out, and Taylor grounded out to third base for the third consecutive time tonight. The Redbirds came up short, losing 2-1, and their eight-game winning streak was over.

The stay above the .500 mark would be short-lived as the Redbirds began packing their duffel bags into the Upstate Tours bus that Olszewski was now warming up in the parking lot. The ball club would return to its hotel in Syracuse with a 23-23 record, leaving the Redbirds two games behind Oneonta in the McNamara Division.

After the players grabbed some food from the concession stand, they began to trickle across the parking lot and tossed their belongings into the storage compartments before staking their claim to a seat inside the bus. When the last player was on the bus, Olszewski would move the bus out of the lot on Nursery Street to begin the short drive to the hotel in Syracuse. Another game had ended, and another night of travel was beginning for Olszewski. The veteran driver knew the routine well, but it did not mean his mind was not wandering to other places.

"Last year, I was away from home 160 nights," Olszewski said. "I have a two-year-old son, and I miss him."

CHAPTER THIRTEEN:

"I'M LOOKING FOR SKIP WEISMAN!"

August 7, 1993—Jamestown, New York

Most of my travels this summer had led me to ballparks located in the center of the New York–Pennsylvania League. Now I was headed for the southwestern corner of the league to watch games in Jamestown, New York, and Erie, Pennsylvania. When I concluded this four-game, three-day road trip, I would only have three more cities in the league to visit: Glens Falls, Oneonta, and Pittsfield.

As I prepared for the weeksend swing through Jamestown and Erie, my accommodation would be at Lake Erie State Park, located south of Buffalo on Route 5 and on the shores of Lake Erie. My first stop on this trip was College Stadium in Jamestown to watch the Expos host the visiting Elmira Pioneers, a rematch of the two ball clubs I had watched earlier in the season at Dunn Field during the invasion of the moths in Elmira. I was detoured on my way to Jamestown when I took Route 394 into the town of Westfield and headed right into a parade. Eventually, I connected to Route 17, a long stretch of highway that ran from the southwestern corner of New York State all the way through the Southern Tier, past

Binghamton, and onward to the state Thruway at its downstate artery located north of New York City. At this western end of Route 17, the traveler got to take in the beautiful views offered alongside Chautauqua Lake. The highway cut right across the lake at a narrow location known as Cheney Point, the bridge spanning the water at a distance high enough to allow for boats to pass underneath.

The Expos played their home games at College Stadium on the campus of Jamestown Community College. The ballpark was a tidy, handsome brick structure which was guarded on the outside by a row of tall trees alongside the first-base side and neatly groomed hedges at the front gate. The park's seating area included the roof-covered brick grandstand that was wrapped around home plate and large bleacher sections that were unattached to the grandstand on each base line.

When I walked through the front gate, I bought a Jamestown program, which had a picture on the cover of Delino DeShields, Wilfredo Cordero, Brian Barnes, Marquis Grissom, Tim Laker, John Vander Wal, and Archi Cianfrocco, all of them wearing Montreal Expos uniforms while gathered at Olympic Stadium. The caption above the photo read, "Seven Ex-Jamestown Players Make the 1993 Montreal Expos Opening Day Roster."

Assistant general manager Chip DeLorenzo accommodated me by opening one of the numerous booths that were attached to the press box atop the roof. The vantage point gave me a quick view of the field dimensions, eccentric to say the least: 335 to left field, 414 in the right-center field alley, and a whopping 353 feet down the line in right. With all this room, I guessed that a lot of the long balls hit at College Stadium would result in nothing more than long outs. Much to my surprise, however, a look at today's stat sheet revealed that the Expos were leading the league in home runs with a total of thirty-six, a figure that was hard to comprehend considering you needed a bazooka to hit it out of the park in this vast field of green. Erie was second in the league with thirty-five home runs, and Elmira was right behind with thirty-three round-trippers. The Jamestown power supply was equally dispersed throughout the roster, and none of the Expos ranked as high as the top four among the league leaders in home runs. Matt Raleigh, a twenty-two-year-old native of Swanton, Vermont, led the team in home runs with eight while designated hitter Robert Henley and third baseman Juan Batista both had six.

The power supply may have been the only compelling aspect of the Expos' season to date. A further look at the stat sheet had the team batting just .248 with thirty-two stolen bases. By comparison, Niagara Falls had 121 stolen bases. The pitching had not been any better, as the Jamestown hurlers had a team earned run average of 4.24. Despite the numbers, the Expos were starting to play some decent baseball, having won three straight games and six of the last seven, a streak that still could not get the ball club out of the Stedler Division basement where it was tied for last with the Erie Sailors, both teams having identical records of 22-26.

The visiting Elmira Pioneers, meanwhile, entered tonight's game experiencing an even more difficult plight. When I had last seen the Elmira ball club, it had taken two in a row against Jamestown on July 11 at Dunn Field to extend a winning streak to five games. The winning streak brought the Pioneers near the .500 mark at 10-12. It had been a struggle since then, however, as the Pioneers had lost seventeen of twenty-five games and were well below the breakeven mark with a record of 18-29, eleven games behind Watertown in the Pinckney Division. Only the Auburn Astros had a worse record, 17-30, and the last place Astros were only one game behind the Pioneers.

The sub .500 record at baseball's port of entry didn't faze the Elmira manager Lynn Jones.

"We're here to develop," said Jones. "Wins are secondary. But it's easier to develop under a winning situation. We have a month left, and we're getting work done and still look to make improvements."

When Jones was asked if his players were beginning to feel the effects of the dog days of the season, he quickly dismissed the idea.

"These guys don't know what the dog days are all about," said Jones. "Their dog days are early morning workouts. That's their idea of a dog day. We've only played forty-something games (forty-seven to be exact). They're used to that."

Tonight, the Expos would flex their muscles once more, knocking two more home runs out of the spacious confines of College Stadium. Physical as well as mental errors, however, would cost the Expos before the night was over. Elmira was clinging to a 1-0 lead entering the top of the eighth inning in a pitcher's duel between the Pioneers' Paul Thornton and Jamestown's Aaron Knieper. In the eighth, Knieper hit the leadoff batter Matt Martinez, who then scored on a triple by Dave Berg. When Jamestown shortstop Jeff Foster made a throwing error to try to get Berg at third base, the Pioneers were ahead 3-0.

Jamestown threatened in the bottom half of the eighth when Jon Saffer led off the inning with a double. Saffer then pulled a move which went against the unwritten rule when your team is trailing by three runs. He tried to steal third base. Berg, the Elmira third baseman, took the throw from the catcher Any Prater, and Saffer was easily tagged out. The Jamestown manager, Tim Torricelli, was noticeably upset while watching this running miscue from an up-close vantage point in the third-base coach's box. Torricelli later confirmed that he did not give Saffer the sign to attempt a stolen base. And one could only imagine what was racing through the mind of the Jamestown skipper moments later when Batista launched a home run over the left-field fence, a solo blast instead of a two-run homer.

The Expos produced one last threat in the ninth inning when Raleigh led off with a home run against reliever Al Walania to cut the margin to one run at 3-2. Vince Lachance then doubled and advanced to third base on a sacrifice bunt by Bobby Henley. Now Torricelli and the Expos had the tying run just ninety feet away and the winning run in scoring position at second base. Both runners would stay right where they were, however, when Tony Marabella popped out in foul territory and Jesus Campos grounded out to end the game, a 3-2 win for the Pioneers. The line score of the game was three runs, five hits, and one error for the Pioneers and 2-8-2 for the Expos. For the record, one of the Jamestown errors occurred in the first inning when the third baseman Batista made his twenty-fifth miscue in forty-eight games.

August 8, 1993—Erie, Pennsylvania

The second day of my weekend swing found me sitting on a park bench in the town square of Westfield, New York, while reading the Sunday newspaper. Westfield was the home of Welch's grape juice plant, where today, striking union employees were picketing while sitting in front of the main gate to the plant and holding signs that expressed their concerns. Today's edition of the *Times News*, the Erie newspaper, had a full-page picture of New York–Pennsylvania League umpire Dan Iassogna in the ready position with hands positioned on knees while working the bases during a recent game. The caption alongside him read, "Making a Play for the Majors: Umpires, like players, pay dues in bush leagues." Inside the paper was a feature story written by staff writer Jeffery Hileman about Iassogna and his partner Mike Cook and their lives as Class A baseball umpires. Iassogna of Shelton, Connecticut, and Cook from St. Clairsville, Ohio, both made their way into professional baseball after attending the Jim Evans Umpire Academy in Florida at a cost of $1,495. The two umpires earned $1,700 per month in salary, twenty-five cents per mile in travel costs, and fifteen dollars per day for a meal allowance. Lodging was paid for by the league, and they were also supplied two pairs of gray umpire slacks, two powder-blue uniform shirts, and a navy-blue cap that read, "NY Penn."

In his story, Hileman wrote that no fans cheered for the umpires and the media did not recognize their achievements. As for the fans, Cook was quoted by stating, "Always friendly when the home team is winning." The two umpires traveled together in Cook's red 1992 Buick Regal, a vehicle that he expected would log five thousand miles for the season. As the umpires looked to climb the minor league ladder, Hileman noted that the salary increased with each step. Umpires working in the long season Class A leagues (Florida State League, Midwest League, Carolina League, South Atlantic League, California League) earned $1,800 per month, while Class AA umpires earned $1,900 per month. There was a more noticeable rise in salary at the Class AAA level, where umpires earned $2,600 per month. In the major leagues, salaries would vary depending on the years of experience. A rookie umpire in the majors earned $60,000, while the top salary was $175,000. Hileman wrote in his article that both Iassogna and Cook would spend the off-season working as substitute teachers back in their hometowns.

"I still wouldn't trade it for anything," Iassogna was quoted by Hileman. "It's a great feeling being able to run a baseball game."

When I finished reading the newspaper, I was on my way to Ainsworth Field in Erie, Pennsylvania. The scouting report that I had on the ballpark was not impressive: short porch in right field, locker rooms located in a nearby school, rocky infield, and a hand-operated scoreboard. The critique was accumulated from a variety of my sources during my travels throughout the league. I was eager to find out if the reports were accurate, because I was especially intrigued with the old, worn-out ballparks than I was with the upscale, sterile, newer renditions.

I was also eager to locate the Erie general manager Skip Weisman, a former classmate of mine at Ohio University, both of us graduating from the Athens school in 1981. Weisman and I met when we worked for the school's radio and TV station, WOUB. Both of us also moonlighted on the weekends by working at WMPO Radio in the Middleport-Pomeroy area alongside the Ohio River in the southeastern corner of the state. Weisman called play-by-play high school football and basketball for WMPO Radio while I was a Saturday- and

Sunday-night disc jockey for the station. The rural station was in a building that I was told used to be an ice cream parlor. In 1980, it was a country-and-western-themed station, which seemed to fit considering that there were horses grazing in the field right behind the building where I tried to keep my sanity while playing one country song after the next. One of the station listeners—I assumed that there was more than one listener—was an elderly woman who would often call me to lend polite critique while suggesting specific country songs I should play on the air. One night, when I was preparing to do my hourly news report, I ripped a story off the Associated Press wire machine that had a Middleport dateline, something that confused me considering I was the local media outlet in this rural outpost. The story read that there was a stabbing in a local bar in the Middleport-Pomeroy area and that the assailant was presently at large while the authorities were in pursuit. I read the story during my report and then quickly made sure that all the doors were locked at the station.

Weisman and I only crossed paths because of our common interest in sports broadcasting. We did not socialize outside the campus TV and radio newsroom and barely talked when we were at the station working on stories. When we finished our undergraduate studies at Ohio University, we went in opposite directions. My journey began in Rohnert Park, California, where I took the job as public address announcer for the Redwood Pioneers of the Class A California League for the 1982 season, seventy games in all for a total of salary of $1,000 ($14 per game) over the span of five months.

With suitcase, duffel bag, and golf clubs in tow, I took up residence in Rohnert Park with a family that agreed with the ball club to house players, and in my case, the public address announcer, at minimal charge. Fortunately for me and Redwood first baseman Darryl Stephens, the rent at my host family home was free of charge. I only had to pay for groceries and long-distance phone bills. I bought a bicycle as my form of transportation, and my host would allow me to use the Lincoln Continental when driving to church for mass on Sunday in nearby Cotati. In order to supplement my income, I umpired high school baseball games and was able to secure a job as the weekend sports anchor at KFTY-TV in nearby Santa Rosa.

As for Weisman, he chose to stay put in Athens to pursue his master's degree in sports management at Ohio University. When he graduated, he climbed his way up the minor league ladder. I tracked his career, reading about his climb in the magazine *Baseball America.* Weisman first worked as an intern with the Charlotte Orioles of the Class AA Southern League before landing a position as assistant general manager for the Anderson Braves of the South Atlantic League. Next, he moved on to the Greensboro Hornets for five years, the last three as the team's general manager. When I parked my car on Washington Place, a residential street in Erie alongside Ainsworth Field, I was certain Weisman would remember me twelve years after I departed the Athens campus.

The Sailors front office was a brick building located behind the third-base bleachers and accessible from Washington Place. I entered the office and introduced myself to the first person—and only person—that I saw inside the building, Kathy Lumbard Cobb, the ball club's assistant general manager.

"I'm looking for Skip Weisman," I said.

Lumbard Cobb directed me to the nearby concession stand and told Weisman that I was here to see him. His reaction was a mix of surprise and confusion. We exchanged pleasantries and I told him why I had come to Erie: another stop on my journey through the New York–Pennsylvania League and my rediscovery of baseball in the bush leagues. Soon thereafter, we retreated to the seats in the home-plate grandstand, talking about topics ranging from Ohio University to minor league baseball. Weisman informed me that after his fifth year in Greensboro, he had a falling out with management. When the 1988 season ended, he was out of baseball and not sure if he and his wife should leave the Greensboro area.

"After the 1988 season, I wasn't sure what I should do," he said. "I didn't want to leave Greensboro. I sold life insurance for three weeks, and then the call from Columbia (Class A South Atlantic League) came. I said, 'See ya!'"

Two years later in 1990, Weisman was on the move once again, this time heading north to the Williamsport Bills of the Class AA Eastern League. And two years later, he packed his bags once more, this time coming to Erie to take the post of general manager and president. With all these moves he had made, Weisman said he was moving backward, going from Class AA to short season Class A here in Erie. Nonetheless, he did not seem to have regrets, as he had equity ownership in his position here with the Erie ball club.

"I'd like to own my own team instead of going to Double A," he said.

While Weisman and I talked in the grandstand seats, I began to take in the scenery at Ainsworth Field, a truly bizarre place to watch baseball. The most imposing sight of all was the large, brown brick building which loomed high above the outfield fence, stretching from center field to the right-field foul line. The structure was the back of the Theodore Roosevelt Middle School, the building backing right up to the fence and only 295 feet away from home plate down the line in right field. The height of the building, including a large brick smokestack, towered over the ballpark behind the fence. To try to prevent a surplus of cheap home runs in the ballpark, the fence was double tiered in right field, and an additional chain-link fence was on top of the wooden fences, making the overall height nearly thirty feet. The added height, insiders have told me, didn't matter, because routine fly balls down the right-field line still resulted in cheap home runs.

The grandstands at Ainsworth Field were very close to the playing field, giving fans proximity to the game in front of them. Even so, the fans were still somewhat removed, because if they tried to reach out and touch the players, they couldn't. The distance between the

front row of the box seats to the playing field was such a long drop
that the youngsters in front of us had to reach low with outstretched
arms while players on the field stood on their toes to accommodate
autograph seekers. As for the dugouts, they were an architectural
design I had never seen before in a ballpark, built right into the
grandstand with the look of a concrete bunker or civil defense fallout
shelter.

"The dugouts are small and cramped, and the overhead is dangerous," Weisman said. "You can hurt your head if you don't duck
when you go in. Everything is antiquated."

The ballpark was owned by the Erie City School District and
was in rough shape every place I looked. The field was far from being
lush, and the infield dirt did not appear to be well groomed. Despite
those deficiencies, one could not take his eye off the large middle-
school building with the high smokestack that overlooked the field
in the right-center. I would learn the next day from Jim Mattis, a
beat writer for the *Erie Morning News*, that the Great Bambino, Babe
Ruth himself, once sent one flying toward that smokestack.

"The claim to fame here," Mattis would later tell me, "is that
Babe Ruth played here in his barnstorming years and hit a home run
over that chimney. I think over the years, the distance of the home
run has increased."

Located on the top of the gymnasium's roof was one of the two
scoreboards in use here at Ainsworth Field. The rooftop version was
electronic, while the scoreboard situated on the Waste Management
sign in left field was hand operated. Another uncommon feature was
that the home clubhouse was in the gymnasium of the middle school
behind the outfield fence. To get to the locker room, the Sailors
walked across the outfield grass to an opening in the fence where the
WXTA Radio Country 98 billboard was in right field. A back entrance to the school was located right behind the fence. Next, players
climbed one flight of stairs to the second floor, where they found
their makeshift locker room, without question the largest in the

league and situated in the form of portable locker cubicles spread out on one half of the basketball court. During a visit later, I was quick to notice that some players were preoccupied during the downtime prior to the opening pitch by playing basketball on the other half of the court. While the facilities for the home team appeared bizarre at best, they were far better than the cramped, dingy quarters the visiting club used on the first-base side inside the concrete bowl of the home-plate grandstand. I asked Weisman what standards Ainsworth Field did not meet regarding the new ballpark requirements for minor league teams.

"It would probably be easier to say what it does meet," he said. "It has grass.

These front row seats should be the best because of the location. But they're not. This walkway in front is the only one (in the grandstand). There's a constant stream of people going back and forth. A guy had an epileptic seizure a few nights ago and hit his head on the concrete. The ambulance crew had a hard time getting through."

If Ainsworth Field was in rough shape now, according to Weisman, it was in even worse shape when he first arrived. The infield was very bumpy, and still was, I was told, and was sunken low in several places. When the 1992 season ended last year, new infield grass was installed during the fall. The school district used the field for high-school baseball games in the spring. Still, school officials refused to sink substantial amounts of money into the facility. The Sailors then renegotiated with the school district, and now the ball club maintained the upkeep of the field.

Despite the numerous downfalls of Ainsworth Field, including a tenant that was playing sub .500 baseball—the Sailors were struggling at 22-27, tied with Jamestown for last place in the Stedler Division—fans were still coming to this ballpark, which sat smack in the middle of a residential section and had street parking only. The Sailors had averaged 1,951 through twenty-five dates, third in the league in attendance behind Glens Falls and Utica.

"This is a great baseball town," said Weisman. "On Friday, there were eight thousand at an all-star football game and two thousand here (for a Sailors game). It's a long winter here. When people can get out in the summer, they take advantage of it."

A new stadium was badly needed in this city which was located on Lake Erie in the northwestern corner of Pennsylvania. Weisman believed that a new stadium would be built soon. A total of $10 million in state funding had been appropriated for Erie. The state would need a local match from Erie, and Weisman was confident it would happen. "The city will build a $5.8 million parking ramp that will hold six hundred cars," he said. "That's up for vote in the next week or two. It's almost a done deal. By building the stadium, the ramp is feasible."

Weisman explained that the remaining fees, nearly $850,000 to $995,000, would come from three groups: the city, the county, and the private sector. He said that Erie residents had appeared serious about keeping baseball in the city. A private organization, Team Erie, was formed three years ago, and Weisman said nearly $300,000 could be raised from the private sector to support a new stadium in Erie.

I was wrong when I thought Weisman was the only familiar face in Erie. Shortly after Weisman walked away from me in the grandstand, a gentleman nearby in the walkway called my name. I was somewhat baffled as I stared at the neatly groomed man wearing casual slacks and a golf shirt.

"Shawn McAnally, remember?" he asked.

Of course I remembered McAnally, who along with Mike Shields were the first two umpires I interviewed this season, back on opening night in June at Auburn's Falcon Park.

McAnally and I talked while the Sailors and visiting Welland Pirates took turns taking infield practice. I told McAnally that he caught me off guard, and that it was surprising to hear someone call my name in a city where the only person I knew—Skip Weisman— had just walked away from me. As we renewed our acquaintance, I told McAnally my travels had gone well, but that life on the road was not an easy task, especially when I experienced twenty-four hours at times without even talking to anyone.

"You've found the secret of minor league baseball," McAnally responded. "The stuff that goes on out on the field is the easy stuff. It's the traveling that's hard. There have been nights where you wake up in a hotel in the night and you don't know what city you're in. The travel and being away from the family are hard. I called my wife today. We usually talk two to three minutes, but today I talked for forty-five minutes. Things have to be done. Bills have to be paid. Things need to be done before we sign a new lease on an apartment."

McAnally had another concern lately besides making sure the bills were being paid back home in Philadelphia. He told me that he and Shields had not been seen by an umpire supervisor since July 4 and 5 when Bill Haller, the former American League umpire, watched them work games in Watertown. Looking back, I was on hand for the second of those two games, a night when I spent most of my time talking to Andy Levinson, the thirty-two-year-old traveling sports agent from Southern California.

While reflecting, McAnally had produced two theories about what was said by Haller following the games in Watertown.

"One, what he said isn't necessarily relevant," began McAnally, "and in the end, you can't tell by what they say, how they view you. Seriously, you can have a great day, but they may rip you. You can never tell what people are thinking."

I could tell what McAnally was thinking right now: he wanted to be observed by a supervisor as soon as possible.

"We want to have a supervisor in town," said McAnally. "It has been so long (without being seen). You have to stay focused. You're doing this so you move up to the next level. When you don't see them for a while, you start to think, 'Am I ever going to be seen?'"

When McAnally was seen, he probably wouldn't know it until after the game. The way it worked, I had been told, was that supervisors typically let an umpire crew know they were in town at the end of the game when they showed up in the umpire's locker room.

"Normally, he'll come in and see one game and won't tell you he was there," said McAnally. "On the second night, after both guys have worked the plate, he'll come in and tell you. Sometimes, you can pick up on whether there's a guy there. We're not watching the stands, but every once in a while you'll see a face or two in the stands."

When I switched topics and asked him to provide commentary on Ainsworth Field, his reply was diplomatic.

"From a fan's perspective, it's probably a good park because the stands come around the plate and you're up high," he said. "But with the wall in right field, you need to be out there to see if the ball hit the wall or his glove. The plate area is hard clay, but the infield itself is good. The locker room facilities are mediocre."

McAnally's favorite ballpark in the league was Dunn Field in Elmira. "Clyde Smoll has done a terrific job there," he said. "The umpire's facility is good. They have a dedicated ground crew. Some ground crews are a couple of guys who own lawn mowers. That might be a slight exaggeration."

McAnally also gave high marks to the ground crew at Sal Maglie Field in Niagara Falls.

"The grounds crew worker in Niagara Falls says he and his crew go out for an hour on stone hunts," said McAnally. "They pick up stones and put them in buckets. You have to respect that."

Another topic we discussed was how umpires spent time away from the ballpark. McAnally said that he and Shields had seen their share of movies at theaters throughout the league.

"We ought to have a league movie review on TV," he joked. "That's fourteen safes for *In the Line of Fire* by the New York–Pennsylvania League umpires."

A check of the league standings today showed that the visiting Welland Pirates continued to struggle along with the Erie Sailors. Welland was 23-26 and just one game ahead of Erie and Jamestown as all three teams were battling to avoid the basement in the Stedler Division. Niagara Falls, meanwhile, was at the top of the division, with St. Catharines right behind. Oneonta entered today two and a half games in front of the Utica Blue Sox in the McNamara Division. The Yankees had just left Erie last night following a three-game sweep of the Sailors. In the Pinckney Division, a Watertown win last night over Batavia combined with a Geneva loss, put the Indians four and a half games in front of the second-place Cubs.

The Welland Pirates were in town tonight, and there was a large crowd on hand to watch two ball clubs that had been struggling all season long. I opted to watch the game from the bleacher section down the left-field line in front of the Erie bullpen. Through four innings, the young female scoreboard operator who sat behind a chain-link fence in the left-field corner near the foul pole had placed nothing but zeroes on the Waste-Management-sponsored scoreboard. That quickly changed in the fifth, however, when the scoreboard operator placed a "2" for the visiting Pirates following a two-run homer by Joel Williamson to left field over the PNC Bank sign.

The Welland lead, however, was short-lived.

When the bottom half of the inning had ended, the scoreboard operator walked out with a "4" in her hand, the damage coming when Erie's Corey Pearson drove in Brian Clark Blair to cut the deficit in half at 2-1, a hit that prompted Welland manager Larry Smith to visit the mound and take the ball from his starter Jason Johnson with two runners aboard. His replacement did not fare any better as Jeff Pickich proceeded to give up a three-run homer to the first batter he faced, Alfred Triplett.

Triplett's home-run ball sailed over the triple-deck sign in right field.

Or did it?

The vantage point from my bleacher seat on the third-base side was not a good one, but the ball may not have cleared the chain-link fence that was the third layer of the triple-deck configuration. Strangely, Smith did not come out to argue. The next day, Welland right fielder Erskine Kelly was talking about the home-run ball that sailed over his head, and he thought the ball went through a hole in the fence. "Above the letter 'I' in the sign," he said.

The home run barrage was not over. Through six innings, the scoreboard operator came out with a "2" in her hand to denote the runs scored via a two-run homer to right-center field by Clark Blair off the Welland reliever Gil Perez. The home run put the Sailors ahead 6-2 and on their way to a 7-3 win. Both ball clubs now had identical records of 23-27. Something would have to happen in the standings tomorrow, however, as both clubs would meet here for a rare Monday afternoon game beginning at 1:05 p.m. Weisman was accurate when he said Erie liked baseball. Despite having a sub .500 record, the Sailors attracted 2,993 fans tonight, and nearly all of them stayed until the final out.

August 9, 1993—Erie, Pennsylvania

Today would mark a first for me during my summer journey through the New York–Pennsylvania League: a two-city doubleheader with the afternoon game in Erie followed by a nightcap in Jamestown. The day of baseball would get underway when my Suzuki Samurai reached the intersection of 24th Street and Washington Place, the intersecting streets directly behind the home-plate grandstand at Ainsworth Field in Erie. When I entered the ballpark, the Welland Pirates were taking batting practice, and the sound of horsehide contacting white-ash wood, pitch after pitch, was worth the return trip to Erie. Adding to the acoustics in this ballpark was the large school building that rose high above the fence in right-center field. With the imposing brick wall standing guard of the outfield fence, the crack of the bat was reverberated in this park more than any other park I had visited in the league.

When I saw Skip Weisman and asked him about access to the Erie locker room out there in the middle-school gymnasium, he assigned me a personal escort, Dave Hough, a summer intern from Robert Morris College. I followed Hough down the right-field line and across the outfield grass toward the WXTA Country 98 sign. While we walked along the warning track, some of the Erie pitchers passed us by while running between the foul poles, a common pregame ritual for pitchers while batting practice occurred. The outfield fence was even worse up close than I had imagined earlier. Hough pointed out numerous holes in the billboards. We passed through the door in the fence, which was cut through the letter "W" on the WXTA sign, and proceeded to enter the middle school where Hough led me up a flight of stairs. He then opened a door and said to me, "Here it is."

In front of me had to be professional baseball's most bizarre location for a clubhouse. The gymnasium looked old, dark, and dreary. A stereo played music while a handful of players were at their respective lockers preparing for the game. An orange carpet was on one half of the gym, taped to the hardwood basketball court. Some twenty-five or more white wooden locker stalls were located at each side of the carpet, while a table sat in the center with Gatorade coolers and bags of bagels on top.

Most of the folding chairs situated in front of each locker stall were unoccupied at the time, and only a few players were in the gym. Lonnie Goldberg, who was eating a bagel while putting his uniform top on, was one of them. Situated at midcourt was a large fan which was directed at the locker stalls. Another fan, located under the basket on the side of the court where the lockers were located, was also facing the stalls to provide air flow from a second angle.

"It is different," said Goldberg of the makeshift clubhouse. "You get used to it. We're lucky to be playing professional baseball. The game doesn't change no matter what the facilities are."

Goldberg added that sometimes players would shoot baskets at the court located at the opposite end of the gym not occupied by the lockers. He said the only competition allowed were games of HORSE. According to Eric Moody, a right-handed pitcher, players were getting too competitive during three-on-three pick-up games, which led manager Doug Sisson to put an end to it.

I found Sisson in his manager's office in the corner of the gym, an office occupied by the physical education teacher during the school year. The room was spacious and came with a desk, shower facilities, and a window that probably provided the best view of Ainsworth Field, a vantage point from high above the right-field fence. A glance out the window at this time offered a view of some of the Erie players stretching in foul ground for the upcoming game.

"You make do with what you've got," said Sisson. "There's no sense complaining. It's not that big a deal. It's better than being jammed in a hole in the wall."

The weather today was ideal for baseball: warm, clear skies, and plenty of sunshine. I was prepared to take in the game from the sun-drenched bleachers but became sidetracked when I picked up today's stat sheet from the press box. I was handed the sheet by Margo Wright, the stadium organist who when providing me the sheet proceeded to ask me for my food order for the second inning. Wright was under the assumption that I was taking in the game from the press box, a decision I quickly opted for when realizing that my other choice for lunch was the peanut butter and jelly sandwich I had stuffed inside my backpack. I would miss a day in the sun, but a hot dog and a Coke would be coming soon, and that was enough to entice me to bunker down in the shade of the press box.

Along with the organist Wright, I joined Joe Mattis, a writer for the *Erie Morning News*, and official scorer Steve Metzler. Metzler confirmed the story about Babe Ruth barnstorming at Ainsworth Field. He told me about a fan who'd brought him a photo last year of Ruth holding a youngster in his arms. Most noticeable in the background, Metzler confirmed, was the imposing sight of Theodore Roosevelt Middle School. Mattis, meanwhile, was quick to make note of the fact that Pete Rose, major league baseball's all-time hits leader, also played here. According to Mattis, Rose came through as a member of the Geneva Red Legs and was inserted in the lineup as a back-up catcher. "I found that in a box score," Mattis confirmed. Rose's son, Pete Rose Jr., also played here as a member of the home-town Erie Orioles in 1989, coincidentally the same year his father was being investigated for alleged gambling activities believed to be connected to baseball.

As Mattis and I penciled our lineups into our scorebooks, we were soon in for a long afternoon, the game starting out at a snail's pace, the incredible total of eight errors committed through five innings not helping matters. Welland second baseman Patrick Gosselin was having the most difficult afternoon of all by committing three errors of his own. In his defense, however, two of those errors were charged to him on ground balls that took bad hops, the ball skipping over his head at the very last moment.

Welland was ahead 5-3 in the bottom of the seventh when Erie's Alfred Triplett led off the inning with a deep fly ball to left field. Welland left fielder Erskine Kelly went back to the fence, braced himself against the wall, and made a leaping attempt to catch the ball. Kelly came close but did not make the catch. The ball and his hat both cleared the fence. As Kelly landed, he inadvertently ripped a piece of the fence from the Elby's Big Boy billboard. Kelly walked to the left-field corner near the foul line, where a fan gave him his hat. He then went back to the Big Boy sign, ripped off the dangling piece of wood, and threw it over the left-field fence like it was a boomerang.

Some of the members of the press box chuckled as they watched this scenario unfold: a simple way, I suppose, of how Ainsworth was showing its age. One writer told Weisman, who had stopped into the booth for a visit, that he would have plenty of time to fix it considering the team was about to embark on a nine-day road trip following today's matinee.

Weisman only laughed at the idea of repairing the fence.

"I'm just going to take it and nail it back up," he said jokingly.

The Sailors, meanwhile, continued to rally in the eighth inning when Osmani Estrada and Cory Pearson both scored to put the Sailors ahead 6-5.

In the ninth inning, Gosselin led off with a walk and the chance to make up for his three fielding errors. Jermain Allensworth and Louis Collier both followed with singles, and the Pirates had the bases loaded and no outs. G. G. Harris followed with a strikeout, but Gosselin tied the game when he scored on a sacrifice fly by Mitch House. Erie escaped the bases-loaded jam by allowing just one run and would try to win the game in the bottom of the ninth.

If the storyline all day long was sloppy defense, that story played out in the bottom half of the inning. With one out, Erie's Estrada reached base when House, the Welland third baseman, misplayed a ground ball, the fourth Pirates error of the day. Welland pitcher Matt Ryan walked the next batter, Michael Hall, which led Welland manager Larry Smith to make a visit to the mound, where he called to the bullpen for reliever Jeff Isom. Smith was in a comparable situation last night when his team was leading 2-1 with one out and two runners aboard in the Erie fifth. At that point, Smith hooked his starter Jason Johnson while opting for reliever Jeff Pickich. The strategy backfired, however, when Triplett hit a three-run homer and a 7-3 Erie win.

This time around, Smith and the Pirates redeemed themselves as Isom struck out Eric Dominow and Pearson, both on called third strikes, and the game plodded along into extra innings, the Pirates and Sailors tied at 6-6.

Following a scoreless tenth inning, Welland broke the game open in the eleventh against Erie reliever Jeff Davis. Louis Collier reached base on a one-out single, advanced to second when House was hit by a pitch and scored what proved to be the winning run on a single to left field by Kelly. John Mitchell added to the lead when he followed Kelly with a three-run homer to left field. Isom then retired the Sailors in order in the bottom of the eleventh, and Welland won the error-plagued game by a score of 10-6. The line score of the game was not pretty:

Welland: Ten runs, thirteen hits, four errors.

Erie: Six runs, six hits, seven errors.

Time of the game: 3:28.

Outside the ballpark on the first-base side, the Pirates were boarding a bus that was parked on 24th Street preparing for the trip back home to Welland. Over in the umpire's locker room, McAnally and Shields were looking forward to having an off night, their next game not until tomorrow night in Batavia. McAnally said they considered spending the night in Buffalo. Mattis, meanwhile, walked by me on Washington Place and would head back to the newspaper to file his story. As for myself, I placed my uneaten peanut butter and jelly sandwich into the cooler in the back of Suzuki Samurai and was on my way to Jamestown where another nine innings of minor league baseball—and maybe more—awaited me at College Stadium, where the Expos were scheduled for an evening game against the visiting Batavia Clippers.

August 9, 1993—Jamestown, New York

I reached College Stadium at 5:50 p.m. and used the extra time to clean out the Suzuki and make a fresh peanut butter sandwich, opting not to eat the sandwich that had spent over three hours in my backpack at Ainsworth Field. Unfortunately, the scorching August heat had turned my peanut butter into liquid form. I made the sandwich nonetheless and was more concerned over the fact that I was running low on my supply of Clearly Canadian sparkling mineral water.

Tonight's game would be a contest between two more lowly ball clubs, and when the day was over, I would have spent it watching the four worst teams in the Stedler Division. Batavia jumped all over

Jamestown starter Thomas Phelps in the first inning, scoring two runs on three hits. Batavia scored more runs in the later innings, pounding out eleven hits against three Jamestown pitchers in a 6-2 win.

The night game here was not as sloppy as the afternoon version played in Erie. Jamestown committed three errors, and the Clippers had one miscue. In all, I had watched twenty innings of baseball in one day, punctuated by a total of *fifteen* errors. Surprisingly, I enjoyed the game in Erie—where eleven of the fifteen miscues were committed—more than the nightcap in Jamestown. Perhaps this was because I just couldn't put my finger on the pulse at College Stadium, a clean facility, but lacking a buzz. The crowd was sparse and extremely quiet. Maybe the relatively quiet atmosphere was a result of the local faithful having little to cheer for as the Expos played sub .500 baseball right out of the gate in June.

The two parks were stark in contrast. Ainsworth Field was sandwiched into a residential neighborhood, being a quirky park with its tight dimensions, the short porch 295 feet away in right field and the brown brick of the middle school, including the tall smokestack, looming in the distance beyond the outfield fence. College Stadium, meanwhile, with all its room, gave the game a completely different twist with dimensions that were bizarre to say the least: 414 feet in straightaway center and 353 feet down the right-field line. How the Expos had managed to lead the league in home runs was beyond my imagination, as College Stadium was a place where doubles went to die in the gloves of outfielders backpedaling to the warning track. When a deep shot tonight found its way to a Jamestown outfielder, a Batavia fan commented aloud, "That's a home run in Batavia."

After Batavia pitcher Pete Agostinelli struck out Jamestown's Chris Grubb to end the game, I headed for the exit to begin the trek home. I watched twenty innings of baseball today in a combined total of five hours and fifty-one minutes. The following morning, the leaders in the three New York–Pennsylvania League divisions

.c Niagara Falls (Stedler), Oneonta (McNamara) and Watertown (Pinckney). My last leg of this summer baseball journey would come later this month with visits to Glens Falls, Oneonta, and Pittsfield. Of the three divisions in the leagues, the standings below on August 10 showed that the McNamara Division was wide open:

Stedler Division

	W	L	GB
Niagara Falls	30	20	---
St. Catharines	30	21	½
Batavia	25	26	5½
Welland	24	27	6½
Jamestown	23	28	7½
Erie	23	28	7½

McNamara Division

	W	L	GB
Oneonta	30	21	---
Utica	26	24	3½
Pittsfield	24	25	5
Glens Falls	25	27	5½

Pinckney Division

	W	L	GB
Watertown	31	19	---
Geneva	26	25	5½
Elmira	19	31	12
Auburn	18	32	13

*A vendor sells programs outside College
Stadium, Jamestown, NY.*

College Stadium as seen from the home plate grandstand.

A young fan watches the action from the home plate grandstand at College Stadium.

The College Stadium grandstand, Jamestown, NY

Fans enter Ainsworth Field, Erie, PA.

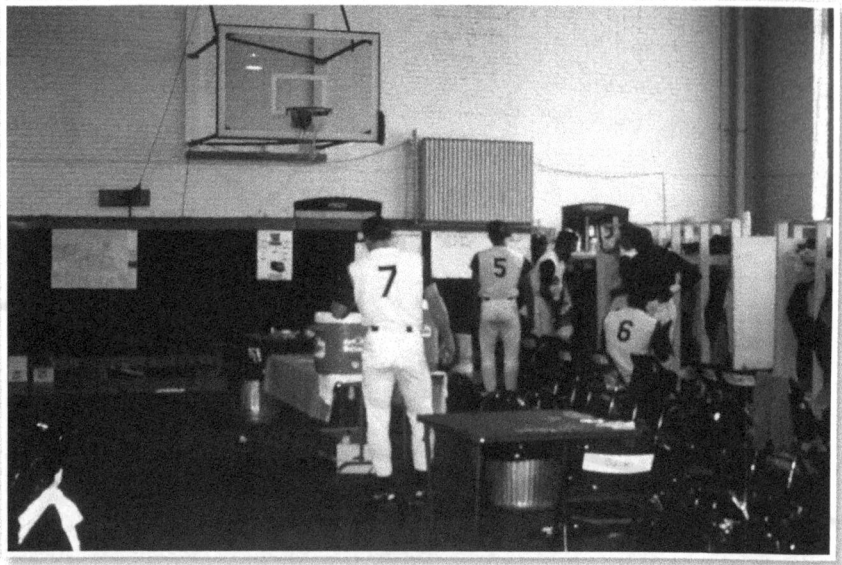

Erie ballplayers can play games of "HORSE" in their locker room.

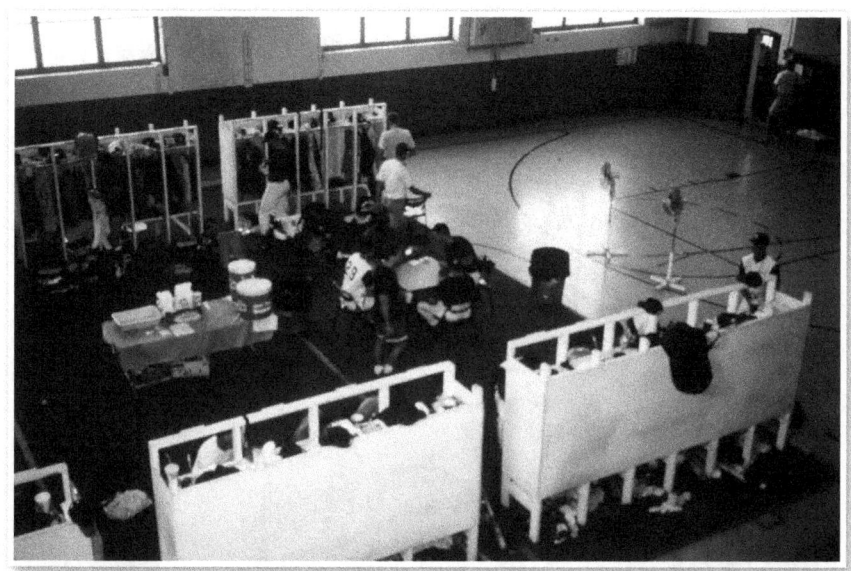

*The Roosevelt Middle School Gymnasium is the
makeshift locker room for the Erie Sailors*

*Umpire Shawn McAnally watches infield
practice at Ainsworth Field, Erie, PA.*

Umpire Shawn McAnally rubs baseballs with Delaware River mud prior to a game at Ainsworth Field, Erie, PA.

Fans enjoy a BBQ meal at Ainsworth Field.

Erie's Cory Pearson signs autographs at Ainsworth Field.

Erie's Ray DeSimone signs autographs at Ainsworth Field.

*Erie's Eric Moody warms up as the starting pitcher
for a game against Welland on August 8, 1993.*

*Erie third baseman Alfred Triplett stands with a Little
League player during the National Anthem.*

The dugouts at Ainsworth Field resemble a bunker.

*Roosevelt Middle School towers over the outfield
fence at Ainsworth Field in Erie, PA.*

The scoreboard in left field at Ainsworth Field is hand operated.

The scoreboard operator at Ainsworth Field

*Kids watch the action at Ainsworth
Field from behind a wire fence.*

CHAPTER FOURTEEN:

JUST PASSING THROUGH

August 25, 1993—Glens Falls, New York

With only twelve games remaining in the New York–Pennsylvania League's regular season schedule, the standings were tight in all three divisions. Since I'd pulled out of College Stadium two weeks ago, two of the divisions had new leaders. In the Stedler Division, St. Catharines had regained first place from Niagara Falls and now led the Rapids by two games. Utica, meanwhile, was on top in the McNamara Division, one and a half games in front of Pittsfield and two games in front of Oneonta. The Watertown Indians still led the Pinckney Division, but their lead had been trimmed by three games as the Geneva Cubs had crept within two and a half games of the division leaders.

The most noticeable changes had occurred in the McNamara Division, where Utica had virtually backed its way into first place while the Oneonta Yankees (32-21) were amid a tailspin by losing five straight games and ten of their last eleven during an August swoon. The slumping Yankees had opened the door for the Pittsfield ball club that just two weeks ago was playing below the .500 mark and trailed the division leaders by five and a half games. Since that

time, the Mets had barely had to play above the .500 mark to surge
ahead of an Oneonta team that couldn't seem to get back on track.

Strangely enough, the hottest team in the league right now was
not even in a pennant race. The Elmira Pioneers had won ten of
their last twelve games but were still below the .500 level with a 29-
33 record in the Pinckney Division.

My decision to visit the McNamara Division teams came with
perfect timing, as Utica, Oneonta, and Pittsfield were only separated
by two games. The fourth ball club in the division, the Glens Falls
Redbirds were six games back at 29-36. When I last saw Steve Turco's
team in Geneva on August 2, the Redbirds were red hot, but they
had cooled off considerably and just snapped a seven-game losing
streak last night with a 5-1 win at St. Catharines, a road trip getaway
game that brought the team back to Glens Falls at 4:30 a.m.

While reading a copy of the *Post Star*, the local newspaper in
Glens Falls, it was reported that the Redbirds starter, Eric Alexander,
took a no-hitter into the sixth inning last night at St. Catharines
and would surrender just three hits through seven innings of work.
Offensively, the Redbirds had a balanced attack, two of the hits
coming off the bat of Greg Almond, the brash catcher I'd met earlier this season at McDonough Park in Geneva when he'd given his
teammates a heavy dosage of friendly banter during batting practice.
Right now, Almond and Matt Matvey were the only offensive spark
in the Glens Falls lineup. Matvey led the team in batting (.310) and
runs batted in (thirty-seven). Almond, meanwhile, was hitting .262
with twenty-eight runs batted in. As a team, Glens Falls was struggling at the plate with a team batting average of .242 along with a
paltry sixteen home runs. Turco would later inform me that the low
productivity stemmed from players being promoted to the next level
in the Cardinals farm system. The pitching staff, meanwhile, had a
team ERA of 4.50, and not a single pitcher had five wins.

It was 4:00 p.m. when I arrived at East Field, the home of the
Redbirds, three hours before tonight's game against the visiting

Oneonta Yankees. When entering the park on Dix Avenue, I made two quick observations: it was the only park in the league with bleachers situated beyond the outfield fence, and the short porch down the left-field foul line measured just 309 feet. Behind the left-field fence was a residential street lined with houses, and the one that was directly behind the foul pole looked within easy reach of home-run balls.

Inside the Redbirds front office, general manager Jack Tracz was keeping a close eye on a nearby television station that was posting the results of races at nearby Saratoga Raceway. Alexandra Stevens, a front-office intern, issued me a media pass and a copy of an updated statistics sheet. Next, I was on my way to the Redbirds clubhouse, located a long walk from the home-team dugout on the first-base side and well beyond the center-field fence in a building known as the East Field Recreation Center. I found Turco in his dark, cramped manager's office. He was wearing blue jeans and a brown muscle shirt, a pair of Docksiders on his feet. Turco was the only one in the clubhouse at the time. His players were informed that there was no batting practice following the early-morning arrival back to Glens Falls. When I had last spoken with Turco, he was beaming with confidence, his ball club riding an eight-game winning streak at the time when entering an August 2 game at McDonough Park in Geneva. The Redbirds lost that game and many more thereafter. At the time, Glens Falls was 23-22, and now, over three weeks later, the ball club was 29-36 after dropping fourteen of twenty games.

"We lost a few players," explained Turco. "I attribute some of it to that. We lost Jeff Berblinger to St. Petersburg, Antoine Henry to Springfield, and Marc Ottmers to Savannah. We're in the process of losing another starting pitcher, Matt Arrandale, to St. Petersburg." To make matters more challenging, pitcher Mike Windham (4-5, 2.65 ERA) had missed his past two starts due to shoulder problems. Despite the August swoon, Turco could find a silver lining in that some of his players were climbing the professional ladder.

"I was talking with (Oneonta manager) Ken Dominguez on the phone the other day," said Turco. "We said that it's our job to get these kids to play a higher level of baseball."

I had heard this view before among managers throughout the league earlier this month when Lynn Jones of Elmira had mentioned it before a game at Jamestown. The trend, however, was that I heard it most often when teams were amid losing streaks. Tonight, it would be Turco and Dominguez matching wits in a game played by two teams that could not find their way out of a slump. Unlike Jones, who groused at my suggestion that the dog days of summer might have been impacting his players, Turco wondered if his players were beginning to wear out.

"You can attribute it to a lot of things," he said. "These kids play fall and spring college baseball, then they come here. They could be getting tired. It has been a combination of things. Just like when we were ten games under .500, we're not getting timely hits. Whether it's starting pitching or relief pitching, we've had areas that have cost us. If we've been anything, we've been a streaky team. We won last night against a tough club. Hopefully, we'll start another streak. We had a meeting the other day, and I mentioned to the players that last impressions are lasting ones. This is a time of year we call Salary Drive Time. It means this is the time to go ahead and play well, so if there is a marginal player and it's the difference between going from one level to the next."

I asked Turco about his own plans for next year, and unlike the players he managed, he did not have the goal of climbing the ladder to the major leagues.

"I enjoy the young guys," he said. "I wouldn't mind staying in short season. I enjoy it. I feel like I have more to offer the younger kids than players at Class AA or Triple-A."

Turco and I wandered outside the recreation center, a building located about 150 feet behind the center-field bleachers. As we stood and talked on the asphalt basketball courts next to the locker-room entrances, the Oneonta Yankees pulled up in their charter bus. Filing out of the bus, the Yankees were dressed in their road-gray uniforms with navy-blue batting practice tops like those worn by their major league affiliate, the New York Yankees. It was a common practice among minor league teams to have the same colors and uniform style of their affiliate, but the Oneonta ball club took it a step further and had the interlocking "NY" on the jerseys, while other players wearing the gray tops had the words "New York" written across the top instead of "Oneonta."

When I caught up with the Oneonta manager Ken Dominguez, he talked about the reasons for his team's subpar play in recent weeks. First, the Yankees were missing their strongest hitter, Ruben Rivera, who was recovering from a hairline fracture in his left hand and was not expected to be back in the lineup until next Tuesday. Rivera was batting .266 and was second in the league with thirteen home runs and fifth in the circuit with forty-four runs batted in.

"It happened in our last game at Geneva (on August 9)," said Dominguez. "He took a pitch up and in and has been out of the lineup ever since."

Dominguez's problems did not end with the Rivera injury.

"Abdiel Cumberbatch hasn't come back like we thought he would," said Dominguez. "He strained a tendon in his left wrist. We got short on pitching. (Clint) Whitworth and (Al) Drumheller both went out with bad elbows. Injuries are going to happen. You play through them. There hasn't been a lack of effort through the losing streak. In fact, they may be pressing. The attitude is upbeat. We're two out with fourteen games left. They feel good about our chances. I do too. I'd be lying if I thought any less. I think they're ready for the challenge."

As Dominguez and I talked, the Yankees continued walking from the street, where the bus dropped them off, and toward the center-field bleachers where there was a gate open in the fence. Along the way, some of the Yankee farmhands were asked for an autograph by a man standing under the bleachers who seemed to be a sports memorabilia collector. Nearly all of the players obliged the fan and continued on their way to the field.

Soon thereafter, batting practice began under the hot sun at East Field. While his teammates took cuts inside the batting cage at home plate, the injured Rivera was off to the side in front of the third-base dugout playing a game of soft toss with Dominguez. The Oneonta manager flipped ball after ball in front of Rivera, who then drove the ball directly into a net in front of him.

Rivera was an imposing figure standing at six-foot-three and weighing 196 pounds. He was twenty-two years old, and his offensive production this year was a vast improvement from a year ago when he hit only one home run and drove in twenty runs in fifty-three games with the Gulf Coast League Yankees. I wanted to talk to Rivera about his nagging injury, but the native of Chorrera, Panama, whose English was not fluent, declined the interview. Instead, he summoned Cumberbatch, who was from Calidonia, Panama, and had a better understanding of English, to function as his interpreter.

"I don't have patience," Rivera said about his injury. "I don't feel good in the dugout watching others. I want to play."

Cumberbatch, who was also an outfielder, could empathize with Rivera. He was also tired of sitting around while waiting to return to the lineup. Cumberbatch was hitting .288 with no home runs and sixteen runs batted in. He led the team with eighteen stolen bases and was tied with teammate Elston Hansen with twenty-nine walks. As his teammates took their swings in the batting cage, Cumberbatch sat in the corner of the dugout soaking his left wrist with a bag of ice. His injury took place simply by swinging at a pitch on July 31 in a game against Jamestown that was played at Doubleday Field in Cooperstown.

"A few days later, I felt pain," said Cumberbatch. "It's tough for me. I don't feel happy for three weeks watching them lose ten of eleven. I take regular batting practice, but it's still sore."

The setbacks to Rivera and Cumberbatch represented op-portunities for other players. Marc Gipner, a catcher, was a re-cent call-up from the Gulf Coast League and had been with the Oneonta ball club for eight days. As he took his cuts, Gipner, a left-handed batter, was hitting line drives to right field on nearly every pitch being offered. When he walked out of the cage to await his next round of pitches, sweat was pouring down his face, the temperature in Glens Falls being somewhere in the low to mid-eighties. Gipner's face appeared young. He was only nine-teen years old but had been playing professional baseball for three years. The promotion to Oneonta, and the opportunity to play in the New York–Pennsylvania League, could not have come soon enough, according to Gipner. In the Gulf Coast League, fifteen teams played a sixty-game schedule, and all the games were played during the day beginning at 12:00 p.m.

"This feels a lot better," said Gipner. "It makes you feel like you're in a league. We rarely had any crowds. We'd have thirty to fifty people, kids from youth clubs, but that's about it. We'd come out and stretch and start batting practice at 9:00 a.m. It feels good to be in a pennant race. I've only had one at bat. He's letting other guys catch. I'll get my chance."

When the Yankees were done with batting practice and infield practice, they would retreat to their visiting clubhouse located in the recreation center for a pregame meal, a ritual I had yet to see among the thirteen other ball clubs in the league. Carl Randolph, the Oneonta trainer, helped coordinate the meal along with the clubhouse manager. "The clubhouse dues in the league are fifteen dollars per player every two weeks," said Randolph. "At the begin-ning of the year, we had a meeting, and we asked if they wanted to pay twenty-five dollars to have food on the road and at home. They agreed. They have sandwiches, peanut butter and jelly, and we make sure they get fruit. Fruit is the first priority. Tim Powell, our club-house manager, is out with the bus right now getting the food. He'll mix a jug of Gatorade and lemonade. It gives them something not too heavy in their stomach."

Juan Nieves was the Oneonta pitching coach, a former left-handed pitcher for the Milwaukee Brewers. It seemed strange that Nieves was here, at East Field in Glens Falls, instead of County Stadium in Milwaukee. Nieves was only twenty-eight years old and appeared to have a promising career ahead of him as a major league pitcher. In three years with the Brewers, he was 32-25, including a no-hitter against the Baltimore Orioles on April 15, 1987, the only no-hitter to date in Brewers history. In 1989, however, problems began for Nieves when he had an operation known as an anterior capsular shift, which deals with instability of the shoulder. The following year would be his last year in professional baseball. A member of the Yankees organization at that time, Nieves was on rehabilitation and placed on the Class AAA roster at Columbus, Ohio. As it turned out, however, Nieves would never pitch for the Columbus Clippers.[40]

"On the last day of spring training, they offered me a coaching job, and here we are," said Nieves. "I knew (playing) baseball would be over. It's bound to happen."

During the time of his rehabilitation stint with Columbus, Nieves considered going back to Puerto Rico to study sports medicine or sports psychology. "But the Yankees made me an offer," he said. "The organization helped me on the downside. I owe a lot to them.

"I'll tell you one thing; everything happens for a reason. These things happen. The problem is genetics and mechanics. The strength of the arm is not there. I didn't have any bitterness. Playing baseball is not forever. It's part of the game. Every professional will get released one day."

40　Nieves, Juan. Wikipedia, *The Free Encyclopedia.* "Juan Nieves." 17 July 2024, https://en.wikipedia.org/wiki/Juan_Nieves

Nieves had it happen to him at an early age, and now the hard part was not being able to take the mound while he watched the young Oneonta pitchers go out there and throw every night.

"It's frustrating not being able to compete," said Nieves. "I miss that the most."

When Nieves spoke to the Oneonta farmhands, he spoke from experience when emphasizing the importance of making the most of every baseball opportunity.

"I need to make them be competitive and understand professional baseball," said Nieves. "They need to deal with failure and understand that failure is nothing. They need to become better pitchers and play the game with pride. Don't go by results. Go by effort. You don't want to take this chance for granted. A lot of things can happen. It can be taken away tomorrow. These kids have been playing for such a long time. They think it's forever. It's not true. We have to take it all with pride. It's a kid's game played by adults, chief!"

Tonight, Nieves would focus his attention on the Oneonta starter Mike Jerzembeck, who led the ball club in wins with a 6-4 record and had a 2.64 ERA. Glens Falls would counter with Dan Pontes, the Geneva, New York, native, who was 1-2 with a 3.55 ERA.

In the first inning, the Yankees got to Pontes right away. It started when leadoff batter Ricky Ledee reached base on a walk and scored the first run of the game on a double to center field by Hansen. In the third inning, Steve Aldridge and Hansen led off with back-to-back singles. Sloan Smith then drove in Aldridge, and Smith scored on a single by Mike Schmitz to make it 3-0, Oneonta.

Jerzembeck, meanwhile, was mowing through the Glens Falls lineup through three innings of play by striking out six batters while allowing no runs and surrendering just one hit. The Redbirds reached him for one run in the fourth when Almond hit a double to bring home Greg Deares, cutting the deficit to 3-1.

In the seventh inning, the Redbirds' Mike Taylor singled and would later advance to third base on a two-out double by John Stutz.

Dominguez then pulled Jerzembeck, the Yankees still ahead 3-1, and brought in reliever Don Leshnock. With the tying run in scoring position at second base, one had to wonder about the decision made by the Oneonta skipper. Leshnock entered the game with shaky numbers, an 0-3 record, and a team-worst 5.56 ERA. Dominguez may have been thinking that Leshnock should be able to handle the first batter he faced, the ninth hitter in the lineup, Osmel Garcia, who was batting .205 with no home runs and just ten runs batted in.

Of course, numbers are not everything, and Garcia responded at the right time by singling off Leshnock on the very first pitch to score both runners. Garcia then ended the inning when he was thrown out attempting to steal second base, but the Redbirds had battled back, and the game was now tied at 3-3.

Oneonta failed to score in the top of the eighth, and in the bottom of the inning, Leshnock found himself in trouble when he gave up a leadoff single to Mark Dean and hit Deares with a pitch. Matvey laid down a sacrifice bunt to push the runners to second and third. Leshnock then intentionally walked the cleanup batter, Almond, to load the bases for Joe Jumonville with one out. Jumonville hit a ground ball back to the mound that was gloved by Leshnock, who threw to the catcher Trimble for one out, and the relay to the first baseman Schmitz was in time for the double play. Just like that, a comebacker to the mound, and Leshnock worked his way out of trouble.

After Glens Falls failed to score in the bottom of the inning, the Yankees regained the lead in the top of the ninth against Rick Croushore, the third Glens Falls pitcher of the night. Croushore entered the game at the outset of the eighth inning and retired Oneonta in order.

In the ninth, he retired Ledee and Aldridge and was one out away from ending the inning, but it would not come easy. Hensen, the third batter in the lineup, reached base on an error by Garcia, the Redbirds' center fielder who had just delivered with his bat when tying the game in the seventh. Croushore then allowed a single to the cleanup batter, Kurt Bierek, and the Yankees suddenly threatened with runners at the corners and two outs. Smith put the Yankees back in front, capping the two-out rally with a double—his second of the night—to score Hansen and give the Yankees a 4-3 lead.

Dominguez pulled Leshnock when the Redbirds came to bat in the bottom of the ninth in favor of Shawn Alazaus, a left-hander from Carrollton, Ohio. This was his first year of professional baseball after pitching in the spring for Mount Vernon Nazarene College in Ohio. Unlike Leshnock, Alazaus had impressive numbers this season as his 2-0 record and team-leading 0.57 ERA could attest.

Alazaus retired the first batter, pinch hitter Vic Llanos, on a groundout to shortstop Brian McLamb. But then the problems started. Alazaus gave up a single to Steve Santucci and issued a walk to Stutz. Garcia went down swinging for the second out, but Dean singled to load the bases. With the bases loaded and two outs, Deares came to the plate with the game on the line, the tying run ninety feet away, the winning run at second base. Deares hit a weak fly to left field, which appeared to be a routine play for left fielder Jason Wuerch. However, at the crack of the bat, Wuerch slipped and fell. He quickly rose to his feet, ran a few steps toward the left-field line, and dove for the ball, but it was out of his reach. The ball landed in fair territory, and Stutz was waved home from second base to score the winning run in a 5-4 win for the Redbirds.

"That's a perfect example of not getting the breaks," Dominguez was quoted as saying in the game story filed the following day by Andrew Gross of the *Daily Star* in Oneonta. "It was a routine fly ball."

Indeed, it was.

Wuerch could have made the play, and the Yankees should have won the game 4-3. Instead, Wuerch and his teammates walked dejectedly toward the gate in the center-field fence and eventually boarded the charter bus waiting nearby in front of East Field

Recreation Center. The walk was a long one for Wuerch, in particular. In fact, when the Oneonta left fielder arose to his feet, he started walking straight for the center-field gate. And then, halfway there, he turned around and walked back to the Yankees' dugout on the first-base side, where he grabbed his bat before making the lonely walk once again.

August 26, 1993—Glens Falls, New York

Wuerch had walked so quickly to the bus following last night's loss that I could not catch up to do an interview. When I found him today before the second game of this series, he was sitting on a folding chair next to the dugout and wearing number thirty on his back instead of twenty-one.

"I pushed hard on my right foot and slipped," said Wuerch of his miscue, which was ruled a double for Deares. "It's as simple as that. And I couldn't recover. That's a big game for us and we need to win. That's the reason why we lost. You have to make that play, but you have to forget about it and get it off your mind."

Dominguez was nearby and within earshot of my interview, something that he did not seem to appreciate at all.

"Hey Wuerchie, let's forget about last night," Dominguez snapped. "It's over and done with."

Despite the defensive mishap, Wuerch and his teammates could take solace in the fact that they actually gained ground on division-leading Utica. The Blue Sox lost a doubleheader last night to the Auburn Astros, the worst team in the league, by scores of 4-3 and 7-6. Pittsfield also lost, dropping a game to Elmira by a score of 5-2. Utica (34-31) was still in first place, one game ahead of Pittsfield (32-31) and one and a half games in front of Oneonta (32-32), a ball club that had now lost eleven of its last twelve games.

"It's kind of weird how baseball works out where you can lose a game and still make up ground on a team ahead of you," said Rob

Trimble, the Oneonta catcher before today's game. "We're only a game and a half out. Baseball is a funny game, and anything can happen. There are winning streaks just like there are losing streaks. We can string a few together here, and I'm sure we'll be all right. The last few days, it seems like there was nothing we could do to win a ball game. It gets tough after a while if you lose so many close games in a row. You kind of get the feeling that we're snake bitten."

Oneonta would try to get back on track tonight when they sent Jason Rathbun to the mound for his fifth start of the season. Rathbun was 1-0 with a 3.31 ERA. The Redbirds would start Alan Benes, the younger brother of Andy Benes, who pitched for the San Diego Padres. The younger Benes had yet to taste victory this season, his record being 0-3 with a 3.24 ERA.

Unlike last night, when I viewed the game from an empty radio booth adjacent to the press box, I would watch tonight's game from the stands. I chose a spot on the first-base side during the early innings, and in doing so, I met Rob Hilliard, part owner of the Redbirds, who settled in alongside me on a wooden bleacher to talk about the future of this franchise in between bites of the hot dog he was eating.

East Field and the city of Glens Falls was nothing more than a temporary stop for Hilliard and his lame duck franchise. The Redbirds were slated to play only the 1993 season here and then it was off to supposedly greener pastures in the form of the *wide-open green pastures* off US Highway 206 in Sussex County, New Jersey, of all places.

Last year, the Redbirds were in Hamilton, Ontario, Canada, where they ran away with the Stedler Division title, finishing at 56-20, a remarkable winning percentage of .737. The Redbirds finished sixteen and a half games ahead of second-place Erie (40-37), but the Redbirds lost to the Sailors, the wildcard playoff team, in the first round of the playoffs. The ball club, which had been in Hamilton since 1988, drew 65,717 fans last year, third in the league behind Utica (73,464) and league-leading Erie (79,245).

Despite success on the field and at the gate, Hilliard and three other partners—Barry Gordon, Marc Klee, and Peter Bardach—had already decided to pull up the stakes and move the team out of Hamilton. When Hilliard and his partners bought the Hamilton franchise in February of 1991 and named it Minor League Heroes, LP, they had plans to move the team to Northwest New Jersey.

"We'll be playing there next year," said Hilliard. "They broke ground down there on June 30."

"There weren't a whole lot of alternatives," said Hilliard regarding the decision to leave Canada for the United States. "Hamilton had allowed the ballpark to decay. We had four rainouts last year where it didn't even rain on the day of the rainout. St. Louis wasn't pleased with the facility or the paperwork of being in Canada. We were well-received when we played a special weekend series here last year. We didn't see it as a lame-duck situation. We've had a good showing here. The league may have another club follow us in. There could be a New York–Penn League team here next year."

According to Hilliard, the new ballpark would be in Sussex County, New Jersey, near Franklin Township with a seating capacity of 4,200. Construction plans called for the inclusion of a baseball museum, an indoor recreation center, and eventually, a restaurant that would overlook the right-field fence.

"It's designed to fit in with the agrarian architecture of northwestern New Jersey," said Hilliard. "It'll be an 'old' new ballpark. The notion is that we want people to feel like they're going through a time warp, but we'll have ten luxury boxes."

The ballpark, said Hilliard, would be near Highway 206, a major thoroughfare from northwestern New Jersey to the Pocono Mountains of Pennsylvania. Hilliard said that 3 million people pass through the area every summer. Franklin Township only had a population of 3,500, but there were 135,000 people living in Sussex County and 3.5 million people living in a thirty-five-mile radius. So, while the neighboring township was certainly not a metropolis,

Hilliard was counting on the notion of attracting the vacationer as well as the regional fan.

"We'll be the big fish in the little pond," he said. "Right now, people eat out at the twenty-four-hour diner and hang out at the Dairy Queen until 12:30 p.m. at night. We've already sold 1,400 season tickets. We're already sold out of the box seats at 850."

While Hilliard painted a promising picture of the near future in a remote area of northwestern New Jersey, professional baseball was living on borrowed time here in Glens Falls. East Field once served as the home to a Double A franchise in the Eastern League beginning in 1980. According to the Glens Falls program, baseball came to the city that season by way of default when the Chicago White Sox failed to get their affiliate into nearby Schenectady, New York, which was in the western shadow of Albany, the capital city of the state. At the time, East Field was nothing more than a high-school baseball diamond. The White Sox came to Warren County nonetheless, even though there were no lights at the facility. Games were played during the day that season until lights were installed midway through the summer. Amazingly, the team drew 85,000 fans in 1980 while playing half of the games during the daytime hours.

One of the most memorable seasons here would have been 1981 when the roster included Greg Walker and Ron Kittle, two players who would both get the promotion to Chicago at the end of the 1982 season and were fixtures in the lineup in 1983 when the White Sox played in the American League Championship Series against the Baltimore Orioles. While playing in Glens Falls in 1981, Kittle fought a chipped bone in his hand along with mononucleosis and influenza, none of which could prevent him from hitting forty home runs and driving in 103 runs. Kittle won the Eastern League Player of the Year honors, and the White Sox attracted 100,000 fans during their second year at East Field.

Twelve years later, fans had been surprisingly supportive of professional baseball in Glens Falls as the Redbirds made their one-year pit stop here before moving to the open space alongside Highway 206 in New Jersey.

Or had they really supported the lame-duck franchise?

I suppose it depended on whether one placed value on the stat sheet that showed the Redbirds second in the league in attendance with 2,238 per game or what you saw by simply sitting in the grandstand. If last night served as an indicator, the attendance figures were questionable, because if 1,657 fans were *really* in attendance, I was not sure where half of them were sitting.

What was even more curious about the lame duck ball club was the letter on page three of the Redbirds program written by Mayor Francis X. O'Keefe. Baseball was now back in Glens Falls after a five-year hiatus, but the welcome letter from O'Keefe to Redbird fans made no mention of a one-year stay. Instead, O'Keefe thanked the Redbird owners for "returning baseball to its home at East Field" and referred to the 1983 season as "the inaugural season of the Glens Falls Redbirds" as opposed to the one and only season.

Oneonta ended two scoreless innings tonight when Hansen hit a pitch over the fence in left-center field in the third inning, a solo shot off Benes for a 1-0 Yankees lead. The Redbirds struck back in the fifth inning when Llanos hit a solo homer to tie the game at 1-1.

Both teams had opportunities to score but came up short each time. In the Oneonta seventh, McLamb doubled with one out, but Wuerch struck out, and Ledee ended the inning when he grounded out to first.

Signs of frustration by the slumping Oneonta ball club were beginning to show. When Ledee returned to center field in the bottom of the seventh inning for his warm-up throws, instead of throwing the ball back to the Oneonta dugout when the inning was ready to begin, he threw the ball over the outfield fence and into the dark evening sky.

Glens Falls failed to capitalize in the bottom of the seventh, and Llanos was on third with one out. Turco gave the sign for a suicide squeeze play with Dean at bat, and Llanos broke for home when Rathbun started his delivery. Dean, however, botched the bunt, popping it up to the first baseman Kurt Bierek, who then fired to third, where the pitcher Rathbun alertly covered the base to complete the double play.

The Yankees may have been struggling at the plate, but they were adept in the field. With the game still tied 1-1 in the ninth, the Redbirds seemed to have the game won with the bases loaded and no outs against Scott Standish, who entered the game in the eighth to relieve Rathbun. Dominguez moved his outfielders close enough to be able to make a throw home to get the runner tagging from third, and his infielders were all hugging the grass. The Redbirds batter, Garcia, found himself at the center of attention once again. He hit a ground ball to third base, where Bierek gloved the ball and threw to the catcher Trimble to get the runner Santucci on the force play.

Dean then struck out swinging for the second out, which allowed the Oneonta defense to pull back to regular depth. Standish proceeded to put out the fire when he forced Deares to hit a fly ball to the center-fielder Hansen for the third out, sending the game into extra innings.

In the Oneonta tenth, the Yankees had started a rally with two outs when Ledee singled against the Redbirds reliever Craig Grasser, who came into the game to relieve Benes in the ninth. Aldridge followed with a double, and just like that, the Yankees had runners at second and third. The rally ended, however, when Grasser escaped the jam by striking out Hansen.

Standish found himself in trouble once again in the tenth when Almond and Santucci singled. Stutz then delivered in the clutch with a two-out single to left field that scored Almond for the winning run in a 2-1 victory, the second night in a row the Redbirds produced a walk-off win.

The two-game series now over, Oneonta and Glens Falls appeared to be two ball clubs moving in opposite directions. The Redbirds

(31-36) were back on track, having won three in a row, while the Oneonta tailspin continued, the Yankees' losing streak now at seven straight games. Even worse, the Yankees had dropped twelve out of thirteen and now found themselves below the .500 mark at 32-33.

"We did everything we needed to do tonight to win except get the clutch hit," Dominguez was quoted by beat writer Andrew Gross in the next day's edition of the *Daily Star* in Oneonta.

The Yankees would try to put an end to their losing streak by returning home to Damaschke Field the following night, where they would begin a two-game series against Watertown. Here in Glens Falls, meanwhile, the Redbirds would try to extend their winning streak to four games when they hosted the Elmira Pioneers. The Redbirds had only six games remaining at East Field, the last game scheduled for September 4 against Pittsfield. The franchise would then pull up the stakes and leave town for that vast open space adjacent to a highway in northern New Jersey. The city of Glens Falls would be without professional baseball once again.

Lorrie Schlake, a member of the Redbirds Booster Club, had a sign hanging from the first-base bleachers that read, "We miss you when you're away from home."

"I'll miss the team, the players," said Schlake. "I've gotten to know them. If not this franchise, there should be another team."

Do not bother telling that to Hilliard and his business partners.

The front office of the Glens Falls Redbirds at East Field

Glens Falls Manager Steve Turco (center) talks with members of the Oneonta Yankees hours before the first pitch.

The Oneonta Yankees have a long walk to the field from their visiting clubhouse located behind the center field fence.

Oneonta Manager Ken Dominguez (left) works with one of his players (14) during batting practice.

*Oneonta players enjoy their pregame meal
at the East Field visiting clubhouse.*

*The Oneonta Yankees gather for PBJ sandwiches,
bananas, and Gatorade in Glens Falls, NY.*

Oneonta pitchers relax in the East Field bullpen prior to a game against the Glens Falls Redbirds.

Fans arrive to East Field to watch the Redbirds host the Oneonta Yankees.

Glens Falls Manager Steve Turco watches
his pitcher warm-up in the bullpen.

East Field has bleacher seats in the outfield, the only
ballpark in the league with seats behind the fence.

CHAPTER FIFTEEN:

BASEBALL IN THE BERKSHIRES

August 27, 1993—Pittsfield, Massachusetts

There was a hidden diamond in the Berkshire Mountains of Western Massachusetts. It was located off Wahconah Street and across a dusty parking lot in Pittsfield. The diamond was surrounded by a blue grandstand, an antiquated structure covered with blue, tin siding on the outside and a roof above. On the front of the grandstand was a large sign that read, "Home of the Pittsfield Mets, Wahconah Park."

A wide ramp cut through the center of the grandstand. The vantage point at the base of the ramp while standing in the parking lot, was a simple view that would have pleased any baseball traditionalist: the grandstand screen, the top of the batting cage, and the treetops far in the distance beyond the center field fence. When I reached the top of the ramp, I was looking at one quaint little ballpark. If there was a ballpark in heaven, I was now standing at the pearly gates waiting for St. Peter to welcome me with a Pittsfield Mets program.

The small wooden grandstand was neatly tucked behind home plate and did not even wrap around on the sides to first and third

base. The box seats were comprised of four rows of folding chairs
that had white cushions with the Pittsfield Mets log atop each seat.
The logo replicated that of the major league affiliate New York Mets.
While the big-league ball club had a design of the Manhattan skyline on a baseball, the Pittsfield logo was the same except that the
background was a sketch of the white-capped Berkshire Mountains.
Above the logo was a slogan that read, "Catch 'Em on the Way Up,"
a reference to watching the Pittsfield prospects before they got a
crack at advancing to Shea Stadium in Flushing, New York.

A narrow walkway separated the box seats from the reserved
seats, which were comprised of two small sections of blue-and-or-
ange wooden benches with back supports. The reserved seats extended a mere two rows high, making the entire grandstand seating, box
seats, and reserved seats combined, a total of only fourteen rows in
all. At the very last row of the seats was a small press box designated
for the visiting radio broadcasters. Directly behind the booth was a
ladder that led to a square cutout in the grandstand roof. Through
the opening, members of the press could gain access to the roof and
the larger press box that sat atop it. Underneath the grandstand roof
hung seven owl decoys. I remembered reading an article not too long
ago in *Sports Illustrated* about the beauty of Wahconah Park and the
purpose of the owls: to keep away unwanted pigeons.

I arrived at Wahconah Park at 3:15 p.m. on this sunny Friday afternoon, long before the 7:00 p.m. game scheduled against the Utica
Blue Sox. Out on the field, Howie Freiling, the first-year Pittsfield
manager, was standing on the pitcher's mound feeding baseballs
into a machine that fired pitches at the young farmhands taking
their turns in the batting cage working on the fine art of bunting.
Occasionally, Freiling would stop to visit the batter and make ad-
justments with the positioning of the bat before returning to the
machine to feed it more balls.

Underneath the grandstand on the first-base side, I found the
Pittsfield front office. The Pittsfield general manager was Rick

Murphy, an outgoing individual who welcomed me to his beautiful ballpark. Murphy introduced me to a young employee named Ethan Wilson, a recent graduate from the University of Massachusetts. It did not take me long to realize that Wilson was the most congenial front office staffer I had met in the entire league. Wilson worked for the ball club as an intern, and his title was Director of Media Relations. When the game began, he took on the role as official scorer from his vantage point in the rooftop press box. Wilson provided me with everything I needed to know about the Pittsfield ball club: updated team and league statistics, game-day rosters, and an official Pittsfield Mets program. The cover of the program was a classic black-and-white aerial view of Wahconah Park, built in 1919 near the banks of the Housatonic River, which flowed behind the outfield fence. Also spread out across the program cover were three other black-and-white photos. On the left was Gene Hasson, the first baseman/manager who led the Pittsfield Electrics with twenty-seven home runs during the 1948 season in the Can-Am League. Freiling was pictured on the right side, and at the bottom of the cover was a team photo of the 1919 Pittsfield Hillies, a club that won the Eastern League Championship. In addition to handing me these helpful resources, Wilson also provided some Wahconah Park history while giving me a walking tour of the ballpark.

"It was built in 1919 before night games were a reality," said Wilson. "The park was built facing west. The sun sets in center field, and it can get in the batter's eyes. We're one of two teams—Bakersfield, California, is the other—that has sun delays. Both teams will go to the dugouts (during the sun delay). Sometimes, players sign autographs during the sun delays. We play songs like 'Sunshine on my Shoulder' or 'It'll be a Bright Sunshiny Day.' We've had three delays this year. It had to be just perfect to get in their eyes. The team had a big black tarp that they draped from that wire hanging between those two poles in center field, but the tarp would rip and blow around. They've decided to live with it. It's part of the baseball allure."

As for the seven owl decoys, Wilson said they were hung from underneath the grandstand roof two years ago. He informed me that the idea had worked and that the pigeon problem had been under control ever since.

I caught up with the twenty-seven-year-old Freiling in the Pittsfield clubhouse, which was attached to the back of the grandstand on the third-base side. The Mets had beaten the Elmira Pioneers 2-0 last night on a combined four-hitter by Tom Engle and Mike Welch. The win, combined with Utica's 4-3 loss in eleven innings against Auburn, gave the Mets (33-31) a share of first place in the McNamara Division with the Blue Sox (34-32), who would come to Wahconah tonight to start a critical two-game series. Oneonta (32-33) was one and a half games behind the co-leaders, and Glens Falls (31-36) was three and a half games behind.

Freiling was sitting in his office at his manager's desk while his twenty-nine-year-old pitching coach, Jeff Edwards, and traveling instructor Rich Garcia sat nearby on a couch. Freiling was originally drafted by the Los Angeles Dodgers in 1987 and played in the Mets farm system, advancing as high as Tidewater in the Triple-A International League.[41] That was three years ago, and now with his playing career behind him, he found himself sitting in first place in one of three divisions in the New York–Pennsylvania League.

"Everybody's excited," said Freiling. "I haven't felt any tightness from them. Even though we're up by a percentage point, that doesn't mean a thing. We're all right together in the pack. Whoever plays the best during these ten games will win the division."

Freiling was not in this position earlier in the year.

The Mets were slow out of the gate and were not able to catch Oneonta, and now Utica, until last night. For most of the season, Freiling's young farmhands had played near the .500 level.

---

41   Freiling, Howie. *Baseball Reference.* "Howie Freiling." 5 August 2024, https://www.baseball-reference.com/register/player.fcgi?id=freili001how

"We started off 2-5, and then we went on to win six straight and went to 8-5," said Freiling. "We actually have only been below .500 for one game since we were 8-5. But we have never been higher than three games above .500. We have done it with good pitching, simply said. Our pitching is second or third in the league. Most of the time, we hit just enough to back up our pitching."

"If we win two or lose two, it doesn't mean we're out of it or have it made," said Freiling when speaking about this short series with Utica. "I think the guys are excited. We have our top two starters (Jason Isringhausen and David Swanson) going today and tomorrow. I think we're going to do all right. At this level, even though some teams have better records than others, it's generally pretty even. The teams are pretty equal. The talent, it's not like one team is up here and the other is down here. It's pretty even."

Utica came into this short series after losing three games to the Auburn Astros (25-41), all the losses by one run, and two of them coming in extra innings. When the Blue Sox pulled into Wahconah Park, I talked with T. J. O'Donnell about his team's recent slump. I had last seen the Blue Sox second baseman on July 3 at Donovan Field in Utica when he was tearing up the league with a .388 batting average, a mark that had dipped since that time but was still respectable at .336.

"We didn't get the big hit when we needed it," said O'Donnell about the Auburn series. "We played some good ball games, but that's just the game of baseball. Sometimes you don't come out on top, and that's what happened. On any given day, anybody can beat anybody. We just happen to be in a situation here where we control our own destiny. We have ten or eleven games left, and they're all within our division. If we play well for the next week and a half, we have a good chance to be on top."

O'Donnell knew the importance of the two-game series here in Pittsfield, but he was also aware that the season would not be decided during these next two days.

"Everybody wants to win," he said. "That's the reason we're here. These are big games, but they're not as big as they possibly could be, like in another week. If it's the same situation, these would be big games. It doesn't matter if you win your division by ten games, or you win by a half-game. You still win it. I still don't think it's a do-or-die situation here."

During batting practice, I met Rafael Hermoso, a beat writer for the *Observer Dispatch* in Utica, who was following the Blue Sox on the road while the pennant race headed into the final stretch. Hermoso, a native of Queens, New York, joined the Utica newspaper in May after working at *Newsday* as an intern. Jeff Leone of WTLB Radio was also at Wahconah Park to broadcast the games back home to the listening audience in Utica. The Blue Sox were the only team in the league to broadcast all their games, home and away. Like Hermoso, this was Leone's debut season in minor league baseball. Leone, a Boston native, was a recent graduate of Syracuse University. His play-by-play partner was Jim Jackson, who stayed back in Utica and was not making the road trip in Pittsfield. According to Leone, Jackson was recently hired as the radio play-by-play announcer for the Philadelphia Flyers of the National Hockey League after calling the action for the Utica Devils of the American Hockey League.

Utica was represented by more than two members of the media during this road trip to Pittsfield. In the concourse area outside the grandstand, I noticed a small group of middle-aged gentlemen wearing Utica Blue Sox hats while eating hot dogs in front of the concession stand shortly before the opening pitch. Fred Neuman, Ed Landesman, John Tarhowski, and George and Ed Schmitt, all members of the Blue Sox Booster Club, had made the trip from Central New York to watch their beloved Blue Sox in the short series against Pittsfield.

The national anthem at Wahconah Park was played on a small organ, which was atop the roof inside the press box. The acoustics of the organ music were impressive. The speakers hung off the roof, and the music rang through the small wooden grandstand. Looking around, I felt as though I had gone back in time.

Was it the organ?

Or maybe it was the coziness of the grandstand where the fans sat close to each other and the field.

Whatever it was, I felt right at home here at Wahconah Park in Pittsfield, and the ten beams that supported the grandstand roof and presented an obstruction of your view of the field, depending on where you sat, didn't bother me a bit.

The playing field here was splendid as well. Most noticeable were the tall green trees which provided the background behind the outfield fence. The infield and outfield grass here were not as lush as some of the better playing fields in the league such as Community Park in St. Catharines. Then again, the home of the baby Blue Jays was not really a ballpark, but instead, just a very well-kept baseball field with aluminum bleachers surrounding it. I had not even seen a pitch here yet, but when I thought of the word *ballpark*, I believed that a picture of Wahconah Park should have appeared next to the definition.

When the national anthem was finished and the Mets began warming up on the field prior to the opening pitch, Scott Snella, the public address announcer, informed the crowd that, "Due to your proximity to the field, be aware of the possibility of foul balls, broken bats, and overthrown balls at all times."

Tonight, I settled into the fourth row of the box seats located behind home plate. Sitting in a chair in front of me was Tom Engle, the twenty-two-year-old right-handed pitcher for the Mets who was a native of Lancaster, Ohio. Engle picked up the win last night while throwing a four-hitter and striking out ten in seven innings of work during a 2-0 defeat of Elmira. Engle improved his record to 7-6 and lowered his ERA to 2.69 in a young career that had been a test of patience. He spent his first two years playing in the Appalachian League for the Kingsport Mets in Tennessee. In 1991, his third season of professional baseball, he tore a ligament in his right elbow that required surgery.

"It was the same operation that Tommy John had," said Engle. "It was done by Dr. Frank Jobe. He took a ligament from my left ankle and put it in my right elbow. Really, it's just like getting started."

That's because Engle then sat out the entire 1992 season. Now, here he was a year later, still in Class A baseball four years after being drafted, but his fresh start had him leading the Pittsfield ball club in strikeouts with ninety through seventy-seven innings of work.

The Pittsfield pitcher second on the team in strikeouts was beginning to warm up out on the mound. Tonight's starter, Jason Isringhausen, fanned eighty-six batters in seventy-eight innings while compiling a 5-4 record and 3.58 ERA. As Isringhausen threw tonight, Engle sat in the stands wearing street clothes while clocking pitches with a Pro Speed professional radar gun.

"They use these in the beginning, middle, and end of the season to make sure the pitchers are maintaining arm strength," explained Engle.

Engle documented the pitches on a chart attached to a clipboard that had columns with headings reading FB (fastball), CB (curveball), SL (slider), and Change. The speed of each pitch thrown by Isringhausen was written down under the appropriate heading. In the first inning, Isringhausen threw a 92-mph fastball, a slider at 87 mph, and a curveball at 77 mph. Isringhausen put the Blue Sox down in order to open the game, ending the inning by striking out Diogenes Baez on a 77-mph curveball. Engle logged the numbers sitting near the grandstand aisle, a location which provided fans an inside look at his notes as they walked by on the way to their seats.

"Most of them are let down because they think everyone can throw ninety-five miles per hour," says Engle. "You say eighty-five, and they say, 'Is that all?' In reality, that's pretty good."

Engle totaled the number of hits, earned runs, strikeouts, and walks each time Isringhausen had completed an inning. When the

Blue Sox were on the field, he put the radar gun in a case, opting not to clock the Utica pitchers. In the bottom of each inning, he had more time to talk. During the early innings, he gave me the perspective of a pitcher's repertoire.

"With a curveball," he said, "you come over the top more. It's like pulling down a curtain shade. A slider is a flick of the wrist at the end. A good curve comes straight down. With the slider, you want a sharp, late break. The slider is tougher to pick up. I don't think your average fan can tell."

The Blue Sox scored first when John Stratton opened the third inning with a walk, advanced to second on a fielder's choice, and scored on a two-out single by Aaron Fuller for a 1-0 lead.

The Mets came right back to tie the game at 1-1 in the bottom of the inning when Randy Warner opened with a single, advanced to second on a wild pitch by Utica starter Dean Peterson, and scored on a double by Charlie Sullivan, the Pittsfield second baseman and ninth hitter in Freiling's lineup.

In the fourth inning, the Blue Sox regained the lead without the benefit of a base hit or a walk. O'Donnell led off and reached base on an error by the Pittsfield shortstop Paul Petrulis. O'Donnell went to second on a fielder's choice and to third base on an error committed by Isringhausen. Dan Collier then hit a sacrifice fly that brought home O'Donnell for a 2-1 Utica lead.

During the fifth inning, Engle was delighted from his press-box seat when a fan walked by and gave him a complimentary plate of nachos with melted cheese on the side.

"I like this," said Engle. "It's a good change. It's good to get up here and eat."

Scott Jones, another Pittsfield pitcher, was also wearing street clothes and sitting near Engle. Jones had suffered from a bout with the flu for a week. Sitting to my left was Jenny Freiling, Howie Freling's wife, and alongside her was Kathy Souza, Engle's fiancée.

The couple, according to Engle, was planning to get married on October 29.

The Mets scored two runs in the fifth inning, the go-ahead run coming when Rafael Hernandez came home on a single by Sullivan, his second hit of the night after entering the game hitless in his last thirteen at bats. Eric Harris ran the score to 4-2 in the seventh inning with a solo homer that prompted Snella to deliver the following message over the public address system: "Ladies and gentlemen, with that shot, Eric Harris will be given fifteen dollars in total cash from the Pittsfield Mets Fan Club."

Isringhausen struck out Nick Ortiz in the eighth but then gave up back-to-back singles to Fuller and O'Donnell. Out of the Pittsfield dugout came Freiling, who pulled his starter after an outing that included three hits, twelve strikeouts, and two walks.

The hard-throwing Isringhausen was replaced by left-hander Steve Grennan, who was 2-0 with a 2.06 ERA to go along with his six saves and forty strikeouts in thirty-five innings pitched.

"This will be a little change of pace," said Engle, who changed his pitch chart sheet while informing me that Grennan's fastball would be in the low eighties. "But he has a sneaky delivery, and it's tough to pick up."

The Utica manager, Dave Holt, countered the pitching change by Freiling with a move of his own. Holt pulled back Baez, a left-handed batter, and brought in pinch hitter Ricky Milligan. The tying run at first base and only one out, the right-handed Milligan dug into the box with a .236 average and only two home runs with eighteen runs batted in.

The move by Holt took away the lefty vs. lefty matchup that Freiling was looking for by entering Grennan.

It did not matter.

Grennan caught Milligan looking at a third strike for the second out of the inning.

Freiling popped out of the dugout once again, taking out Grennan after facing just one batter to bring in right-hander Brandon Newell to pitch to the right-handed Collier, Utica's cleanup hitter. Collier was batting only .239, but had fourteen home runs and forty-four runs batted in. Even more impressive was his .333 average against Pittsfield for the season along with four home runs against Mets pitching. Collier, like Milligan, went down swinging—according to Engle, on a curveball clocked at 85 mph—and the Utica rally ended in an inning that had three Pittsfield pitchers each record a strikeout.

With one inning remaining, Engle was done for the night as he began to pack up the radar gun and compile his notes before leaving for the Pittsfield clubhouse. "It's missing pitches," he said of the radar gun. "The batteries are dying. Plus, I'm mainly concerned with starters."

Pittsfield still led 4-2 entering the ninth when Utica designated hitter Joe Hayward reached base on a walk to begin the inning. Eric Ford entered the game as a pinch runner for Hayward and advanced to second base when Joe DePastino grounded out. Ford would be stranded in scoring position, however, when Newell retired Stratton and Mark Senkowitz to end the game, picking up his second save of the season. With the 4-2 win now secured, so was sole possession of first place in the McNamara Division for the hometown Mets.

The win improved Isringhausen's record to 6-4, and when interviewed by writer Howard Herman of the *Berkshire Eagle*, the league's strikeout leader (ninety-eight) called it his best performance of the season. "I was pumped up tonight," he said. "I had a lot more jitters."

Outside the visiting clubhouse on the third-base side of Wahconah Park stood Stratton. Teammates were filtering out of the clubhouse, still wearing their uniforms, while walking toward the nearby bus, opting to shower back at the hotel instead of the cramped quarters of the clubhouse. Stratton, however, was not in a big hurry to get on the bus, talking instead to friends from his native Stratford, Connecticut, who had come to watch him play in tonight's game. The loss was Utica's fourth straight, by a combined total of five runs, and the Blue Sox were now one game behind the division-leading Mets.

"It's frustrating," said Stratton of the losing streak. "You're right there, neck and neck. You're battling as hard as you can. It's tough to lose a game like this. We need to get it going."

August 28, 1993—Pittsfield, Massachusetts

The incredible decline of the Oneonta Yankees continued last night, and their season was unraveling at a rapid pace. After spending most of the season atop the McNamara Division, the Yankees dropped their eighth in a row last night in a 14-2 loss to the Watertown Indians at Damaschke Field in Oneonta. The Yankees had now lost thirteen of their last fourteen games and found themselves two and a half games behind Pittsfield.

I arrived at Wahconah Park today at 5:05 p.m. and talked with Utica manager Dave Holt about the tight pennant race in the McNamara Division. With a win tonight, the Blue Sox could leave town in the same position as when they arrived: tied for first place. Holt had just come off the field after throwing batting practice and giving way to his pitching coach Garry Roggenburk. Holt grabbed a towel to dry off while settling into the first-base dugout, his gray Utica T-shirt soaked in sweat.

"It doesn't take a brain surgeon to figure out what's at stake here," said Holt about the two-game series. "It goes without saying that the games are crucial."

When Roggenburk came off the field after finishing batting practice, he, too, was drenched in sweat. The daily routine of throwing batting practice for the Red Sox hopefuls, day after day, took its toll in the late stages of the season. The Blue Sox had been at it for sixty-seven days now, and the end of the seventy-eight-game regular season schedule was eleven days away.

"I've lost ten pounds from being out in the heat throwing and sweating," said Roggenburk. "It keeps me going. You see the end in sight. You plug away and you try to be consistent. You get a rainout, and you get a day off. It wears on you."

When Roggenburk, Holt, and their counterparts throughout the league threw batting practice before a game, a protective L-shaped screen was placed on the grass in front of the mound to protect the manager or coach from getting hit by line drives. The pitcher stood in the front of the mound as opposed to pitching off the rubber, making the distance shorter than a game situation.

"To throw from that rubber every day," said Roggenburk, "I couldn't get it up there (to the plate). They want the ball up there quicker. It makes them quicker."

Tonight, I decided to watch the game from the cramped quarters of the press box that sat atop the grandstand roof. To get there, I walked to the fourteenth row of the grandstand, where I then climbed up the iron ladder that led into the small hole in the rear of the grandstand roof. The ladder resembled a fire-escape ladder, and while climbing it, one needed to be careful while holding the side rails. It was tough to carry duffel bags and the like through the small opening at the top, which was a wooden hatch. On the top of the roof, a walkway led to the press box, which was painted blue and orange, the team colors of the Pittsfield Mets as well as the parent ball club. The press box was divided into two equal sections separated by a wall in the middle, both sections accessible by two different back doors to the booth. One press box housed the scoreboard operator, official scorer, and public address announcer. In the other booth, there was room for me and two other writers, Howard Herman of the Pittsfield *Berkshire Eagle* and Rafael Hermoso of the Utica *Observer Dispatch*. All three of us were positioned on stools while looking down on the field from behind a wire fence that covered two open flaps to the booth. There was limited space on the ledge in front of us, just enough for me to lay out my scorebook, notebook, and journal. It was also dark in here, so much in fact that I could barely read my scorebook and notes. Behind Hermoso and me, there might have been enough space for two or three people to stand, but that was it. Herman told me that actor Bill Murray once stood right here, behind where we sat, during a rain delay in the late 1980s. Murray was then a part owner of the ball club that was a Chicago Cubs affiliate in the Class AA Eastern League.

Left-hander Kurt Bogott would get the start for the Blue Sox along with the task of putting an end to the four-game losing streak. Bogott came into the game with a 1-5 record, a 4.70 ERA, and opposing batters were hitting .277 against him. The Mets would counter with left-hander David Swanson, who was 6-2 with a 2.49 ERA.

The Mets wasted little time jumping all over Bogott, scoring two runs in the first inning when leadoff batter Gary Collum singled and advanced to second on an error by Senkowitz. Collum scored the first run when Cesar Diaz singled, who then proceeded to steal second before scoring on a single by Tad Smith.

In the second inning, Warner walked, Hernandez doubled, and both runners scored on a triple by Sullivan to put the Mets in front 4-0. During the past two nights, Sullivan had produced from his ninth slot in the batting order, driving in four runs with three hits in his last four at bats. Holt stayed with Bogott, and his patience paid off, the lefty settling down and not allowing a run over the next four innings while giving up just one hit. Utica, meanwhile, began to claw its way back into the game, the big hit coming in the fourth when Stratton hit a two-run double.

In the sixth inning, the Blue Sox reached Swanson again. Ortiz, who had struck out three times last night, reached base for the third time tonight when he opened the inning with a single. DePastino drove home Swanson with a single of his own and tied the game at 4-4 when he scored on a triple by Senkowitz.

The Mets answered in the seventh and eighth innings for three runs, the go-ahead run scoring on a single by pinch hitter Benny

Agbayani, to regain the lead at 7-4 heading into the ninth inning. The Blue Sox were not going down quietly against Pittsfield closer Mike Welch, who came into the game with a 3-1 record, 1.55 ERA, eight saves, and thirty strikeouts over twenty-nine innings pitched. The ninth hitter, Baez, greeted Welch with a double to start the inning and scored on a one-out single by O'Donnell to cut the score to 7-5. Ortiz then collected his third single of the night and advanced to second on an error, the miscue sending O'Donnell to third base. The cleanup batter, Collier, followed with a groundout that scored O'Donnell, and the Red Sox cut the gap to one run at 7-6 with Ortiz advancing to third base.

The tying run ninety feet away with two outs, DePastino came to bat with three singles on the night in four at bats. Welch prevailed, striking him out to pick up his ninth save while preserving a 7-6 win. Utica left town dropping both games, putting the Blue Sox two games behind the Mets. Dave Holt's ball club had now lost five straight games by a combined total of six runs.

August 29, 1993—Pittsfield, Massachusetts

I returned to Wahconah Park for a third straight day, this time for a Sunday afternoon contest against the Glens Falls Redbirds with the opening pitch scheduled for 3:00 p.m.

Elsewhere around the McNamara Division, something would have to give at Donovan Field in Utica later tonight when the Blue Sox and Oneonta Yankees squared off in a contest of two teams mirrored in late season losing streaks: five straight losses for the Blue Sox and nine straight for the struggling Yankees. Oneonta had lost again last night, a 6-4 decision against Watertown, marking the team's fourteenth loss over the last fifteen games. On August 10, the Yankees were 31-21 and in first place. Today, the team was 32-35 and three and a half games behind front-running Pittsfield with ten games to play.

A glance around the league had Niagara Falls producing a 3-2 win over Erie last night in thirteen innings. The Rapids (42-27) were now a half-game behind St. Catharines (43-27) in the Stedler Division pennant race. In the Pinckney Division, Watertown (41-28) had the largest lead of any first-place team in the league, the Indians three and a half games in front of Geneva (37-31).

Today, Pittsfield would play the Glens Falls ball club that had now reeled off five straight wins entering the Sunday matinee after losing seven in a row. The manager of the team, Steve Turco, was right about his team when I spoke with him recently at East Field and he described the Redbirds (33-36) as streaky. Glens Falls, tied for third with Oneonta in the division standings, still had a chance to make the playoffs, and with four of its last eight games against Pittsfield, could even steal the division title.

I caught up with Howie Freiling in the Pittsfield clubhouse at 1:45 p.m. and found him tinkering with his lineup card with a little over an hour to go before the opening pitch. When he was finished, he had Benny Agbayani as the leadoff hitter for the Mets and playing center field, a decision that meant Freiling would have used three different players to bat leadoff in the past three games.

When I walked out of Freiling's office, it was 2:00 p.m., and it struck me as odd that the Glens Falls bus had yet to pull into the parking lot at Wahconah Park for a game that was to start in exactly one hour. Coincidentally, this was the same team that showed up with little time to spare on August 2 for a game at McDonough Park in Geneva against the Cubs. A few minutes went by before the Redbirds' team bus pulled into the dusty parking lot and the players filed out, dropping off their duffel bags in the visiting dugout before heading to the right-field corner for a team stretch. I caught up with Turco to inquire about the late arrival and learned that the Redbirds were on their way to Pittsfield, but turned back to Glens Falls because the meal money for the players was back in his office at East Field.

After spending Friday night watching Tom Engle clock pitches for Pittsfield from the box seats and Saturday night in the press box with writers Herman and Hermoso, I was back in the box seats once again for today's afternoon contest. This time, I was just to the right side of home plate, three rows up from field level where I introduced myself to Dick Teed, a sixty-seven-year-old scout for the Los Angeles Dodgers. Teed informed me that he played for the Brooklyn Dodgers in 1953 and had been scouting for a total of twenty-five years. Later, a check on Teed in the *Baseball Encyclopedia* showed that the Springfield, Massachusetts, native was hitless in his one and only at bat for the Dodgers in 1953, striking out in his only experience playing at the big-league level.[42]

Teed lived in Windsor, Connecticut, and he scouted high school and college baseball throughout New England. When those seasons ended, he became an organizational scout. This year, he was scouting Pawtucket in the Class AAA International League, Albany-Colonie and New Britain in the Class AA Eastern League, and Glens Falls in the New York–Pennsylvania League. Last year, Teed covered the Boston Red Sox and New York Yankees organizations from the Class AA level to the major leagues.

"If there is a trade in the major leagues, and it concerns a player out of the minors, they'd contact me and ask which players I like in the trade," said Teed. "That way, you don't have to go to three or four scouts. I should know the Yankees and Red Sox players as well as anybody."

Teed drove a Ford Taurus leased to him by the Dodgers organization and logged 25,000 to 30,000 miles every year while blanketing New England to cover high school and college baseball. "If there's a pitcher I need to see in Orono, Maine, I go see him," he said.

The life of a scout was all about travel and loneliness. Teed, however, informed me that he had ways to beat this aspect of the job. As

---

42   Teed, Dick. Wikipedia, *The Free Encyclopedia*. "Dick Teed." 2 July 2024, https://en.wikipedia.org/wiki/Dick_Teed

one example, when he recently stayed over in Glens Falls to watch
the Redbirds play the Elmira Pioneers, he awoke at 6:30 a.m. and
grabbed his golf clubs for a round at Bay Meadows Golf Club in
Glens Falls. "I got paired up," he said. "That's what's good about
golf, you get paired up and they enjoy playing with you."

Lunch, however, was often spent alone.

"You're lonely by yourself," he said. "You don't have anybody to
eat with you. When you're by yourself, you eat quick and get back
to the hotel."

At about 2:00 p.m. at the hotel, Teed said he went through his
reports. He had to grade players from other organizations on pitching, throwing, running, fielding, and hitting. He sent his reports
after seeing all the pitchers on a particular team, and they were received by Terry Reynolds, the Los Angeles scouting director.

"He (Reynolds) gives it to the farm director, and they put it on
a file in a computer," said Teed. "They'll call me up and might say,
'We're interested in so-and-so.'"

Following the midafternoon paperwork tasks, Teed got ready for
dinner around 4:30 p.m., and then it was off to the ballpark, arriving
nearly two hours before the start of the game. The early arrival was
a must for Teed, who needed to assess players' skills while watching
them during batting practice and infield practice.

"You watch batting practice, and you see if they have power,"
said Teed. "Then you see infield practice and outfield practice. You
may not ever see an outfielder throw during a game."

Today, Teed began to do his pregame work with a radar gun
nearby and a yellow score sheet on his lap. The sheet contained the
lineup for both teams tonight with a box for each player's position
and five rectangular spaces to mark the results of their at bats. A
larger space existed at the end of the row for him to write comments
about each player. Teed had completed a card from last night's game
at Glens Falls, but he would not let me see his comments when I
inquired.

"It's too personal," he said. "I don't want anybody knowing what I'm saying about these players."

As the Mets took the field in the first inning, the starting pitcher, Eric Ludwick, began to throw his warm-up pitches. Ludwick entered today's game against the Redbirds with a 2-4 record and 3.68 ERA.

"He's throwing 90 or 91 (mph)," said Teed after a few pitches were thrown by Ludwick.

The early numbers may have sounded impressive, but as Teed explained, the velocity of the fastball was not the only criteria he was looking for in a pitcher.

"Basically, does his breaking ball have good bite?" Teed commented. "You should study him. You watch him, and you see what his best pitch is."

The radar gun could gauge velocity, but it could not reveal the pitcher's mental makeup. This was a part of scouting, according to Teed, that could be more challenging for him and his counterparts throughout the game.

"The only thing you can pick up on is whether he has got a little bulldog in him," said Teed. "Does he come at you?"

In the first inning, Ludwick showed plenty of bulldog by striking out the Redbirds in order. Then in the second inning, Greg Almond came to bat to lead things off for the Redbirds. Normally the team's catcher, Almond was penciled into Turco's lineup today as the designated hitter.

"He can hit the fastball, but he has been struggling the past few games," said Teed of Almond, who entered the game batting .286. "He has a short stroke."

Almond struck out against Ludwick, and when teammate Victor Llanos also followed with a whiff, the Pittsfield hurler had struck out the first five batters of the game. When the next batter, Steve Santucci, stepped into the box, Teed had a hunch that the string of strikeouts was ending.

"Santucci will hit his fastball," said Teed. "He's a fastball, first ball hitter."

Sure enough, Santucci did hit the offering from Ludwick, but it was on the ground to third baseman Josh Haggas, who threw Santucci out at first to end the inning.

"When you watch the batter," said Teed, "you look for a quick bat, power, and the strike zone. A short, quick stroke is the best. Number 19 in right field (Greg Deares of Glens Falls) has a long stroke. He can get by, but I'd rather see a guy with a short stroke. You have better control of the bat."

Ludwick stayed in a groove, not allowing a runner past first base until the fourth inning when Deares hit a single and then proceeded to steal second base.

"He's throwing hard, 90 to 93 miles per hour," said Teed of Ludwick. "You don't find too many who can do that." Later, Teed would share with me that Ludwick did not have much of a breaking ball.

Eric Alexander, the starting pitcher for Glens Falls, was also throwing well today. He did not allow a hit until the fourth inning and kept the Mets scoreless through six innings while the Redbirds held on to a 1-0 lead after Santucci singled in the fifth and would eventually score on a sacrifice fly by Mark Williams.

As the game wore on, the topic shifted to defense, and Teed emphasized the need for speed and the importance of being steady with the glove up the middle (catcher, shortstop, second base, center field).

"Everybody is looking for speed, especially with infielders," said Teed. "The shortstop, second baseman, and center fielder, they've got to be able to run. The right fielder should have the best arm, and the left fielder is your power hitter. Most catchers can't run. That is why they're catchers, because they can't run. I was a shortstop, and they converted me to a catcher. I could run, but after three years of catching, it slowed me down."

Another tool Teed had within his repertoire was the stopwatch. He would use it to gauge the arm strength of a catcher, clocking a throw from home to second base when a runner was attempting to steal a base. He started the watch from the moment the ball hit the catcher's mitt and stopped it when the second baseman or shortstop caught the ball.

"If you get it at 2.2 or 2.1, you've got a good arm," said Teed. "If you're 1.9 or below, you'll throw anybody out. If you're 2.4 or 2.5, you won't get anybody out."

As for the speed he looked for when a hitter ran from the batter's box to first base, the numbers, he said, should be 4.2 seconds for a lefthanded hitter and 4.1 for a right-handed batter.

When asked who the best players were that he had signed, Teed mentioned John Franco and Eric Young. According to Teed, years ago, scouts used to get a little bonus if a player they signed to a contract reached the major leagues, but no such bonus came with the job today. When I asked Teed if he could forecast whether some of the players in front of us today would make it to the majors, he hesitated.

"That's hard to do," he said. "It's the first time they've played every day, the first time they play all their games under the lights, and their first time away from home. It's hard. It's ridiculous to guess that, yeah, he'll pitch or catch in the big leagues. In Class AA or Class AAA, I might be 80 percent accurate."

Whether he could predict a major league career for a Class A player or not, Teed still had the job of answering a tough question on a player's scouting report. It was the section which asked whether the scout considered the player a prospect and at what level he should play the following season.

The congenial Teed did not seem to mind my company while the pitching duel between Ludwick and Alexander unfolded in front of us at Wahconah Park. Had he been sitting with another scout, however, Teed informed me that he would not be so talkative.

"Scouts don't talk to each other about who they like or don't like," said Teed. "It's just a rule about scouting. I don't want anybody to know what I'm thinking about a player."

Next year, Teed said, would be his last year of full-time scouting. Following the 1994 season, he said he would go into the Dodgers' Hall of Fame Retirement Plan: a three-year format that allowed him to work less games as the years progressed. By 1997, his last year, he would receive 25 percent of his normal salary. By then, it would be time for him to pack away the radar gun and stop putting all those miles on the car while combing through diamonds across New England watching high school and college baseball games. Three years from now, he would have been associated with the game of professional baseball for a total of fifty years.

It had been a career that had brought more than miles on the company car. Teed had numerous fond memories of his association with the national pastime and was the owner of three championship rings, all of them while working as a scout with the Dodgers: the 1978 National League Championship Series, the 1981 World Series, and the 1988 World Series. Teed, however, said he did not wear any of the rings.

"I'm saving them for my grandkids," he said.

Teed's off-season began in mid-October and extended through the winter until the beginning of March. During those five months, he watched his grandchildren play sports. He had four daughters, the oldest being forty. Teed gave credit to his wife, Virginia, for supporting his profession as a scout.

"She's understanding," said Teed, who would celebrate his forty-fourth wedding anniversary on September 3. "You couldn't find a better one. She became an independent woman. Most of the things that went wrong with the kids or the appliances were when I was on the road."

While Teed was sharing insight about his profession, the afternoon clipped along while Alexander and Ludwick stayed locked in a pitcher's duel. Ludwick allowed one run while striking out seven batters through seven innings. Alexander had not allowed a run while throwing a one-hitter through six innings and striking out eight batters.

In the seventh inning, Pittsfield opened with a walk by Smith and a double by the designated hitter, Kevin Lewis. With runners at second and third and nobody out, Turco came out of the dugout, and that was the end of the day for Alexander. The relief pitcher, Rich Croushore, retired Warner on a groundout to the shortstop, but Smith scored on the fielder's choice to tie the game, 1-1, while Lewis advanced to third.

Freiling, who was working out of the third-base coaching box, called time-out and met the next batter, Rafael Hernandez, in foul ground to talk strategy before his plate appearance. Hernandez then proceeded to execute a perfect sacrifice bunt to score Lewis for a 2-1 lead. Ludwick then gave way to the reliever Welch in the eighth inning, who shut the door in both innings to pick up the save in a win that put the Mets four and a half games in front of the Redbirds.

The next stop on my itinerary was a visit tomorrow night to Damashke Field in Oneonta. Teed, meanwhile, wouldn't be eating dinner by himself tonight. He was packing up his gear for the return trip home to Windsor, Connecticut.

"I told my wife I'd be home for a 7:00 p.m. dinner," he said. "It's only about an hour-and-a-half drive."

The Utica Blue Sox bus arrives in Pittsfield, August 27, 1993.

*Blue Sox players, like all ballplayers in the
minor leagues, carry their own bags.*

*Blue Sox players head to the visiting clubhouse
at Wahconah Park, Pittsfield, MA.*

*When I entered the parking lot at Wahconah Park, I
knew I was about to enter a baseball treasure.*

The exterior of Wahconah Park, Pittsfield, MA.

A view of the Wahconah Park grandstand which includes owl decoys hanging from the rafters to keep away pigeons.

Pittsfield Manager Howie Freiling uses a pitching machine during bunting practice.

Pittsfield Mets players take batting practice

Pittsfield players wait their turns around the batting cage.

*Pittsfield Manager Howie Freiling teaches
a player bunting techniques.*

Young fans seek autographs prior to a Pittsfield Mets game.

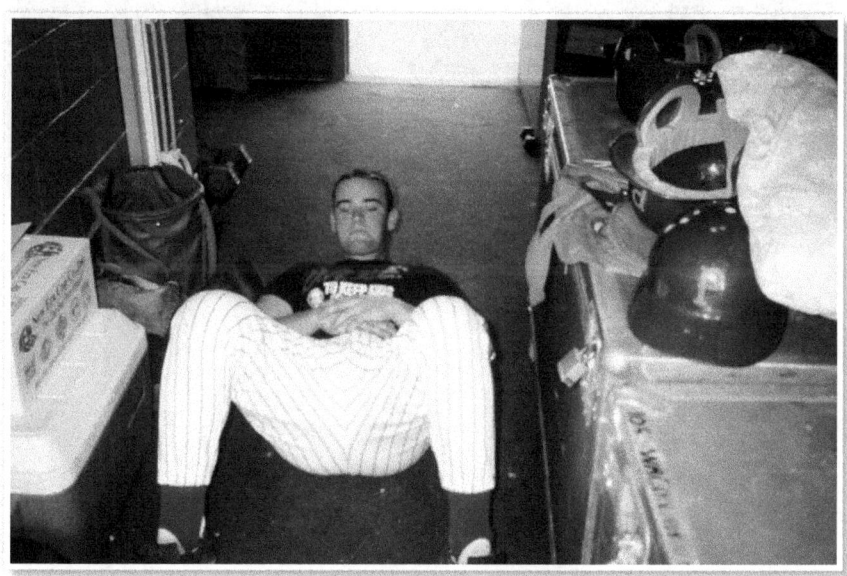

A Pittsfield player does abdomen exercises in the home clubhouse.

*Utica Blue Sox players take a rest outside
their clubhouse at Wahconah Park.*

CHAPTER SIXTEEN:

SAM NADER, DEAN OF THE NEW YORK– PENNSYLVANIA LEAGUE

August 30, 1993—Oneonta, New York

Southwest of Albany, and in the northern foothills of New York State's Catskill Mountains, sat the city of Oneonta, home of Damaschke Field and the Oneonta Yankees. I had been looking forward to my visit to this city and the ballpark, the place where Elmira fan George Levering said a tree branch hung over the right-field fence and the place where countless Yankee farmhands passed through on their way to Yankee Stadium and the major leagues. It was also the place where Sam Nader had been the owner of the franchise since 1968 and had watched Yankee farmhands win a total of eleven New York–Penn League championships in 1968, 1969, 1971, 1974, 1977, 1979, 1980, 1981, 1985, 1988, and 1990.[43]

43   List of New York-Penn League Champions. Wikipedia, *The Free Encyclopedia.* "List of New York-Penn League Champions. 30 October 2023, https://en.wikipedia.org/wiki/List_of_New_York%E2%80%93Penn_League_champions

When I pulled my vehicle into the parking lot, my first task was to find the legendary dean of the New York–Pennsylvania League. In search of the Oneonta front office, I was in disbelief when a worker directed me to a small brown shack that was alongside the grandstand and near the third-base side of the ballpark. The structure looked like a storage shed for lawn tools or a farm stand alongside a country road. I was even more surprised to find out that Albert "Sam" Nader, president and general manager of the Oneonta Yankees, wasn't there. It was 4:15 p.m., a time on game day when most general managers were making sure that all was well in preparation for the first pitch. I would catch up with him later, certain that the seventy-four-year-old icon would have stories aplenty to share with me.

The Oneonta losing streak continued last night when the Yankees lost their tenth straight and fifteenth of their last sixteen games in a 5-1 loss at Utica against the Blue Sox. Utica's Chad Renfroe struck out ten Yankees and allowed only one run, a solo homer by Ricky Ledee. The Yankees were now 32-36, four and a half games behind Pittsfield.

I caught up with Oneonta manager Ken Dominguez while the Yankees were working out on the field. Mark Newman, the organization's minor league coordinator, was in town and was currently working with the Oneonta third baseman.

"It's frustrating for everyone concerned, no doubt," said Dominguez. "You have to be professionals and play through it. The kids aren't letting down, but there is a sense of frustration."

If there was hope for the Oneonta ball club, it would come in the form of four games remaining against Pittsfield of the nine games remaining, a pair of back-to-back doubleheaders on Thursday and Friday later that week at Wahconah Park.

"There's still a chance," said Dominguez. "We have to start winning tonight. We can't afford to lose any games."

The Yankees were playing hurt.

Dominguez said Ruben Rivera, the team's leader in home runs and runs batted in, may be in the lineup tomorrow after rehabilitating an injured wrist. Abdiel Cumberbatch went to Albany today to have his injured hand examined and it was likely that he'd be out of the lineup for the remainder of the season.

"It wears on you after a while," said Oneonta reliever, Greg Resz, of the ten-game losing streak. "Tomorrow, we get Rivera in the lineup. He still leads the team in runs batted in. We try to keep on plugging. The key is to sweep Pittsfield right there (at Wahconah Park)."

Sam Nader was now on the premises, and when I told him about my purpose as a freelance writer traveling throughout the league, he gave me a copy of the lineups and stat sheets but told me I would have to buy my own program for one dollar at the souvenir stand. At the time, he was too busy to talk, informing me that it was Hartwick College Night and that he was busy with pregame preparations. During my brief stay in his office, I noticed that the walls were covered with Oneonta Yankees memorabilia: program covers, pictures, posters, and pennants. A framed picture of the current manager of the parent New York Yankees, Buck Showalter, was among the numerous artifacts.

The view beyond the outfield fence at Damaschke Field was the most picturesque of all the ballparks in the league. The rolling foothills of the Catskill Mountains provided the backdrop to a ballpark that looked like a makeshift operation. A small, rickety, old grandstand sat far behind home plate, and an odd collection of portable bleachers, spread out from one section to the next, were located down both baselines. One of the nicest features was the new Oneonta clubhouse located behind the first-base bleachers: a cinder block building with the Yankees logo painted on the front. Adjacent to the clubhouse and further down the right-field line was an odd-looking structure to see at a ballpark: a long, green trailer, the kind that was pulled by a semi down a highway. On the side of it was a sign that read, "Sports Mobile." The structure was a trainer's room, the place where the young "O Yanks" went to get arms rubbed along with a variety of treatments from Carl Randolph, the team's trainer. I found Randolph inside the trailer, which looked far better on the inside than it did on the outside. In the center was a trainer's table, and alongside the walls were several storage lockers, a total of thirty-six in all. Most of the lockers were filled with medical equipment, but others contained brand new Louisville Slugger bats.

"It's unique," said Randolph, who would enter his senior year at the University of Maine next week. "People like this. This is my own room. I'm not stuck in a little closet."

Randolph said he would begin giving treatments to players two hours before they had to be on the field. During home games, players needed to be dressed and on the field for stretching at 4:00 p.m., which meant that Randolph started seeing players as early as 2:00 p.m. for treatments. Oneonta catcher Rob Trimble was in the Sports Mobile while I met with Randolph, but instead of getting treatment, Trimble was there to check on the wood of a new bat.

"They get two bats at the start of the season," said Randolph. "When they break a bat, they hand in the broken one and get a new one."

When Trimble left, in walked Shawn Alazaus, a relief pitcher who came asking for a rubdown.

"Flexall or Albolene?" asked Randolph.

Randolph was referring to the type of product Alazaus would prefer to be rubbed on his arm. Alazaus selected Albolene, which according to Randolph was a liquefying cleanser that allowed him to make the muscle move so he could try to loosen it.

"Flexall is a heating agent that keeps them warm on the mound," said Randolph.

"I've been sick," said Alazaus, "and I've been lying in bed all day. I'm trying to get my muscles stretched."

"The air conditioning on the buses makes them susceptible to colds," said Randolph.

His treatment from Randolph now complete, Alazaus was in and out of the Sports Mobile in just over five minutes.

Shortly after departing the Sports Mobile, I recognized familiar faces across the parking lot at Damaschke Field. Two distinguished-looking gentlemen were crossing the street toward the ballpark carrying garment bags. Shawn McAnally and Mike Shields, the two umpires I met on opening night at Falcon Park in Auburn, had arrived to work tonight's game between the Yankees and Utica Blue Sox. I followed them into the umpire's locker room, the former Oneonta clubhouse that was located underneath the wooden home-plate grandstand. The facility was small for a baseball team but spacious for a two-man umpiring crew. The two umpires had more than an hour before the start of the game and began to get settled into a room that was filled with weights and video equipment.

"Our season is going well," said McAnally. "We've finished seeing our supervisor. Bill Haller was at Erie on August 9. After that, we saw Denny Craig on the tenth and eleventh at Batavia. He (Craig) mentioned a couple of things. He said to slow things down on the bases and that my timing was too quick. When you're making a call, you want to make sure you wait for everything to happen."

Shields mentioned an incident that happened last Thursday, August 26, during a night game at Niagara Falls. Shields was working the bases in a game that the Rapids were winning, 3-0, against the Batavia Clippers. With two outs and runners on second and third for the Clippers in the top of the ninth, the Batavia batter checked his swing after a pitch with two strikes.

Or did he?

McAnally, working behind the plate, did not call it a strike, but the Niagara Falls catcher asked for help because he thought the batter swung. McAnally looked to his partner asking for help.

"Strike three!" signaled Shields.

The game ended, and the Rapids won 3-0. But Batavia manager Al LeBoeuf disagreed, and he let Shields know about it.

"He kept me from leaving the field," said Shields. "We made contact. He bumped me and poked me in the cheek."

"I tried to step in between them," said McAnally. "I put my arm in front of him. He went after me too for a while."

With the LeBoeuf incident behind them, the two umpires were focused on the present and the near future. Both received assignments to umpire the upcoming New York–Pennsylvania League playoffs. Shields accepted, but McAnally declined the offer. Instead, he would use the time off to rest up before going to the Florida Instructional League, which would begin on September 16.

I chose to watch tonight's game from the press box, which was located on the top of the grandstand roof. Next to me in the booth was the WTLB Radio broadcast team of Jim Jackson and Jeff Leone, there to send the play-by-play account of the game back to the listening audience in Utica.

"A pleasant good evening, Jim Jackson and Jeff Leone from Damaschke Field in Oneonta, welcome to the dugout show," said the thirty-year-old Jackson as he began the broadcast of his pregame show. As Jackson continued, he quickly mentioned that Oneonta was a team trying to end a ten-game losing streak. "This team was 31-21," Jackson commented, "and now they're four and a half games back. Quite frankly, their pennant hopes are fading fast."

Following some live commentary about the Yankees and Blue Sox at the top of the broadcast, Jackson introduced an interview segment that was prerecorded. Leone was on tape interviewing the Utica shortstop Nick Ortiz. During this portion of the show, Leone and Jackson could pull off their headsets and talk in the press box. They were both graduates of Syracuse University, but Jackson had been in the field much longer than the twenty-one-year-old Leone.

"Jim is the grizzled veteran," said Leone. "The business is so much who you know. Jim doesn't really know anybody, but he has made it to the Philadelphia Flyers."

Leone was referencing what he mentioned to me over the weekend in Pittsfield when he told me that Jackson would be announcing play-by-play radio for the Flyers beginning that fall. He gained his hockey experience by announcing games for the Utica Devils, a farm team for the New Jersey Devils in the American Hockey League.

"I did every single game they played, 499," said Jackson. "I never made it to the five hundredth game, because they lost in the playoffs. So, my five hundredth game will be Pittsburgh against Philadelphia."

Jackson and Leone honed their craft at WAER Radio at Syracuse, which Leone referred to as "the Cradle of Sportscasters." Among the names of sportscasters as SU graduates, he listed Marv Albert, Bob Costas, and Sean McDonough.

The dugout show ended, and when a commercial was finished, Jackson was back live on the air, once again wearing his headphones with a microphone attachment.

"A pleasant good evening and welcome to Utica Blue Sox Baseball on WTLB," began Jackson, "brought to you by the Utica National Insurance Group."

When the game began, it was Jackson doing the play-by-play and Leone providing the color analysis. They would reverse the roles during the middle innings and then switch back to Jackson as the lead announcer for the final three innings. The accommodation for the two broadcasters at Damaschke Field was mediocre at best. Brown paneling lined the walls of that cramped room which was separated by a door from the other portion of the press box that housed writers, the public address announcer, and the scoreboard operator. In between innings, Jackson continued to open that door because of the extreme heat in the tight quarters on the grandstand roof. Jackson later told me that he would prefer to keep the door open for the entire game, but that his microphone would pick up the background noise being made by the occupants of the other half of the booth. Even the air conditioner in the radio booth remained off, because it would create too much noise that would be heard over the airwaves.

Jackson and Leone had only one alternative: sweat it out!

Their view from the rooftop perch was not much better. The windows attached to the front of the booth cranked open from the bottom, causing a portion of the window frame to come into their field of vision when looking at home plate. Even with the windows now open, the broadcasters still had to look at the field from behind a wire fence that also covered the open window frame.

The first pitch was getting closer, and much to my surprise, Damaschke Field was host to an egg toss, a hokey pregame event that I thought for certain would not click with Sam Nader's traditional baseball standards. Making matters worse, the event took place on the field grass. When the mess was cleaned up, the Yankees took the field with Mike Jerzembeck (6-4) getting the start against Utica's Eric Cormier (7-3). In the first inning, the public address announcer told the fans that the owner of the dirtiest car in the parking lot would receive a coupon for a free car wash at a local sponsor.

The announcement prompted Jackson to mention on the airwaves, "All I care about is that I don't have the car in the parking lot with the shattered windshield."

Jackson and Leone did not normally have to worry about shattered car windows, because they traveled to road games on the team bus. But with Utica being just an hour away, tonight they commuted to Oneonta in Jackson's car. Jackson was a New York–Pennsylvania League veteran, having announced Blue Sox baseball since 1985. It was not until 1990, however, that all the games were broadcast both at home and away. During his on-air delivery, Jackson did not hesitate to offer criticism. On the topic of the lighting at the ballpark, Jackson said, "Jeff, I don't know about you, but center field looks a little dark." As for the playing field, Jackson said, "The infield is dry and hard. It will yield bad hops." He did not shy away from critiquing the umpires either. When Cormier appeared displeased about some pitches that were not called strikes, Jackson quipped, "Cormier is trying to find the plate and Shawn McAnally's strike zone."

As the game wore on, the Utica broadcasters were in the process of calling a classic pitcher's duel, the game being scoreless through the first five innings. Jerzembeck was throwing a two-hitter and struck out six batters. Cormier, meanwhile, was also spinning a two-hitter through five innings and had survived two Yankee threats. In the second inning, Oneonta's Sloan Smith hit a one-out triple but was stranded at third base. Two innings later, Cormier battled his way out of a bases loaded jam with one out when he struck out Trimble and forced Mike Schmitz to fly out to the Utica center fielder Aaron Fuller.

While the pitching duel unfolded in front of me, I took some time to become familiar with the Oneonta franchise by leafing through the program that Nader told me I would need to purchase for one dollar. On the cover was a black-and-white photo of a game taking place at Damaschke Field with the foothills of the Catskills looming in the background. According to a story inside the program, Oneonta was the smallest city in the league and the fourth smallest city among the more than two hundred cities in professional baseball. Oneonta entered the league in 1966 as an affiliate of the Boston Red Sox and became affiliated with the Yankees one year later. This year marked the twenty-eighth consecutive year of professional baseball in Oneonta, twenty-seven of them in partnership with the parent New York Yankees, a streak that no other team in the league came close to matching.

Most impressive about the program was that it listed all the Oneonta team rosters dating back to 1966. Ken Brett, George Brett's brother, was a member of the 1966 team, and so was Amos Otis, who would go on to play center field with the Kansas City Royals. A few pages later, the publication listed where many of the Oneonta alumni were located today. Brett was an announcer with the California Angels, and Otis was a coach with the Colorado Rockies. John Elway, the quarterback for the Denver Broncos, played here in 1982. Elway was still a student at Stanford at the time and never made it to the major leagues. Several players, however, had once called Oneonta home before climbing the minor league ladder to the major leagues, a total of 110 players in all: Jim Beattie, Jim Deshaies, Mike Ferraro, Cesar Geronimo, Roberto Kelly, Al Leiter, Jim Leyritz, Kevin Maas, Don Mattingly, Willie McGee, Mike Pagliarulo, Dan Pasqua, Rafael Santana, Buck Showalter, J. T. Snow, Bob Tewksbury, and Bernie Williams, to name a few.

The Oneonta faithful had had the pleasure to watch quality players on the rise during four decades of a winning tradition. According to the program, last year's edition of the O Yanks was 37-38, only the fourth time in twenty-eight years that the franchise had fielded a team with a sub-.500 record. In twenty-eight years, the Yankees had had the best record in the league ten times. Two standout years were 1985 and 1986 when Showalter, currently the New York Yankees manager, was penciling the lineup card here at Damaschke Field. The 1985 ball club finished the year at 55-23 and won the league championship against Geneva. The next year, Showalter's O Yanks were even better, posting a 59-18 record. Despite the record, the team fell victim to the "one and done" format in the first round of the league playoffs, losing the one and only game against Newark, a team that had eighteen less wins than the Yankees over the course of the regular season.

By far, the best stretch of success occurred during a five-year span from 1977 to 1981 when the manager was Art Mazmanian, who won five division championships and four league championships with teams that included McGee (1977), Mattingly (1979), Pagliarulo (1981), and Tewksbury (1981).

This year's edition of the O Yanks was writing a destiny of their own until the wheels came spinning off during this current ten-game losing streak, dropping the team out of first place in the McNamara Division. Tonight, with the game still scoreless in the bottom of the sixth inning, the Yankees went ahead when Elston Hansen led off the inning with a walk and scored on a triple by Kurt Bierek for a

1-0 lead. Bierek then scored on a wild pitch by Cormier to give the Yankees a 2-0 lead entering the seventh.

Jerzembeck was undoubtedly on a tight pitch count, because when the Yankees took the field in the seventh, Jerzembeck was done even though he was throwing a two-hit shutout. Enter the reliever Scott Standish, and later, Shawn Alazaus, two pitchers who joined Jerzembeck on the night to combine for a five-hit shutout and a 2-0 win over the Blue Sox.

The ten-game Oneonta losing streak was now history.

"It feels pretty good," said Smith, the Oneonta right fielder. "Baseball in the minor leagues is a job. You have to come to the park every day with the mentality that 'I'm going to give it my all.' You always come to win. I think we've been focused. We just had some tough luck the last couple of games. Everything that could go wrong has gone wrong."

August 31, 1993—Oneonta, New York

A visit to Oneonta would also mean a visit to nearby Cooperstown and the National Baseball Hall of Fame and Museum.

This last day of August began on a bright, sunny Tuesday at Gilbert Lake State Park, where I spent the night in my Eureka dome tent. This accommodation was an upgrade from the smaller, cramped, pup tent that I had used earlier in the season when making overnight trips to ballparks throughout the league. My ride from the village of Laurens to Cooperstown covered a stretch of some of the most scenic landscapes in New York State; winding roads, hills, thick woods, and old barns were the norm.

Arriving in Cooperstown, the Farmer's Museum sat across the road from the southwest corner of Glimmerglass Lake. At Leatherstocking Golf Course, a lush layout stretched across both sides of Route 80 and along the corner of the lake. The crown jewel, however, at this point of entry to the village, was the Otesaga Resort

Hotel, a huge brick structure with white pillars at the front entrance and a huge veranda in the back that overlooked the south end of the lake. The National Baseball Hall of Fame and Museum was located right on Main Street and in the heart of the village.

My parents took my brother, Benny, and me here in the late 1960s, and I bought a Baltimore Orioles hat at the souvenir store next to the Hall of Fame. Today, the same souvenir store remained, but the difference in the village since my childhood was that souvenir stores dotted the landscape of the entire Main Street. There were restaurants, bars, and places to buy ice cream, but one must wonder where the residents went to get a haircut or to buy a pair of shoes.

Also, in the heart of the village, just beyond the statue of Sandlot Kid, sat Doubleday Field, the birthplace of baseball and one of the grandest little ballparks you would ever see. Just like the souvenir store I saw in the 1960s, nothing had changed at this tiny brick stadium where, like Wahconah Park, it had a ramp running through the center of the roof-covered grandstand that led right up to the screen protecting the box seats. Over twenty-five years ago, I ran the bases on this field with Benny during our visit as little kids, and my dad took a picture of us while sitting on the handheld scoreboard above the outfield fence.

The annual Hall of Fame game was played here every year, an exhibition game between an American League and National League team to highlight the Induction Weekend ceremonies. The ballpark was locked in by a parking lot to the front of it and houses behind the outfield fences. There were not any lights at Doubleday Field, and I doubted there ever would be. Author Roger Kahn, who wrote among his numerous publications *The Boys of Summer*, wanted to bring a franchise to this tiny village and ballpark as a member of the New York–Pennsylvania League. It would seem fitting that the birthplace of baseball would have a minor league entry, but the village residents blocked Kahn's bid because they were opposed to the installation of lights due to the proximity of the houses. Instead,

Kahn ended up in Utica in 1983, where he wrote *Good Enough to Dream*, a memoir of a season spent with the Utica Blue Sox.

I had lunch at the Doubleday Café where I enjoyed a grilled chicken breast sandwich and a garden salad, fine dining for someone who had spent the past three months eating hot dogs, peanuts, and Coca Cola during my travels throughout the league.

Two tight races were taking place, in the Stedler Division and in the McNamara Division.

A glance at the sports section today showed St. Catharines one game in front of Niagara Falls after the Blue Jays routed Geneva last night, 17-2. Adam Melhouse led the "Baby" Jays with four hits, two of them for home runs, and four runs batted in. The Blue Jays picked up the one-game lead when Niagara Falls lost 2-1 against the Batavia Clippers.

Watertown was now five and a half games in front of Geneva in the Pinckney Division. In the McNamara Division, Pittsfield remained two games in front of Utica after losing to Glens Falls, 2-0. The Mets were shut out by the Rapids' Dan Pontes, the Geneva native, who struck out seven batters in six innings of work.

Tonight, the Yankees would be at home against Glens Falls while the Blue Sox host Pittsfield in a doubleheader at Donovan Field in Utica. When I arrived at Damaschke Field later in the day, I saw Oneonta manager Ken Dominguez, who grinned while walking by me on his way to the clubhouse.

"Good to get that monkey off our back," said Dominguez.

I caught up with Sam Nader, the seventy-four-year-old president and general manager of the Oneonta ball club, and this time, he was able to talk.

"I brought the club here in 1966 when I was mayor," he said. "After 1966, the Red Sox said they'd return, but they pulled out in spring training when the league decided to go to a short season schedule."

According to Nader, at the time, the team was owned by Joe Buzas, who played one season in the major leagues, a thirty-game career with the New York Yankees in 1945 while compiling a .262 batting average.[44] As time went on, Buzas would become known for his work as a minor league entrepreneur while purchasing franchises in several minor league cities. Nader put together a group which purchased the club from Buzas for the price of $7,500. The Yankees then became the parent club in 1967 and had been ever since. By 1971, Nader became the majority owner and had seen his share of prospects come through the system.

He arose from his chair at this desk and grabbed a copy of the 1986 program that showed Don Mattingly and Willie McGee on the cover.

"At one time, Mattingly and McGee were most valuable players in their respective leagues (American and National), and we had both of them here in Oneonta," said Nader. "How about that!"

John Elway played here for a total of forty-two games as an outfielder in 1982. His season was cut short in August because he needed to return to Stanford University to begin football practice. Of course, Elway would end up choosing football over baseball, but Nader believed he would have had a legitimate shot at making a career in major league baseball.

"He was a real prospect," said Nader. "He could have made it. He had power, he was coachable, fast, had a good arm, and had a good attitude."

Nader looked up the numbers on Elway, which were placed in a binder from the 1982 season: a .318 batting average, four home runs, and thirteen stolen bases.

"He played with Orestes Destrade, Dan Pasqua, Jim Gorsi, and Jim Deshaies," said Nader. "Not too bad!"

I was quick to figure out that Nader was a down-to-earth guy: no nonsense and a baseball traditionalist. Damaschke Field didn't serve

---

44   Buzas, Joe. Wikipedia, *The Free Encyclopedia*. "Joe Buzas." 4 July 2024, https://en.wikipedia.org/wiki/Joe_Buzas

beer, and as long as Nader was involved with the ball club, the beer ban would remain in effect.

"We try to sell this as a family-type operation," said Nader. "I feel the sale of beer is not conducive to that type of atmosphere. We never had a Marlboro man billboard here. Didn't want it. I used to like a cigar. I drink a beer, but I don't want to sell it."

Nader was known as an outspoken executive throughout the league. He had been at the business longer than anyone else in the league and was set in his ways. Damaschke Field was a nice place to watch baseball without the carnival atmosphere found at almost every minor league ballpark in the country.

"I tell it the way I believe it," said Nader. "If they (other general managers) don't like it, too bad. You can disagree without being disagreeable."

Owning and operating the Yankees had often been a family affair for Nader. In 1982, his daughter Suzanne was the general manager. Nader's thirty-seven-year-old son, John, was currently listed as the general manager of the team, although it appeared to me that they were sharing the duties. John had a full-time job as an economics professor at nearby Delhi Tech. The elder Nader had received offers through the years from prospective buyers. These people, he said, were from other cities, and wanted to come in and purchase the franchise.

He refused them every time.

"I love baseball," said Nader. "I'm opposed to entrepreneurs who come into the community. They move on. They're not in it for the love of the game. They're in it for money. Oneonta is the fourth smallest city in organized baseball. Our population is eleven thousand in the summer. We hold our head above water (financially). As long as we can stay in the black, we're all right."

Walking out of Nader's office, I noticed that the sky had darkened considerably and that the lights were already on at a time of the afternoon when infield practice was taking place. During this pregame routine, I sat once again with Shawn McAnally, who was working the bases tonight while his partner, Mike Shields, would call balls and strikes. This was the third city in the league—Auburn and Erie being the other two—where I had had the pleasure to talk baseball during infield practice with the umpire, McAnally.

No sooner had McAnally stood up to go to the locker room to get ready for the game was he back in the grandstand, informing me that he had just met with Nader and Dominguez and that a decision had been made to push back the starting time from 7:15 p.m. to 7:30 p.m. with the hope that the oncoming storm would pass.

At 7:15 p.m., the sky was colored purple, and a fierce wind was blowing at Damaschke Field. It looked as though a tornado was about to engulf this tiny little ballpark at any minute. Choosing to ignore the oncoming storm was a small group of Latin ballplayers from Oneonta and Glens Falls that had gathered behind home plate. Five minutes later, Dominguez and Steve Turco, the Glens Falls manager, were now on the field talking with McAnally and Shields.

The 7:30 p.m. starting time came and went without the first pitch being thrown. At 7:34 p.m., those purple skies opened with a flourish. The rain came down heavily, and the strong wind blew with lightning striking nearby. The bleachers on both the first- and third-base sides had been left vacant by the few fans that were there to begin with. Most of the fans had headed for their cars in the parking lot, conceding to the notion that baseball would not be played in Oneonta tonight. There were only seventy-four fans by my count, all of them huddled together in the home-plate grandstand, trying to stay clear of the bottom rows so they didn't get drenched by the blowing rain that was blustering through the backstop screen and into the box seats.

The rain was not letting up, and by 7:49 p.m., there was standing water on the field. This was by far the worst storm I had seen at any ballpark in the league this summer—worse than the downpour in June that wiped out a game at Community Park in St. Catharines during the first week of the season. And worse than the downpour that seemed to make the press box shake and rattle at Dwyer Park in Batavia in late June.

A few minutes later at 7:51 p.m., and in the middle of this thunder and lightning storm, someone walked onto the field in foul territory on the first-base side. Braving the elements and drenched within seconds was groundskeeper Lenny Sutliffe, who was taking a slow walk to right field.

I was not quite sure what Sutliffe was going to accomplish in conditions that appeared risky, if not dangerous.

Sutliffe walked to the warn track in right field, where he picked up a large branch that had fallen onto the field from one of the trees that overhung the fence. Public address announcer Dick Cavanagh asked the sparse crowd to give Sutliffe some applause. And on cue, a loud crack of lightning struck nearby.

At 7:57 p.m., the field was now underwater, and there was absolutely no way a baseball game was going to be played tonight. McAnally and Shields had emerged from their locker room to survey the damage, and three minutes later, Cavanagh announced that the game had been cancelled and would be made up tomorrow as part of a doubleheader that would begin at 6:00 p.m.

At that point, I went to the Oneonta locker room to catch up with Dominguez, who was trying to shuffle a pitching staff that may now be without the services of Shawn Alazaus, the relief pitcher who visited Randolph in the Yankees' Sports Mobile for a rubdown yesterday and then picked up the save in the 2-0 win over Utica. Now Dominguez was informing me that his reliever had strep throat.

In no order, Dominguez needed healthy players, sunshine, and a little bit of luck.

"I'd hope for us to sweep Glens Falls and Utica to sweep Pittsfield," said Dominguez.

In the event such a scenario was to occur the next day, Oneonta would pull within one and a half games of first-place Pittsfield.

"These are all crazy scenarios," continued Dominguez. "We have a better chance because we have four games with Pittsfield."

The Yankees would need to get their rest tonight while preparing for three doubleheaders in the next three games, against Glens Falls tomorrow and at Pittsfield on Thursday and Friday: six games in three days against two teams and an opportunity to regain control of the McNamara Division.

I left Damaschke Field and made my way for Main Street, where I enjoyed two slices at Sal's Pizzeria while the rain continued to fall outside onto the streets of Oneonta. As I ate the slices, I watched a special ABC TV report about Hurricane Emily that was causing severe damage along the coastline of North Carolina. My evening without baseball was then substituted with an evening at the Oneonta Theater a few blocks away on Chestnut Street, where I watched *Sleepless in Seattle* starring Tom Hanks and Meg Ryan.

*The ticket booth at Damaschke Field
includes a list of promotions.*

*Sam Nader is the owner of the Oneonta Yankees and the
dean of executives in the New York–Pennsylvania League.*

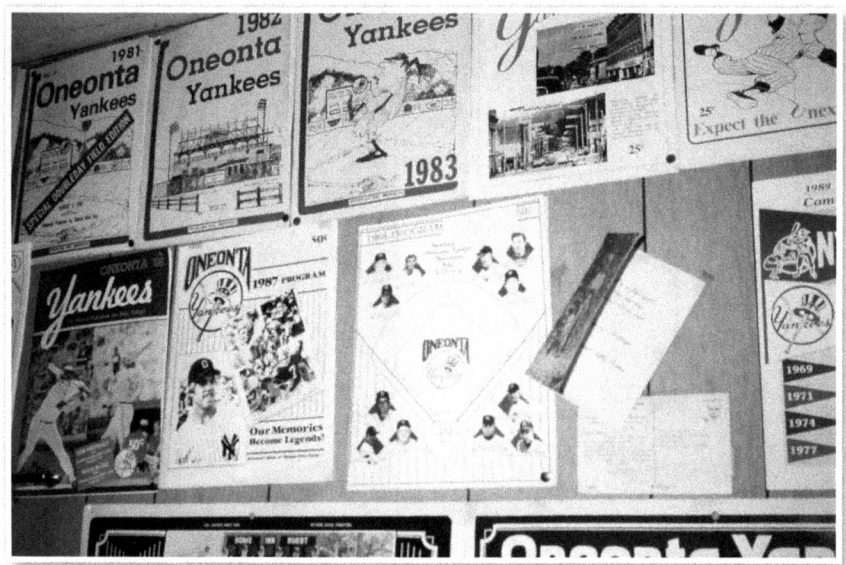

Sam Naner's Office resembles a minor league baseball museum.

*The home plate grandstand at Damaschke Field
is one of the smallest in the league.*

The Oneonta Yankees stretch prior to a game.

*The Catskill Mountains provide the background while
Oneonta players stretch at Damaschke Field.*

An Oneonta player enjoys a sandwich in the home clubhouse before a game in August 1993.

Oneonta players rest outside the home clubhouse before a game.

Oneonta Trainer Carl Randolph does his work before home games at the Sports Mobile, a trailer parked outside Damaschke Field.

Oneonta Catcher Rob Trimble gets a new bat from the Sports Mobile.

The author talks baseball with NY-P League Umpire Shawn McAnally in the Damaschke Field grandstand.

Oneonta pitcher Chris Cumberland warms up in the bullpen under the watchful eye of Juan Nieves, Oneonta Pitching Coach. Nieves, at age 22, was the second-youngest pitcher to throw a no-hitter when he did so for the Milwaukee Brewers in 1987 against the Baltimore Orioles.

Oneonta's Chris Cumberland takes his cuts in the batting cage.

*Utica Blue Sox Baseball is on the air with Jeff Leone (left)
and Jim Jackson providing the radio play-by-play coverage
of a game at Damaschke Field on August 30, 1983.*

The author ditched his small pup tent and upgraded his accommodation with a Eureka dome tent at Gilbert Lake State Park, Laurens, New York while making visits to Damaschke Field in nearby Oneonta.

CHAPTER SEVENTEEN:

HEADING HOME

September 1, 1993—Utica, New York

The 1993 regular season now in its final days, my journey through fourteen cities in three states and one province would not be complete without a visit to the league office at 1629 Oneida Street in Utica. The New York–Pennsylvania League Office was in a small building next to Julian's Laundromat and across the hallway from the law office of Bob Julian, an attorney who also happened to be the president of the league.

Vonda Bonham, who recently began the position of public relations director, greeted me when I entered the league office, informing me that Julian was out of town on business in Binghamton. The main office of the New York–Pennsylvania League was smaller than some of the cramped umpire locker rooms I had visited during the past three months. The office contained a desk that was surrounded by numerous stacks of cardboard boxes containing wrapped sets of New York–Pennsylvania League baseball cards produced by ProCards. A closet was filled with boxes that were stacked high, each one of them containing a dozen baseballs.

Bonham handed me a copy of a letter recently written by Julian and addressed to the league's general managers, informing them that the playoff format would not consist of a three-game format in the first round. Instead, the first round would consist of a one-game playoff with the championship round to be determined in a three-game series.

After taking in a few sights in Downtown Utica, I arrived at Donovan Stadium at the same time the Pittsfield team bus was unloading. The Mets and Blue Sox were originally scheduled to play a three-game series here, but with last night's game rained out, tonight's doubleheader reduced the series to a two-game set. The schedule for the remainder of the season did not allow any room for the third game to be played between the Mets and Blue Sox. As a result, Pittsfield benefitted from Mother Nature as the rainout last night kept the two-game division lead intact.

A Utica sweep of the twin bill tonight, however, would lock the Blue Sox and Mets in a tie for first in the McNamara Division.

"It's an unfortunate thing that happened," said Utica utilityman John Walker in reference to last night's rainout. "We just have to keep on winning. That's our problem. We worry about who's behind us or how many we have to catch up instead of worrying about the game that night."

"It puts us in a situation that we have to win both games today," said Utica shortstop Nick Ortiz. "We don't have a third game to rely on. We're pretty confident that we can come on the winning side of the doubleheader today. If not, we just have to play it day by day. We just have to play our game and try to win every game we have left."

Jim Rice, the former outfielder who spent his entire sixteen-year major league career with the Boston Red Sox, was in town today to work with the young Blue Sox hitters. Rice, who turned forty this past March, was one of three minor league roving instructors with the Boston Red Sox. The other two instructors within the system were Steve Braun and another Boston favorite, former shortstop Rico Petrocelli. Rice compiled a .298 career batting average while hitting

382 home runs. He played in two American League Championship Series and one World Series. Rice was playing left field for Boston in 1986 when the Red Sox were one out away from winning the World Series during Game Six at Shea Stadium against the New York Mets. The third out never came, however, and the Red Sox would lose Game Seven and the Series.[45]

I approached Rice to talk while he was standing in the corner of the third-base dugout at Donovan Stadium getting a drink from the water cooler. I introduced myself, we shook hands, and then Rice started to walk away. When I then asked if we could talk, he said he had to go to the outfield where some Blue Sox outfielders participated in pregame activities and he kept on walking.

Later, during the first game of the doubleheader, I was confused why Rice, as a roving instructor, spent the game in front of the groundskeeper's garage, located in foul ground down in the right field corner near the Utica clubhouse, instead of conversing with the Blue Sox players who were seated far away in the third base dugout. Perhaps this was a better view for him to assess the defensive skills of the Blue Sox outfielders. If so, I still had a hard time thinking that this was a better vantage point to assess the Utica players when they dug into the batter's box, located some 330 feet from the groundskeeper's garage.

Pittsfield sent Tom Engle to the mound in the first game of the doubleheader. The Mets starting pitcher, whom I sat with in the Wahconah Park box seats while he clocked pitches last Friday, would be opposed by Utica's Shawn Senior. I watched Senior make his league debut back on July 3 against Oneonta right here at Donovan Stadium with his parents in attendance after they made the drive from New Jersey. It was a debut that I was sure the left-hander would have liked to forget, the Yankees knocking him out after just five

45   Rice, Jim. Wikipedia, *The Free Encyclopedia*. "Jim Rice." 30 July 2024, https://en.wikipedia.org/wiki/Jim_Rice

innings when they scored five runs on nine hits. Senior also walked three batters, threw two wild pitches, and committed one balk.

Since then, Senior had put together a 6-2 record with sixty-eight strikeouts in sixty-nine innings of work. Tonight, he started out in total command on a hot, muggy night in Central New York, allowing one run through the first four innings while striking out six batters. Utica gave Senior a 1-0 lead when Dan Collier hit a solo homer in the second inning over the right-field fence. The Mets scored their run in the third inning when David Zuniga doubled, advanced to third on a fielder's choice, and came home on a sacrifice fly by Paul Petrulis.

The game remained tied through four innings until Utica broke it open against Engle in the fifth inning, scoring four runs on four hits. The key hit was a three-run homer to right field by John Stratton, who had struck out in both of his prior at bats, to give the Blue Sox a 5-1 lead.

Following the Stratton home run, Pittsfield manager Howie Freiling made a visit to the mound to talk with Engle. While he was out there, he became engaged in a long-range shouting match with the home-plate umpire Jason Gibbons. Based on the way the argument transpired, I had to believe that Freiling's intention was not so much to talk with his starter, but instead, to stir things up with Gibbons. Freiling went too far with his commentary, and Gibbons tossed him, sending the Pittsfield manager for the long walk to the visiting clubhouse in the right-field corner.

The Mets scored again in the seventh, which was the last inning of the game for a minor league doubleheader, but Senior caught pinch hitter Kevin Lewis looking at a called third strike for the final out and a 5-2 Utica win in the opener.

"Winning the first one gives us a chance to pick up two instead of coming out even," said Senior in between games of the doubleheader. "I just wanted to keep us close early. I knew we'd been struggling with the bats a little bit. I felt if I could hold them down for the first three or four innings and give our team a chance to get on a roll—which they did—I could finish it off."

In the second game, Pittsfield bounced back and knocked the Utica starter, Dean Peterson, out of the game in the third inning. The Mets scored four runs off Peterson on three hits, two of them coming on a two-run single by Benny Agbayani. The Blue Sox came right back in the bottom of the inning and scored two runs to cut the lead to 4-2. Jason Isringhausen, the Pittsfield starter, would throw shutout baseball the rest of the way and cruise to a win with plenty of offensive support. The Mets scored eight more runs against three other Utica pitchers, Jeff Johnson, Leif McKinley, and Jim Telgheder, for a 10-2 win and a split of the doubleheader.

Time was now running out on the Blue Sox and the rest of the contenders in the McNamara Division trying to catch the Pittsfield Mets, who left town in the same position in which they arrived: atop the division and two games ahead of second-place Utica.

As I pulled out of the parking lot at Donovan Stadium, my summer-long baseball road trip was approaching the late innings. With the completion of tonight's doubleheader in Utica, I had concluded a swing through the four cities of the McNamara Division and visited all fourteen ballparks in the New York–Pennsylvania League. The calendar had flipped to September, which meant that the playoffs were around the corner, scheduled to start in less than a week.

CHAPTER EIGHTEEN:

PLAYOFF BASEBALL

September 7, 1993—Watertown, New York

The regular season ended on September 5, and the Pittsfield Mets held on to their slim lead to win the McNamara Division by two and a half games over the Utica Blue Sox (38-38) with a final record of 40-35. Glens Falls (37-40) finished in third place, four and a half games behind, while the Oneonta Yankees, the team that led the division for most of the season, finished in last place, four and a half games behind. The Yankees, who were 31-22 on August 11, posted a 5-18 record during their last twenty-three games to finish the season at 36-40.

As the final 1993 standings below indicate, St. Catharines (49-29) had the best record in the league while edging Niagara Falls (47-31) by two games in the Stedler Division, and Watertown (46-32) was equally impressive while winning the Pinckney Division.

Stedler Division

	W	L	GB
St. Catharines	49	29	---
Niagara Falls	47	31	2
Batavia	38	39	10.5
Erie	36	41	12.5
Welland	35	42	13.5
Jamestown	31	46	17.5

McNamara Division

	W	L	GB
Pittsfield	40	35	---
Utica	38	38	2.5
Glens Falls	37	40	4
Oneonta	36	40	4,5

Pinckney Division

	W	L	GB
Watertown	46	32	---
Geneva	43	34	2.5
Elmira	31	44	13.5
Auburn	30	46	15

The playoff format consisted of the division winner with the best winning percentage, St. Catharines, playing the wildcard team, Niagara Falls, in a one-game series. The other division winners, Watertown and Pittsfield, would also play in a one-game series, with the two winners advancing to the league championship best-of-three game series.

With both one-game series scheduled for Labor Day, the Mets and Indians were rained out at Duffy Fairgrounds in Watertown. The Blue Jays and Rapids also had rain in St. Catharines last night, but the game was played nonetheless on a soggy Community Park field. St. Catharines led the game 1-0 entering the ninth inning, but Niagara Falls scored two runs to grab a 2-1 lead. The Blue Jays tied the game, 2-2, in the bottom of the ninth, and the game went into extra innings. In the bottom of the twelfth inning, St. Catharines had the bases loaded with two outs but failed to score. Then in the top of the thirteenth, the Rapids' Del Marine hit a three-run homer off relief pitcher Dilson Torres. In the bottom of the inning, Mike Richardson, the Niagara Falls relief pitcher, finished off the Blue Jays with a 5-2 win in a game that ended at 12:22 a.m.

The Rapids would get a day of rest today before hosting the first game of the New York–Pennsylvania League Championship Series tomorrow against either the Pittsfield Mets or the Watertown Indians. Just one game into the post season, St. Catharines, the team with the best record during the seventy-eight-game regular season, fell victim to the one-game playoff format. It was just a year ago when the Hamilton Redbirds also took a quick exit after an impressive regular season record of 56-20.

Here in Watertown, Mike Young, the manager of the Indians, had opted to bypass two of his pitchers who were ranked among the top ten league leaders in earned run average. Casey Whitten was 6-3 with a 2.42 earned run average while Roland de la Maza was 10-3 with a 2.52 ERA. Instead, Young was handing the ball to Daron Kirkreit, and the pitcher who also just happened to be Cleveland's number one selection in the 1993 June Amateur Draft. Kirkreit (4-1, 2.23 ERA) had won four games in a row, and tonight, he would be opposed by Pittsfield's ace, Jason Isringhausen (7-4, 3.29 ERA), who led the league with 104 strikeouts.

Bob Sutton, the beat writer who covered the Indians for the *Watertown Daily Times*, noted in his playoff story during today's edition of the newspaper that the Indians had not played a full nine-inning game in a week. This situation, according to Sutton, was the result of doubleheaders (seven-inning games) and rainouts. Incredibly, the Indians' last eight games were parts of doubleheaders, the last twin bill being Sunday when they swept the Auburn Astros, winning both games by the identical scores of 2-0. The sweep left the Indians with a 46-32 regular season record, the second-best in franchise history since the 47-30 mark that was set by the first installation of a Cleveland farm club here in 1989.

The big bat in the Watertown lineup for Insringhausen to contend with would be the first baseman Greg Thomas, who compiled a .307 average while leading the league in runs batted in with a total of sixty-three.

Kirkreit, meanwhile, would face a Pittsfield lineup that would be best described as balanced. A glance at the league's batting statistics did not include a Pittsfield player among the top five hitters in four offensive categories. The Pittsfield pitching staff, meanwhile, ranked fourth among the fourteen teams with a 3.37 earned run average.

I noticed familiar faces today as soon as I entered the Duffy Fairgrounds. Over at the concession stand, eating a slice of pizza, was Howard Herman, the Mets' beat writer from the *Berkshire Eagle*. Standing next to him was Ethan Wilson, arguably the league's most outgoing public relations director.

Prior to the opening pitch, I had a brief visit with Howie Freiling, the Pittsfield manager, who was not too thrilled about his team having to spend two nights at the Watertown Days Inn while waiting to play this game. "I feel like we were ready to play yesterday," said Freiling, who spent the rainout playing pinball at an arcade inside the nearby Salmon Run Mall. "Nobody likes sitting around."

I asked Freiling if he would manage tonight's game in a different manner considering it was a win-or-go-home one-game playoff.

"We have everybody available," he said. "We might go to the bullpen quicker, but just because you go to the bullpen doesn't mean you'll get out of the jam. You've got to be careful not to treat this so differently. We worked hard all year to get here. We should enjoy it."

I walked into the dingy Watertown clubhouse at 6:30 p.m. and found manager Mike Young sitting in his office. Young played baseball in the Netherlands after his college career and was now managing in his third organization following stints as a Class A manager in the Blue Jays and Orioles organizations prior to hooking on with Cleveland to lead the Watertown Indians in 1993.[46]

The last time I saw Young was in July before a game at McDonough Park in Geneva. Prior to that midsummer contest against the Geneva Cubs, Young would not talk with me.

Tonight was not much of an improvement.

Young greeted me by saying, "This isn't a good time, a half-hour until the ball game."

In Young's defense, he was right.

It was understood throughout professional baseball that interviews with players and managers should not take place within thirty minutes of a game. I explained to him that I had just made a two-and-a-half-hour drive, but that I would leave if he wanted me to do so. Young said I could stay, but he was brief, giving me quick, sharp responses. My biggest takeaway from this exchange was him stating, "You just do what got you here."

I settled in for tonight's game in the makeshift, aluminum bleacher section on the first-base line behind the visiting dugout and introduced myself to the person sitting next to me, Erton Sipher, a seventy-two-year-old retired dairy farmer from the nearby city of Gouverneur. Sipher told me that he was at Duffy Fairgrounds for only the third time this season. He said he watches a lot of baseball, but most of it was Toronto Blue Jays baseball on television. Sipher was wearing an odd-looking baseball cap with a San Francisco Giants logo on one side of the front and an Oakland A's logo on the other side, a souvenir he said that was sent from his son who resided in the San Francisco Bay Area.

---

46   Young, Mike. *Baseball Reference.* '"Mike Young." 31 January 2023, https://www. baseball-reference.com/bullpen/Mike_Young_(manager)

"There were probably only two of these east of the Mississippi," said Sipher, "and the other one, my son gave to the Baseball Hall of Fame."

Pittsfield scored first when Preston Wilson walked to open the second inning, advanced to second base when Kirkreit balked, and came home on a single by Charlie Sullivan for a 1-0 lead. The lead was short-lived as the Indians loaded up the bases against Isringhausen in the third and tied the game when Mike Neal scored on a sacrifice fly to center field by Robert Lewis.

During that inning, the big concern for the Mets came after the Watertown batter, Steve Hodson, swung and missed at a pitch by Isringhausen, who then suddenly appeared injured, prompting a visit from Freiling to check on his pitcher.

When I later caught up with Isringhausen after the game outside the visiting clubhouse, I inquired about this incident, and he explained to me that his left knee gave out. Isringhausen would remain in the game after the visit from Freiling, and as the game progressed, he and Kirkreit became locked in a pitcher's duel, the game still tied at 1-1 through six complete innings of play.

Midway through the game, I noticed a Mets fan whose name was Bill Measick. He was wearing a camera around his neck and a T-shirt that had a team picture of the Pittsfield Mets on the front, the caption reading, "1993 McNamara Division Champs." Measick was sixty-eight years old and a member of the Pittsfield Mets Fan Club. He told me that the souvenir shirts were just printed the other day.

Measick was a resident of Germantown, New York, located along the Hudson River, and as he described it, a forty-eight-minute drive to Wahconah Park in Pittsfield. Still, despite the distance, he identified himself as a Pittsfield Mets season-ticket holder.

"This is the way baseball should be," said Measick of the minor league version. "Either way, this is a good ball game. Whoever pulls it out will earn it."

Measick was traveling with his wife, Ruth, whom he described as "not a baseball fan."

I asked Measick if he and Ruth would make the trip to Niagara Falls for the League Championship Series if the Mets were to win the game tonight.

"Not tonight, but in the morning we would (travel)," said Measick. "The team would go tonight. Not me. I'm too old for that."

In the top of the seventh inning, Measick might have needed to begin travel plans to Niagara Falls instead of going back to Germantown. That was because the Mets broke the tie ball game by scoring three runs off Kirkreit, two of them coming on a single by Eric Harris that drove in Wilson and Matt Terrell.

Isringhausen left the game after pitching seven complete innings, allowing just one run while throwing a two-hitter, and his team ahead 4-1. His replacement, reliever Jeff Tam, did not fare quite as well, allowing a solo homer to Robert Lewis, the second batter he faced in the eighth.

It would be the last time the Indians would score.

Pittsfield scored one run in the ninth, and Freiling brought his closer, Mike Welch, into the game in the bottom half of the inning with hopes of slamming the door on the Indians. Welch responded, and the Mets won the game 5-2 to advance to the New York–Pennsylvania League Championship Series against Niagara Falls.

After the game, the Mets were abuzz in their steamy and cramped visiting clubhouse. Right next door, the Indians clubhouse was silent. Neal, the Watertown shortstop who walked three times and struck out once, was dressing quickly while trying to put the sudden-death playoff loss into perspective.

"That's the thing about baseball, having a dominant pitcher," he said. "Their starter had a real good night."

Aside from allowing just one run while throwing the two-hitter through seven innings, Isringhausen also lived up to his billing as the league's whiff king by striking out nine Indians.

"All it takes is a pitcher like that do his job," said Neal. "He shut us down, and we couldn't hold on. He was throwing hard and hitting spots well. He kept us off-balance."

Neal, who played his college baseball at Louisiana State University, was in a hurry to leave Watertown tonight. The Indians had spent the past two weeks residing in the Watertown Days Inn because they had to leave their campus-area housing. Neal planned to drive through the night back home along with teammate Chris Plumlee.

"I'm going to start heading home," said Neal. "It's a twenty-three-hour drive to get back to Louisiana. We'll split the time driving. I'll spend some time with my family and my girlfriend."

His time in the Bayou State would be short-lived, because Neal and fifteen of his Watertown teammates would go to Winter Haven, Florida, later this month to begin a six-week stint in the Florida Instructional League.

"We put up a good season, and it comes down to one game," said Neal. "If we could have had a series, we could have come out on top."

Walking across the grassy parking lot at Duffy Fairgrounds, I crossed paths again with Measick and his wife, Ruth, on the way to my car. I told him I would see him tomorrow at Sal Maglie Stadium in Niagara Falls. I also gave him one recommendation about Niagara Falls: a visit to the Press Box Lounge, where he would find the best and largest hamburger waiting for him in the form of the famous "Pittsburgher."

September 8, 1993—Niagara Falls, New York

When I arrived at Sal Maglie Stadium, my first item of business was not to go to the field, but instead, to check out the pool.

The last time I was here, during the opening weekend of the season in mid-June, the large built-in city pool located at the very front of the stadium lay empty without water. At that time, it was just a big cement rectangle with some standing rainwater in the deep end. Today, it was a different story. The pool was filled to the top, and I could not wait to see a splashdown from a foul ball!

I found Larry Parrish, the Rapids manager, sitting in his office before the game. I asked him about the one-game playoff win two nights earlier at St. Catharines when his team beat the Blue Jays in thirteen innings thanks to the three-run homer by Del Marine.

"It was a great baseball game," said Parrish. "We feel like we had a good ball club, and so did they. Being in a one-game playoff, we pulled out all the stops."

"The guy (Torres) left a good pitch out over the plate for me, and I just did what I could with it," said Marine of his home run. "It really felt good. He threw me a slider. He threw me two sliders before that, and I pulled them foul, one for a foul-ball home run. He threw me a third one, out over the plate a little more for me, and I just got extended on it and got a good swing. We were matched up perfectly. We had the same pitching staff, one and two (in team ERA) throughout the year. It brings out everything in you to play a game like that. A lot of people were all concerned about when we were going to get home (for the off-season), and not really thinking about the game. But once the game came around and we were in a battle with them, I don't think anybody on the team was thinking about going home. We wanted to play to win, and that's what we did. And we're here to win this too."

Tonight, Parrish would throw left-hander John Rosengren, who was 7-3 with a 2.41 earned run average during the regular season. Rosengren, who was fifth in the league in earned run average, was the Rapids' strikeout leader with a total of ninety-one. Even more impressive was the fact that Rosengren held opposing hitters to a .183 batting average. In his last fourteen innings, he had allowed just one run, but surprisingly, had little to show for his efforts during that stretch with a record of 0-1.

Rosengren and his teammates would oppose Pittsfield right-hander Tom Engle, who finished the regular season at 7-7 with one hundred strikeouts in eighty-four innings of work.

The Mets scored first tonight in the second inning, when Randy Warner reached base on a two-out walk and came home on a double by Cesar Diaz, the ball landing just inside the foul line before bouncing into foul territory in the right-field corner.

In the bottom of the third inning, Malvin DeJesus led off with a walk and scored on a two-run homer by Mike Wisely, the ball just clearing the Wendt Dairy sign in center field to put the Rapids ahead 2-1.

As the game progressed, I found myself having to move around from seat to seat in the press box. First, I moved to make room for beat writer Ken Fox of the *Niagara Gazette* and eventually ended up in the far-left end of the press box, a portion of the booth that was unoccupied and unlit and where members of the media went to get their complimentary soda from a machine.

It was here, in this darkest portion of the press box, that I met Jon Goodfellow, the head groundskeeper at Sal Maglie Stadium. Goodfellow was a math teacher at nearby Grand Island Middle School and had spent his summer months as the stadium grounds-keeper during all or portions of the 1989, 1992, and 1993 seasons. I had heard stories about Goodfellow from Shawn McAnally, the umpire who cited Goodfellow as one of the best in the league. I remembered McAnally specifically telling me about Goodfellow's habit of taking rock hunts through the Sal Maglie infield dirt.

"If you have a pebble that big," he said, while making the size of a quarter with his finger, "I want it out of there. The kids that work for me, their job is to walk around with pop cups and have a rock hunt. We'll do it for fifteen minutes. If it rains, it takes the dirt downward and rocks will appear. They seem to rise and settle at the top and are very visible as they rest on top of the dirt."

Goodfellow had developed a faster way of collecting the rocks. Instead of constantly bending over to pick them up, he used the sand wedge from his golf bag and hit the rocks into a dustpan that had a long handle.

Rocks were not Goodfellow's only problem.

Feathers presented a challenge to him as well, the culprits being flocks of seagulls that hovered over the field.

"We go on feather hunts," he said. "I'll tell them, 'We're going after feathers in the infield.' It's tough to hang onto them. We have a creek outside the stadium. They're attracted to that body of water."

Feathers and rocks were not the only objects he collected at Sal Maglie. He also found chicken wings, sometimes as many as five a day.

"We have restaurants in the area," said Goodfellow. "The birds must scavenge, hit garbage cans, and fly them in. I pick them up and put them in my pocket. If I had one, I'd show you."

Goodfellow wanted to share more with me than chicken wings. He told me that he would be glad to show me the collection of rocks that he and his ground crew staff had collected this season. The rocks, I was told, were stored in his groundskeeper quarters, located under the stadium and next to the umpire's locker room. That was where he also said he kept his "wonder tool," which he said looked like a hoe and was used to edge the lips around the bases.

In the top of the seventh, the Rapids were ahead 2-1 when I found it to be coincidental listening to Goodfellow talk about his manicuring habits just as Pittsfield's Randy Warner hit a ball that was chopped in fair territory, but then bounced foul.

"That should go foul, and it did go foul," said Goodfellow. "And that pleases me."

"What pleases me," he continued, "is if we get a bunted ball on dirt and it starts out fair, I want it to stay fair. You want it to be level. If it goes foul, I'm cheating that kid."

Goodfellow could not stop offering his stories about being a groundskeeper and his view about baseball.

"I like white lines, and I like them straight," he said. "We lost a patch in front of the mound during the World University Games.

If you look, I cut out sod from the third-base coaching box to re-place it.

"There has not been a bad hop through seven innings. I hope this 2-1 game isn't influenced by a bad hop."

Goodfellow would get his wish.

The two-run homer by Wisely in the third inning was all the scoring the Rapids would need as they held on for a 2-1 win behind the two-hit pitching of Rosengren and reliever Brian Moehler.

The win gave the Rapids a 1-0 lead in the best-of-three games series with Game Two scheduled for tomorrow night at Wahconah Park in Pittsfield. If necessary, Game Three would also be played in Pittsfield.

Only one thing was certain at the end of the game.

Goodfellow would be turning out the lights for the last time at Sal Maglie Stadium this season, the Rapids to finish the playoffs on the road whether they won or lost the series. The groundskeeper was fine with the season ending.

"My arms and shoulders hurt so much," he said. "If you're physi-cally unable to put your arm around your wife, you have to question your job."

The Mets would pull their bus out of Hyde Park and make the long drive on the Governor Thomas E. Dewey Thruway across New York State to Pittsfield, Massachusetts. The Rapids, on the other hand, had chosen to stay home overnight and would make the drive to the Berkshire Mountains tomorrow morning.

"It's basically minor league baseball," said Parrish about avoiding an extra night on the road. "If we win tomorrow night, we don't have to pay for a motel. There's no doubt, we would've rather liked to see Watertown win, because we wouldn't have as long a ride."

I found Rosengren, the winning pitcher, in the cramped Niagara Falls clubhouse. Parrish lifted him after seven innings because he had reached his maximum pitch count of one hundred, a mark that the manager was required to follow with orders coming from the parent Detroit Tigers.

"We stayed on that (pitch count) all year," said Rosengren. "We're the only team that didn't have a complete game all year. It has been like that all year. I expect it. I have no problem with it. He (Parrish) wants to keep our arms fresh."

Tomorrow night's fresh arm would come in the form of Gary Goldsmith, who was 4-2 with a 2.30 earned run average during the regular season.

Rosengren liked his team's chances in Game Two.

"Goldie's throwing," said Rosengren. "He's the man. We're going to win it tomorrow."

Rosengren predicted correctly.

The following night at Wahconah Park, the two teams were locked in a pitcher's duel once again, playing scoreless baseball through nine complete innings. The Rapids went ahead in the top of the tenth when Mike Wisely scored from third base on a surprise two-strike drag bunt by teammate Glen Barker off Mets' reliever Mike Welch. The game had been delayed for an hour due to rain, and Barker's bunted ball slowed down in the wet grass. Goldsmith threw six scoreless innings and relievers Mike Richardson and Gabe Sollecito held off the Mets the rest of the way for a 1-0 win to capture the 1993 New York–Pennsylvania League Championship.

My journey through the league included thirty-six baseball games in fourteen cities. I kept a scorebook for every game, bought a program in every ballpark, and ate countless hot dogs as well as that soggy hamburger on opening night at Falcon Park in Auburn when I tripped in the bleacher seats and spilled my soft drink.

Some ballparks were better than others, and my favorite was Wahconah Park in Pittsfield.

Other ballparks, such as Falcon Park, needed to be leveled.

No matter how good or bad the ballpark was, however, I was thrilled to visit every one of them. Last winter, my objective was to put my finger on the pulse of minor league baseball during the summer months.

My travels complete, I had found the heartbeat of baseball in the bush leagues to be as strong as ever.

The view outside the grandstand at Sal Maglie Stadium

Niagara Falls native, and former Major League Pitcher Sal Maglie, is honored outside the stadium in Hyde Park.

Manager Larry Parrish led the Niagara Falls Rapids to the 1993 New York–Pennsylvania League Championship.

EPILOGUE

Eric Danapalis of Niagara Falls led the New York–Pennsylvania League in batting with a clip of .341, while T. J. O'Donnell, the Utica Blue Sox player who was the league leader during my visit to Donovan Stadium in July, finished second with a mark of .329.

Wes Shook of Erie was the league leader in home runs with seventeen, while Dan Collier (Utica) and Matt Raleigh (Jamestown) finished tied for second with fifteen each. Five members of the Jamestown Expos would go on to play in the major leagues, but Raleigh was not among the group. His nephew, however, would accomplish this task, as Cal Raleigh is currently a catcher with the Seattle Mariners.

John Neese led the league with the most wins as the Niagara Falls hurler posted a record of 12-3. Alsonso Beltran of St. Catharines was 11-2, teammate Edwin Hurtado was 10-2, and Adam Meinershagen rounded out an impressive trio of Blue Jays pitchers with a mark of 8-1. Roland de la Maza, the Watertown pitcher who passed over to start the one-game playoff against Niagara Falls, was 10-3.

Jason Isringhausen of Pittsfield finished the season with a 7-4 record and led the league with 104 strikeouts. Two years later, in 1995, he made his major league debut with the New York Mets and would record 300 career saves—thirtieth on the all-time list— over the course of a seventeen-year career while playing for six major league teams. He recorded thirty-three saves for the St. Louis Cardinals in 2006 but missed the playoffs due to a hip injury. His Cardinals teammates went on to win the World Series that season against the Detroit Tigers. Isringhausen led the National League in saves in 2004, played on two all-star teams, and recorded 830 career strikeouts.[47]

I never saw Billy Wagner, the Houston "Bonus Baby," pitch during the 1993 season, and his name is nowhere to be found in any of the top pitching statistical categories. For the record, he was 1-3 with the Auburn Astros with a 4.08 earned run average. He started seven games and struck out thirty-one batters in twenty-eight innings pitched. The numbers in Class A baseball, however, are not always an indicator of what will happen over the course of time for pitchers as well as position players. Such was the case for Wagner, whose career took off when he was converted to a reliever while playing Triple-A Baseball in Tucson in 1996. He played his first full major league season with the Astros in 1997 in a career that saw him play with five teams over the course of thirteen years. While his numbers were not noticed in the New York–Pennsylvania League, he would finish with 422 major league saves, ranking him in eighth place on the all-time list. He had a 47-40 record, a 2.31 earned run average, and played in seven All-Star games. In 2003, while pitching for the Astros, he was the sixth and last pitcher to combine for a no-hitter in a game against the New York Yankees. Wagner retired in 2011 and is currently the coach of the baseball team at the Miller School of Albemarle in Virginia, where he has guided his teams to two state independent school titles.[48]

---

47   1993 New York-Pennsylvania League. *Baseball Reference*. 5 August 2024, https://www.baseball-reference.com/register/league.cgi?id=d7b1ceaa

48   Wagner, Billy. Wikipedia, *The Free Encyclopedia*. "Billy Wagner." 24 July 2024, https://en.wikipedia.org/wiki/Billy_Wagner

A total of fifty-three players who were on the fourteen teams during the 1993 New York–Pennsylvania League season would play in the major leagues. The roster included the following:

- **Auburn**: Billy Wagner, Mike Grzanich
- **Batavia**: Tony Fiore, Wayne Gomes, Kevin Sefcik
- **Elmira:** Dave Berg, Marc Vlades, Andy Larkin, Billy McMillon, Bryan Ward
- **Erie:** Eric Moody, Marc Sagmoen
- **Geneva:** Alex Cabrera, Jon Ratliff, Brendon Donnelly
- **Glens Falls**: Jeff Berblinger, Alan Benes, Rich Croushore
- **Jamestown**: Alex Pacheco, Tommy Phelps, Antonio Alfonseca, Bobby Henley, Neil Weber
- **Niagara Falls**: Brian Moehler, Jorge Valendia, Glen Barker, Eddie Gaillard
- **Oneonta:** Mike Jerzembeck, Ricky Ledee, Sterling Hitchcock, Ruben Rivera, Frank Lankford
- **Pittsfield:** Jason Isringhausen, Preston Wilson, Eric Ludwick, Allen McDill, Mike Welch, Jeff Tam, Benny Agbayani
- **St. Catharines:** Shannon Stewart, Edwin Hurtado, Adam Melhouse, Dilson Torres
- **Utica**: Joe DePastino
- **Watertown:** Roland de la Maza, Steve Kline, Travis Driskill
- **Welland:** Ramon Morel, Jermaine Allensworth, Jason Jonnson, Jason Phillips, Chris Peters, Lou Collier[49]

A strange footnote to this list is the inclusion of Sterling Hitchcock of the Oneonta Yankees. He made his major league debut a year prior in 1992, when he was 0-2 with the parent New York Yankees. He pitched one inning for the Oneonta Yankees in 1993

---

49   1993 New York-Pennsylvania League. *Baseball Reference.* 5 August 2024, https://www.baseball-reference.com/register/league.cgi?id=d7b1ceaa

while facing three batters and spent most of that season with the Columbus Clippers of the Triple-A International League.[50]

Ruben Rivera of Oneonta would recover from the injury in August of 1993 that limited his playing time during the pennant drive. He reached the major leagues with the New York Yankees in 1995 and was on their active roster in the American League Championship Series. Considered a top prospect by the Yankees in 1993, Rivera played with four other major league teams while compiling a .216 batting average in a career that ended in 2003.[51]

Rivera's teammate, Ricky Ledee, the Oneonta outfielder who threw a ball over the center field fence out of frustration at East Field in Glens Falls amid his team's late-season skid and fall from first place, made his major league debut with the New York Yankees in 1998 and was part of that World Series championship team that beat the San Diego Padres in the World Series. The 1998 Yankees team was 114-48 during the regular season and considered by many to be the best Yankees team in history. Ledee had six hits in ten at bats in the World Series against the Padres. His former Oneonta teammates, Rivera and Sterling Hitchcock, were members of the opposing San Diego ball club. Ledee also was a member of the Yankees team that won the 1999 World Series against the Atlanta Braves. He played with six more teams in a career that concluded in 2007 as a member of the New York Mets. He was a member of the "fictional" New York Yankees in the Hollywood movie titled *For the Love of the Game* starring Kevin Costner and Kelly Preston that was released in 1999.

Shannon Stewart batted .279 for St. Catharines in 1993. He was with the parent Toronto Blue Jays two years later for the beginning of what turned out to be a thirteen-year major league career that included a .297 batting average and 115 home runs.

---

50   Hitchcock, Sterling. *Baseball Reference.* "Sterling Hitchcock." 5 August 2024, https://www.baseball-reference.com/register/player.fcgi?id=hitchc001ste

51   Ledee, Ricky. Wikipedia, *The Free Encyclopedia.* "Ricky Ledee." 1 August 2024, https://en.wikipedia.org/wiki/Ricky_Led%C3%A9e

Manny Acta, the Auburn manager and the first of the fourteen managers I met with that summer, managed seven more years in the minor leagues, winning a league championship in the Class A Florida State League with Kissimmee before taking a third-base coaching job with the Montreal Expos under manager Frank Robinson. He would become a major league manager with the Washington Nationals in 2007, a position he held for three years before taking over as skipper of the Cleveland Indians from 2010 to 2012. Acta is still in the game today as the third-base coach for the Seattle Mariners. In addition to his success and longevity in the game of baseball, he has raised thousands of dollars to help provide students in the United States with college scholarships through his ImpACTA Kids Foundation.[52]

The start of the 2024 season marked the thirty-seventh year of coaching in professional baseball for Al LeBeouf, the former Batavia Clippers manager. In 2012, doctors found a cancerous spot on his hip, and he was diagnosed with the disorder POEMS syndrome, which damages nerves in the leg. He underwent chemotherapy, a stem cell transplant, and at one point, was in a wheelchair. His recovery has allowed him to stay in the game of baseball, and he is currently in his fourth consecutive season as the batting coach for the Triple-A Nashville Sounds.[53]

Steve Turco, the Glens Falls manager, followed through on the career vision he shared with me by staying at the lower levels of minor league baseball to instruct young players. In 1994, he returned to the place where his professional managing career started, in Johnson City, Tennessee, where the Cardinals had an entry in the Class A Appalachian League. He stayed in that post for six years before

52   Acta, Manny. Wikipedia, *The Free Encyclopedia*. "Manny Acta." 18 July 2024,
      https://en.wikipedia.org/wiki/Manny_Acta
53   LeBeouf, Al. *milb.com*. "Al LeBeouf." 30
      November 2017, https://www.milb.com/news/
      colorado-springs-sky-sox-hitting-coach-al-leboeuf-beats-adversity-stay-262524256

switching to a scouting position with the Cardinals organization. Turco had the itch to be back in the dugout and went to the port of entry in baseball in 2009 to manage for the St. Louis farm club in Florida's Gulf Coast League. Turco won a league championship in that league in 2016. He was awarded the Mike Coolbaugh Award at the 2018 baseball winter meetings, an award given to an individual for knowledge of the game of baseball and mentoring young players. Following a forty-year career in professional baseball, Turco retired from the game in 2018.[54]

Larry Parrish, the Niagara Falls manager, climbed the ranks within the Tigers organization following the 1993 season. His travels took him back to the major leagues, where he became the bench coach for Detroit. In 1998, Parrish took over as manager of the Detroit Tiger and was replaced by Phil Garner for the 2000 season. He returned to the minor leagues, and throughout his career, he managed championship teams at all three levels: Class A (Niagara Falls), Class AA (Jacksonville), and Class AAA, where he won back-to-back Governor's Cup Championships with the Toledo Mud Hens.[55]

Erie manager Doug Sisson became the first-base coach for the Kansas City Royals and was later a roving minor league instructor. He also had coaching stints at the college level at Georgia and Auburn.[56]

Watertown manager Mike Young managed two more years of minor league baseball, his best season coming the next year in 1994, when he led the Columbus RedStixx of the South Atlantic League to a first-place finish with a record of 87-51. He would become

54   Turco, Steve. *ballparkdigest.com*. "Steve Turco." 7 November 2018, https://ballpark-digest.com/2018/11/07/steve-turco-wins-mike-coolbaugh-award/

55   Parrish, Larry. Wikipedia, *The Free Encyclopedia*. "Larry Parrish." 20 July 2024, https://en.wikipedia.org/wiki/Larry_Parrish

56   Sisson, Doug. Wikipedia, *The Free Encyclopedia*. "Doug Sisson." 23 July 2024, https://en.wikipedia.org/wiki/Doug_Sisson

instrumental in the baseball movement in Australia and was a key figure in the development of the Australian Baseball Academy.[57]

Jamestown manager Tim Torricelli left the Expos organization and became a coach and manager in the Tigers minor league system before returning home to Springfield, Illinois, to become a home loans banker.[58]

J. J. Cannon of St. Catharines continued working in the minor leagues for the Blue Jays and three other organizations as a manager and coach for eleven seasons. In 2001, he guided the Lexington Legends to a league title. Cannon would later mentor teenage boys at a group home in Versailles, Kentucky.[59]

Dave Holt, the Utica manager, spent one more year in the Red Sox organization and would eventually open a baseball academy in Salinas, California. In 2005, he returned to his hometown of Visalia, California, and coached the team where his baseball journey began, Mt. Whitney High School.[60]

Howie Frieling continued managing and coaching in the Mets organization and later became a scout for the Mets as well as the Philadelphia Phillies.[61]

Ken Dominguez of Oneonta would spend eleven years managing and coaching in the Yankees organization and continued his career in professional baseball as a coach with the White Sox, Dodgers, Phillies, and Brewers minor league systems.[62]

57   Young, Mike. *Baseball Reference*. '"Mike Young." 31 January 2023, https://www. baseball-reference.com/bullpen/Mike_Young_(manager)

58   Webster, Brian. *The State Journal-Register*. "Torricelli put family ahead of baseball coaching career." 27 -February 2026, https://www.sj-r.com/story/ sports/2016/02/27/torricelli-put-family-ahead-baseball/32466591007/

59   Cannon, Joe. Wikipedia, *The Free Encyclopedia*. "Joe Cannon." 5 July 2024, https:// en.wikipedia.org/wiki/Joe_Cannon_(baseball)

60   Holt, Dave. *Coachandplaybaseball.com*. "Dave Holt." (2008-2023). https://www. coachandplaybaseball.com/Dave-Holt.html

61   Frieling, Howie. *Thegreatest21days.com*. "Howie Frieling." 6 June 2019, https://www. greatest21days.com/2019/06/howie-freiling-appreciated-that-11.html

62   Dominguez, Ken. *Baseball Reference*. "Ken Dominguez." 20 April 2020, https:// www.baseball-reference.com/bullpen/Ken_Dominguez

Elmira manager Lynn Jones returned to the major leagues in 2001 and would be a coach for a total of four different organizations. In 2004, he was the first-base coach for the Boston Red Sox when the team ended an eighty-six-year World Series drought by winning the Fall Classic against the St. Louis Cardinals. In 2013, he returned to Thiel College in Greenville, Pennsylvania, where he graduated in 1974 and is currently a volunteer assistant coach for the baseball team.[63]

The baseball resume of Jerry Weinstein is remarkable as well as lengthy. His coaching career began long before he was manager of the Geneva Cubs in 1993. Weinstein first coached in 1966 for the UCLA freshman team. His positions as a coach and manager have been in the professional and college ranks. In 2017, he managed Israel in the World Baseball Classic. Weinstein was still managing as recently as 2019 for the Wareham Gatemen of the Cape Cod Summer League. He has created articles, videos, and books about coaching baseball and is eighty years old.[64]

Larry Smith also has a lengthy baseball resume, and most of it occurred at the college level prior to him becoming manager of the Welland Pirates in 1993. Smith would spend two more years in the minor leagues and would work as a baseball scout for the Pirates, Reds, and Rangers organizations.

Ellen Harrigan-Charles, the general manager of the St. Catharines Blue Jays, didn't take long to accomplish her goal of reaching the big leagues. Toronto general manager Pat Gillick hired her and took her with him when he assumed the same role with the Baltimore Orioles in 1996. Today, she is in her twenty-fourth season with the Los Angeles Dodgers and is currently the team's vice president of baseball administration.[65]

---

63   Jones, Lynn. Wikipedia, *The Free Encyclopedia.* "Lynn Jones." 30 July 2024, https://en.wikipedia.org/wiki/Lynn_Jones

64   Weinstein, Jerry. Wikipedia, *The Free Encyclopedia.* "Jerry Weinstein." 15 March 2023, https://en.wikipedia.org/wiki/Jerry_Weinstein

65   Osborne, Cary. *Dodger Insider.* "A front-office game changer." 21 December 2023, https://dodgers.mlblogs.com/a-front-office-game-changer-6766da2cccaf

Skip Weisman, my classmate from Ohio University and the general manager for the Erie Sailors, was a baseball executive for five different minor league teams before shifting careers in 2002 when he opened a business consulting company. Since then, he has become a speaker, and most recently, a fiction writer.[66]

Jim Jackson, the radio play-by-play voice of the Utica Blue Sox who I shared a cramped press box with at Damaschke Field in Oneonta, has been a play-by-play announcer for the Philadelphia Flyers since 1993. He spent his first two years as the radio voice and the past twenty-eight as the lead TV broadcaster.[67]

Rafael Hermoso, who covered the Blue Sox for the Utica *Observer Dispatch*, went on to continue his craft as a major league baseball writer for the *New York Times* and *New York Daily News*.[68]

Dan Iassogna, the umpire who was featured by writer Jeffery Hileman in the Erie newspaper the *Times News*, made his major league debut in 1999 as a fill-in umpire for umpires who were on vacation or injured. He became a full-time major league umpire in 2004 and is still working in the big leagues today. Iassogna has been a part of a World Series umpire crew in 2012, 2017, and 2022.[69]

Leo Pinckney's wish came true when moments after the 1994 season ended, a bulldozer crashed through the center-field fence of Falcon Park in Auburn to begin demolition before the eventual re-building of a new ballpark.[70]

The 2019 season was the last year of baseball for the New York–Pennsylvania League. Major league baseball downsized the minor

66   Weisman, Skip. *skipweismanauthor.com*. "Skip Weisman." (2024). https://www.skip-weismanauthor.com/about-me

67   Jackson, Jim. Wikipedia, *The Free Encyclopedia*. 14 July 2024, https://en.wikipedia.org/wiki/Jim_Jackson_(sportscaster)

68   Hermoso, Rafael. *The Kent State University Press*. "Rafael Hermoso." (2016). https://www.kentstateuniversitypress.com/author/rafael-hermosa/

69   Iassogna, Dan. Wikipedia, *The Free Encyclopedia*. "Dan Iassogna." 5 August 2024, https://en.wikipedia.org/wiki/Dan_Iassogna

70   Falcon Park. Wikipedia, *The Free Encyclopedia*. "Falcon Park." 5 May 2023, https://en.wikipedia.org/wiki/Falcon_Park

leagues after the 2020 NY-P League season was cancelled due to the COVID-19 pandemic. The league would cease to exist in 2021. The remaining teams in the league in 2019 from my journey through the league in the summer of 1993 were Auburn and Batavia. The league started in 1939, and the last chapter was written when the Brooklyn Cyclones became league champions in 2019. The Oneonta franchise won the most league championships with a total of twelve.[71]

When the 1993 season ended, I returned to teaching elementary students at Allendale Columbia School in Rochester. Following teaching positions in the Rochester City Schools and the Pittsford Central School District, I embarked on a nineteen-year journey in 2002 as a school administrator, six years as a principal, and thirteen years as a superintendent of schools at various districts throughout New York State. Along the way, I began doctoral studies at the University of Rochester, and eventually received my doctoral degree in Educational Leadership from Manhattanville College in 2020.

In addition to Hillary, my wife Mary Beth and I had two more children with the births of Kevin and Abigail. As time marched on, I took the family to numerous Rochester Red Wings ball games at Silver Stadium, and later, to the new Frontier Field in Downtown Rochester. My children had the opportunity to also watch games there with my mother, an avid baseball fan—especially of the New York Yankees—who followed the team on the YES Network up until her passing at the age of 101 in 2023.

All three of my children graduated from Duquesne University in Pittsburgh. Mary Beth and I are proud of their accomplishments at this school, along with the work they currently do in their respective careers. I also enjoyed sitting with them at PNC Park beginning in 2010 while watching Pittsburgh Pirates games and taking

---

71   List of New York-Penn League Champions. Wikipedia, *The Free Encyclopedia*. "List of New York-Penn League Champions." 30 October 2023, https://en.wikipedia.org/wiki/List_of_New_York%E2%80%93Penn_League_champions

in the beauty beyond the outfield fence which features the Roberto Clemente Bridge and the downtown Pittsburgh skyline.

In 2021, Mary Beth and I moved to South Carolina, and I would return to the classroom as a teacher in 2022 when I taught fifth grade at Blessed Sacrament School in nearby Savannah, Georgia. I managed to share my interest in our national pastime with students by teaching them how to play Strat-O-Matic baseball, a statistical board game that I sensed many of the students could have spent hours playing. At recess, I pitched to them during wiffleball games at nearby Daffin Park, and our boys' and girls' Wiffleball World Series games are memories that I will forever treasure.

Since moving to South Carolina, I jump-started my passions as a high school and youth baseball umpire and basketball referee. I began umpiring and officiating in 1982 in Santa Rosa, California, and have now umpired baseball in five states: Ohio, California, New York, South Carolina, and Georgia.

In May of 2024, I had the pleasure to sit next to my three-year-old grandson, Teddy, along with his mother, my daughter Hillary, her husband Casey, and my son Kevin at PNC Park in Pittsburgh while watching the Pirates beat the Colorado Rockies in a rain-soaked game. In coming years, I have hopes to teach Teddy how to keep score during a ball game, a lost art among fans as a glance around any major or minor league ballpark will surely indicate.

I continue to watch games in minor league ballparks, and when Mary Beth and I visited historic McCormick Field in Asheville, North Carolina, in June of 2024, it marked the fiftieth minor league ballpark I had visited. It could not have been a better choice. This beautiful little ballpark has a warm, welcoming vibe and is nestled into a hillside with a right-field fence standing thirty-six feet high, which helps to prevent cheap home runs from occurring. The distance to the fence at the foul line in the right-field corner is just 297 feet from home plate. The parking was free, the tickets cost ten dollars each, and Mary Beth and I enjoyed the game on Dollar Hot Dog Night.

The author and his family at Yankee Stadium in 2008.
(left to right) Mary Beth, Hillary, Kevin, and Abigail.

ACKNOWLEDGMENTS

I am thankful for the opportunity to have interviewed so many individuals during my travels through the New York–Pennsylvania League in the summer of 1993. Those people were gracious and kind to share their insights about the game of baseball from their varying perspectives.

I want to thank the editorial, design, and publishing staff at Palmetto Publishing for the publication of my manuscript, a process led by Project Manager Elizabeth Stallman. Special thanks to Roy Francia, Palmetto Publishing Executive Consultant, a fan of minor league baseball, who believed in my work following my 31 years of rejections from publishers and literary agents across the nation.

I am most appreciative of my loving wife, Mary Beth, who I met in 1984. One of our first dates was watching a Rochester Red Wings game at Silver Stadium, a place she had never visited despite being a Rochester native. She is still amazed that I can remember that the Richmond Braves were the team in town that day to play the Red Wings.

Mary Beth was patient and understanding when I took my journey visiting fourteen ballparks for a total of thirty-six games in 1993. Since then, she has been patient and supportive, while encouraging me to continue the pursuit of publishing my manuscript.

ABOUT THE AUTHOR

Martin D. Cox, Ed.D., is a passionate follower of minor league baseball, having frequented 50 ballparks, beginning in his native Rochester, New York. His career spans over three decades in New York State's educational system, including roles as a teacher, principal, and superintendent of schools. His education includes a BS degree in Communications from Ohio University, a Master of Elementary Education degree from Nazareth College, and a doctoral degree in Educational Leadership from Manhattanville College. He lives in Bluffton, South Carolina with his wife Mary Beth. They are proud parents of three children: Hillary, Kevin, and Abigail. His book, *Behind a Wire Fence*, is a testament to his lifelong love for baseball.

9 798822 957343